MULTICULTURAL EDUCATION SERIES

James A. Banks, Series Editor

IMPROVING ACCESS

TO

MATHEMATICS

DIVERSITY AND EQUITY
IN THE CLASSROOM

Edited by

Na'ilah Suad Nasir
Paul Cobb

TEACHERS
COLLEGE
PRESS

Teachers College
Columbia University
New York and London

Published by Teachers College Press, 1234 Amsterdam Avenue, New York, NY 10027

Several of the chapters in this volume were published in previous versions in *Diversity, Equity, and Mathematical Learning* (2002), a special issue of *Mathematical Thinking and Learning* (Volume 4, Issues 2 & 3), edited by Na'ilah Suad Nasir and Paul Cobb. Copyright © 2002 by Lawrence Erlbaum Associates. Used by permission. The original titles of these chapters, as well as the page numbers from the journal, follow.

Chapter 1: "Research, Reform, and Equity in U.S. Mathematics Education" by Sarah Theule Lubienski, pp. 103–25.

Chapter 2: "Paying the Price for 'Sugar and Spice': Shifting the Analytical Lens in Equity Research" by Jo Boaler, pp. 127–44.

Chapter 3: "Enabling the Practice of Mathematics Teachers in Context: Toward a New Equity Research Agenda" by Rochelle Gutiérrez, pp. 145–87.

Chapter 6: "A Situated and Sociocultural Perspective on Bilingual Mathematics Learners" by Judit Moschkovich, pp. 189–212.

Chapter 9: "Identity, Goals, and Learning: Mathematics in Cultural Practice" by Na'ilah Suad Nasir, pp. 213–47.

Chapter 11: "A Relational Perspective on Issues of Cultural Diversity and Equity as They Play Out in the Mathematics Classroom" by Paul Cobb and Lynn Liao Hodge, pp. 249–84.

Library of Congress Cataloging-in-Publication Data

Improving access to mathematics : diversity and equity in the classroom / edited by
    Na'ilah Suad Nasir, Paul Cobb.
        p. cm. — (Multicultural education series)
    Includes bibliographical references and index.
    ISBN-13: 978-0-8077-4729-2 (cloth : alk. paper)
    ISBN-10: 0-8077-4729-7 (cloth : alk. paper)
    ISBN-13: 978-0-8077-4728-5 (pbk. : alk. paper)
    ISBN-10: 0-8077-4728-9 (pbk. : alk. paper)
    1. Mathematics—Study and teaching—United States.   2. Multicultural
education—United States.   3. Educational equalization—United States.   I. Nasir,
Na'ilah Suad.   II. Cobb, Paul.
    QA13.I467 2007
    510.71'073—dc22

                                                                      2006024976

ISBN-13:   ISBN-10:
978-0-8077-4728-5 (paper)   0-8077-4728-9 (paper)
978-0-8077-4729-2 (cloth)   0-8077-4729-7 (cloth)

Printed on acid-free paper

Manufactured in the United States of America

14   13   12   11   10   09   08   07   8   7   6   5   4   3   2   1

Contents

Series Foreword

The nation's deepening ethnic texture, interracial tension and conflict, and the increasing percentage of students who speak a first language other than English make multicultural education imperative in the 21st century. The U.S. Census Bureau (2000) estimates that people of color made up 28% of the nation's population in 2000 and predicts that they will make up 38% in 2025 and 50% in 2050 (El Nasser, 2004).

American classrooms are experiencing the largest influx of immigrant students since the beginning of the 20th century. About a million immigrants are making the United States their home each year (Martin & Midgley, 1999). More than five million legal immigrants settled in the United States between 1999 and 2004 (United States Department of Homeland Security, 2006), most of whom came from nations in Latin America and Asia (Riche, 2000). A significant number also come from the West Indies and Africa. A large but undetermined number of undocumented immigrants also enter the United States each year. The influence of an increasingly ethnically diverse population on the nation's schools, colleges, and universities is and will continue to be enormous.

Forty-two percent of the students enrolled in the nation's schools in 2003 were students of color (National Center for Education Statistics, 2005). This percentage is increasing each year, primarily because of the growth in the percentage of Latino students (Martinez & Curry, 1999). In some of the nation's largest cities and metropolitan areas, such as Chicago, Los Angeles, Washington, D.C., New York, Seattle, and San Francisco, half or more of the public school students are students of color. During the 2003–2004 school year, students of color made up 67.5% of the student population in the public schools of California, the nation's most populous state (California State Department of Education, 2006).

Language and religious diversity are also increasing among the nation's student population. In 2003, about 18.7% of the school-age population spoke a language at home other than English (National Center for Education Statistics, 2005). Harvard professor Diana L. Eck (2001) calls the United States the "most religiously diverse nation on earth" (p. 4). Islam is now the fastest-growing religion in the United States. Most teachers now in the classroom and in teacher education programs are likely to have students from diverse ethnic, racial, language, and religious groups in their classrooms during their careers. This is true for both inner-city and suburban teachers.

An important goal of multicultural education is to improve race relations and to help all students acquire the knowledge, attitudes, and skills needed to participate in cross-cultural interactions and in personal, social, and civic action that will help make our nation more democratic and just. Multicultural education is consequently as important for middle-class White suburban students as it is for students of color who live in the inner city. Multicultural education fosters the public good and the overarching goals of the commonwealth.

The major purpose of the *Multicultural Education Series* is to provide preservice educators, practicing educators, graduate students, scholars, and policymakers with an interrelated and comprehensive set of books that summarizes and analyzes important research, theory, and practice related to the education of ethnic, racial, cultural, and language groups in the United States and the education of mainstream students about diversity. The books in the *Series* provide research, theoretical, and practical knowledge about the behaviors and learning characteristics of students of color, language minority students, and low-income students. They also provide knowledge about ways to improve academic achievement and race relations in educational settings.

The definition of multicultural education in the *Handbook of Research on Multicultural Education* (Banks & Banks, 2004) is used in the *Series*: Multicultural education is "*a field of study designed to increase educational equity for all students that incorporates, for this purpose, content, concepts, principles, theories, and paradigms from history, the social and behavioral sciences, and particularly from ethnic studies and women's studies*" (p. xii). In the *Series*, as in the *Handbook*, multicultural education is considered a "metadiscipline."

The dimensions of multicultural education, developed by Banks (2004) and described in the *Handbook of Research on Multicultural Education*, provide the conceptual framework for the development of the books in the *Series*. They are *content integration, the knowledge construction process, prejudice reduction, an equity pedagogy,* and *an empowering school culture and social structure.* To implement multicultural education effectively, teachers and administrators must attend to each of the five dimensions of multicultural education. They should use content from diverse groups when teaching concepts and skills, help students to understand how knowledge in the various disciplines is constructed, help students to develop positive intergroup attitudes and behaviors, and modify their teaching strategies so that students from different racial, cultural, language, and social-class groups will experience equal educational opportunities. The total environment and culture of the school must also be transformed so that students from diverse groups will experience equal status in the culture and life of the school.

Although the five dimensions of multicultural education are highly interrelated, each requires deliberate attention and focus. Each book in the series focuses on one or more of the dimensions, although each book deals with all of them to some extent because of the highly interrelated characteristics of the dimensions.

The chapters in *Improving Access to Mathematics* are timely, important, and instructive. They were written by authors who are on the cutting-edge of theory, research, and development in mathematics education. Mathematics is one of the gatekeeper subjects in schools. Scores on math tests are often used to justify and reinforce existing power arrangements related to race, ethnicity, social class, and gender within educational institutions and the larger society. With the passage of the No Child Left Behind Act in 2001 and the standardization and testing that have been implemented in response to this act (Sleeter, 2005), the stakes in mathematics performance have escalated. Disparities in the math performance of some groups of Asian American and White students and the performance of students of color such as African Americans and Mexican Americans remain wide, perplexing, and intractable. An aim of this significant book is to uncover and describe the causes and processes that underlie inequities in mathematics achievement using a cultural lens. The chapters are unified by how the authors analyze inequities in mathematics achievement using cultural, social, and political concepts and paradigms.

The engaging and carefully researched chapters in this book contain novel and important insights, data, and interpretations that will stimulate a productive dialogue about ways to address the serious inequities in mathematics achievement. Some of the refreshing interpretations in this book challenge existing paradigms—such as the cultural difference explanation of the achievement gap—that are well established and largely unquestioned in the multicultural education literature. Several of the contributors to this book caution that the cultural difference explanation may result in essentializing the characteristics of racial, ethnic, and cultural groups as well as locating the problem of underachievement within individuals or groups rather than within the social, political, and economic structures (Anyon, 2005).

Other original interpretations and conceptualizations in this book problematize established assumptions and paradigms and will stimulate productive and needed deliberations about gender, culture, and educational inequities in mathematics. The concept of gender as a response rather than a characteristic of individuals, viewing math classrooms as communities of practice, and different ways of viewing culture are among the exciting and stimulating ideas in this engaging and illuminating book. The contributors describe two ways of viewing culture, as the way of life of a bounded community, and as localized, dynamic, improvisational, and co-constructed (Geertz, 1983). The contributors to this book conceptualize culture as the latter.

This book contains helpful and thoughtful discussions of mathematical knowledge and power, teaching mathematics for social justice, and the ways in which math teachers can use the knowledge and experience of their students' families to enrich their teaching. The discussion of mathematics education as a political process and of how issues of power are manifested inside and outside of the mathematics classroom is informative and discerning. The analyses of the relationship between identities, power, culture, and math education makes this book unique and especially welcomed. The discussion of the need to uncover the cultural assumptions of our pedagogical practices and their relationship to maintaining and reinforcing the existing power arrangements within schools and society is refreshing.

The thoughtful chapters in this book go beyond describing and analyzing the problems of teaching mathematics to diverse groups of students. It provides visionary, trenchant, and practical guidelines that can guide action and increase equity in mathematical learning for all students. I am pleased to welcome this incisive, well-researched, and significant book to the *Multicultural Education Series*.

James A. Banks
Series Editor

REFERENCES

Anyon, J. (2005). *Racial possibilities: Public policy, urban education, and a new social movement*. New York: Routledge.

Banks, J. A. (2004). Multicultural education: Historical development, dimensions, and practice. In J. A. Banks & C. A. M. Banks (Eds.), *Handbook of research on multicultural education* (2nd ed., pp. 3–29). San Francisco: Jossey-Bass.

Banks, J. A., & Banks, C. A. M. (Eds.). (2004). *Handbook of research on multicultural education* (2nd ed.). San Francisco: Jossey-Bass.

California State Department of Education. (2006). Public school summary statistics 2003–04. Retrieved April 14, 2006, from http://www.cde.ca.gov/ds/sd/cb/sums03.asp

Eck, D. L. (2001). *A new religious America: How a "Christian country" has become the world's most religiously diverse nation*. New York: HarperSanFrancisco.

El Nasser, H. (2004, March 18). Census projects growing diversity: By 2050: Population burst, societal shifts. *USA Today*, p. 1A.

Geertz, C. (1983). *Local knowledge: Further essays in interpretive anthropology*. New York: Basic Books.

Martin, P., & Midgley, E. (1999). Immigration to the United States. *Population Bulletin*, 54(2), pp. 1–44. Washington, D.C.: Population Reference Bureau.

Martinez, G. M., & Curry, A. E. (1999, September). *Current population reports: School enrollment, social and economic characteristics of students* (update). Washington, D.C.: U.S. Census Bureau.

National Center for Education Statistics (U.S. Department of Education). (2005). *The condition of education 2005*. (NCES 2005-094). Washington, D.C.: U.S. Government Printing Office.

Riche, M. F. (2000). America's diversity and growth: Signposts for the 21st century. *Population Bulletin*, 55(2), pp. 1–43. Washington, D.C.: Population Reference Bureau.

Sleeter, C. E. (2005). *Un-Standardizing curriculum: Multicultural teaching in the standards-based classroom*. New York: Teachers College Press.

United States Census Bureau. (2000). *Statistical abstract of the United States* (120th edition). Washington, D.C.: U.S. Government Printing Office.

United States Department of Homeland Security. (2006). *Yearbook of immigration statistics: 2004*. Washington, D.C.: U.S. Department of Homeland Security, Office of Immigration Statistics.

Preface

This book grew out of a set of meetings in 2001 that brought together scholars to focus on issues of culture and mathematics achievement. These meetings included not only scholars in mathematics education, but also people who studied culture and race in other academic domains, and in education more broadly. We discovered early on that while we shared a common set of concerns, we frequently had difficulty in understanding one another, for our terms and constructs were often quite different. As the meetings evolved, we came to realize that sociocultural theory (including discussions of relationships, memberships in communities of practice, and issues of identity) provided us not only with a common language, but also with a tool kit of ideas that potentially offered important insights into long-standing equity and diversity issues in mathematics education. These ideas represented a departure from the purely cognitive approach that many in mathematics education were using at that time, and caused a number of participants to think about our work in new ways.

A special issue of the journal *Mathematical Thinking and Learning* (2002), also edited by Nasir and Cobb, was the first product of these meetings, and the articles in that special issue became the first drafts for six of the chapters in this volume. Additional chapters were solicited from leading scholars doing cutting-edge theoretical and pedagogical work on equity and mathematics education, and the result is the current 11 chapters.

As use of sociocultural theory sometimes appears to be driven primarily by ideological commitment, it is important to stress that all the chapter authors take care to ensure that the ideas they discuss actually do useful work in supporting equity in students' mathematical learning. This volume is unique in providing extensive theoretical treatments of culture, race, and diversity in mathematics education and in illustrating the kinds of practices that these theoretical accounts might lead us to designing, to directly address and challenge inequity in mathematics classrooms. The chapters in this volume enable us to understand the multiple ways in which race and culture interact to influence the learning opportunities that different groups of students are afforded in the mathematics classroom. Collectively, the chapters reframe the "problem" of unequal achievement and course-taking by race and gender in mathematics, and thus what we as a field have to offer as potential solutions.

We are grateful to the National Science Foundation for supporting the meetings that led to this book, under grant number REC 9902982. We are also grateful to Carol Lee and Lynn Liao Hodge for serving as co–principal investigators on the grant and for playing pivotal roles in organizing these meetings. In addition, we acknowledge the important contributions of the participants in these meetings, among them Michael Apple, David Bloome, Wanda Chambers, Marta Civil, Jose Luis Cortina, Chrystal Dean, David Dennis, Ellice Forman, Michele Foster, Juan Guerra, Kris Gutierrez, Paula Hooper, Francis Jackson, Ido Jamar, Gloria Ladson-Billings, Jacqueline Leonard, Jerry Lipka, Kay McClain, Kimya Moyo, Marcela Perlwitz, and Erna Yackel. We would be remiss if we failed to acknowledge our colleagues and graduate students at Stanford and Vanderbilt who have helped shape many of the ideas addressed in this book (Michael Heimlich, Victoria Hand, Tesha Sengutpa, Nikki Cleare, Jo Boaler, Grace Atukpawu, Jim Greeno, Bryan Brown, Aisha Lowe, Arnetha Ball, Alfredo Artiles, Rich Milner, Lucius Outlaw, Jana Visnovska, and Qing Zhao); those who graciously agreed to review drafts of the chapters; the series editor, Jim Banks; editorial staff at Teachers College Press Brian Ellerbeck and Adee Braun; and, last but not least, our families (for Nailah: my husband, Baayan, and my children, Leya, Ase, Sajdah, and Ajeyei; for Paul: my wife, Jenny).

Introduction

NA'ILAH SUAD NASIR & PAUL COBB

The chapters in this book are all concerned with how issues of diversity and equity play out in the mathematics classroom. This focus is motivated in large part by analyses of school achievement, course-taking patterns, and standardized-test data that reveal prevalent patterns of inequity in students' access to significant mathematical ideas. The marginal performance in mathematics of minority students; language-minority students; poor students; and, to some extent, girls has led a number of scholars to raise concerns about the opportunities for members of these groups to compete in an increasingly technological world (Oakes, 1990). These achievement patterns are, however, not a recent phenomenon. Differences in mathematics achievement have remained relatively stable in the 20 years since inequitable achievement patterns first became the focus of public debate in the United States (Lockheed, Thorpe, Brooks-Gunn, Casserly, & McAloon, 1985; Reyes & Stanic, 1988; Secada, 1992).

Ladson-Billings (1997) captures the general viewpoint reflected in this book when she observes that much of the literature on equity in mathematics education and related fields falls short by summarizing achievement gaps and proposing solutions without first developing a conceptual grasp of the underlying problems and issues. As she observes, research has frequently focused on the design and assessment of instructional materials and strategies designed to help remedy achievement gaps (e.g., Masingila & King, 1997; Peressini, 1997; Silver, Smith, & Nelson, 1995; Sleeter, 1997; Strutchens, Thomas, & Perkins, 1997). These explorations of issues of equity from a variety of methodological and theoretical perspectives are interesting and informative, and we can learn much from them. However, well-intentioned investigations of this type typically propose solutions to what Secada (1995) referred to derisively as "the equity problem" without first attempting to understand the underlying sources of inequities. On one level, the problem is indeed simple: Poor and minority students are not doing as well as we would like in mathematics. But on another level, we know very little about how the multiple dimensions of race, class, culture, language, power, and knowledge play out in mathematics classrooms to generate inequities. Only a relatively small number of studies in mathematics education have responded to widespread inequities by seeking to explain the patterns of success and failure in mathematics of poor and minority students (e.g., Apple, 1995a; Lubienski, 1997; Walker & McCoy, 1997). The contributors to this book all seek to provide a grounding for interventions through understanding the processes by which inequities in students' access to significant mathematical ideas continue to be regenerated.

In foregrounding issues of race, class, culture, power, and knowledge as they relate to mathematics learning, the chapter authors make explicit the inherently political nature of all research (and indeed teaching) in mathematics education (see Mellin-Olsen, 1987; Skovsmose, 1994). Moses, Kamii, Swap, and Howard (1989) bring this political dimension to the fore when they when they note:

> At the heart of math-science education issues . . . is a basic political question: If the current technological revolution demands new standards of mathematics and science literacy, will all citizens be given equal access to the new skills, or will some be left behind, denied participation in the unfolding economic and political arena? (p. 423)

In posing this question, Moses and colleagues ask us to confront the gatekeeping role of school mathematics in delimiting some students' but not others' *access* to future educational and economic opportunities. In everyday discourse, the notion of access is closely related to that of admittance, in the sense of gaining access or being admitted to a particular activity or event. To avoid misinterpretation, it is therefore important to stress that access, as the chapter authors use the term, is not restricted to whether students are admitted to key gatekeeping mathematics courses, but also concerns the content of those courses as it is actually realized in the classroom and experienced by students. The authors would, for example, question whether mathematics instruction is equitable if certain groups of students but not others construe the instructional context as one that required them to assimilate mainstream beliefs and values at the expense of their cultural identities. This perceived requirement of assimilation to the mainstream serves to delimit certain groups of students' access to the unfolding economic and political arena referred to by Gibson (1988) and Moses and colleagues (1989). The contributors to this volume conceptualize access in this broad sense even as they recognize the need for students to develop a range of mathematical competencies that enable them to participate in what Delpit (1995) terms the culture of power.

It is important to note that research in mathematics education is also political in a further sense, one that concerns the process by which the field establishes what is central and what is peripheral. Secada (1995) draws on his experiences in the mathematics education research community to assert that research on equity has been marginalized. His concern is not merely that, with the possible exception of gender, research on equity is underrepresented in the mathematics education literature (cf. Lubienski, 2002). He also seeks to clarify why the limited number of studies with an equity focus have, for the most part, been constituted as peripheral to the field. In describing this process of marginalization, Secada notes that mathematics education has traditionally appropriated theoretical constructs from psychology. His basic claim is that research that is not cast in what he terms the dominant psychological "Discourse" is viewed as marginal to the concerns of the field. Analyses that focus on issues such as race, class, culture, power, and identity therefore come to be seen as peripheral because they necessarily violate the norms of this dominant Discourse.

We are more hopeful than Secada about the possibility that research on equity might come to be seen as central to the field. Our optimism stems from developments that have occurred in the years since Secada first presented his analysis. Although it is true that mathematics education has traditionally looked to psychology for theoretical insight, perspectives that are rooted in other disciplines have come to be seen as increasingly legitimate in recent years (cf. De Corte, Greer, & Verschaffel, 1996). Foremost among these are perspectives, such as situated cognition and distributed intelligence, that employ constructs derived from sociocultural theory. This is encouraging from our point of view given that the chapter authors draw on sociocultural theory and on situated and distributed approaches to develop theoretical tools. We therefore have some confidence that their work might be viewed as relevant to the central concerns of the mathematics education research community.

The contributors' use of sociocultural constructs is both reasonable and potentially productive in light of the mounting evidence that the culturally based interpretations that students bring to the mathematics classroom can profoundly influence both how they learn and indeed what they define as learning (Abreu, 2000; Eisenhart, 2001). These approaches rest on the idea that students construct various forms of mathematical knowledge as they participate in socially and culturally organized activities in a range of settings, including the mathematics classroom. These activities are socially and culturally organized in that they involve values, norms, goals, artifacts, and conventions. In taking this stance, the authors here focus both on the systems of schooling in which students participate and on the diversity in that participation. Their analyses therefore implicate the organization of students' mathematics education in the production of success and failure (Martin, 2000). In addition, most of the contributors focus on inequitable social structures, the relationships of power, identity, and language, as they relate to mathematics learning and teaching. These issues are often not addressed in the mathematics education literature on equity and diversity but prove to be critical to the experiences of underserved students. As Lee (1995) and Gutiérrez at al. (1999) observe, these issues are also underrepresented in the sociocultural literature. Of necessity, the contributors therefore adapt constructs from sociocultural and related perspectives in order to make them appropriate to the problems of mathematics education.

As a group, the eleven chapters in this book have the potential to help us reframe issues of equity in mathematics education and to enrich our understandings of the process by which "diverse" learners experience mathematics education. Several of the chapters are theoretical in orientation and offer insights into how we might develop a sociocultural approach to equity in math education. Others rely on close analyses of mathematical learning in and out of the classroom to understand the construction of "equity" at level of classroom social interactions. Chapters 1 and 2, by Lubienski and Boaler, respectively, offer perspectives on current treatments of equity in the mathematics education literature and point to both the need for and the promise of new theoretical approaches. In her chapter, Lubienski summarizes and critiques current treatments of equity and its relation to mathematics reform, arguing for the use of sociocultural approaches that can uncover ways in which cultural issues relate to mathematics learning. Boaler, for her part, focuses specifically on research on gender and mathematics learning in order to tease out lessons for research on equity more generally. In doing so, she takes issue with traditional conceptions of equity and argues that researchers should be careful about locating conceptions of inequality in individuals or groups without exploring the broader environments within which people learn.

In Chapter 3, Gutiérrez questions not only the explanatory power of several prevalent accounts of equity, but also the very definitions of equity that underpin these accounts. She elaborates a new definition of equity that foregrounds issues of social justice both by considering what equity might look like locally and by articulating the implications of her view for the nature of the mathematics that students might learn. Gutstein, in Chapter 4, also isolates unjust social structures as a primary source of inequities in the mathematics education of students of color and low-income students. He draws on his efforts to foster a problem-posing environment in his middle school classroom to illustrate what teaching mathematics for social justice might mean in both theory and practice. In Chapter 5, Davis, West, Greeno, Gresalfi, Martin, Moses, and Currell also explore the elements of effective mathematics teaching for social justice, in their analysis of Algebra Project classrooms. They use different lenses to examined social interactions in Algebra Project classrooms, focusing on both the learning of mathematical content and on how students are positioned in relation to their mathematics learning.

Moschkovich, in Chapter 6, highlights the importance of building on students' cultural and linguistic knowledge in her analysis of mathematics learning in bilingual classrooms. In doing so, she develops a model that incorporates situated and sociocultural perspectives of mathematics learning and mathematical communication. In the viewpoint that she presents, mathematics learning is characterized as a process of becoming better able to use multiple resources for participation in mathematical discussions. Civil extends this focus on students' cultural and linguistic resources in Chapter 7 by reflecting on her work in low-income, mostly Latino communities over more than 10 years. Her goal is to clarify the challenges that arise for both teachers and researchers as they attempt to pursue mathematical agendas by capitalizing on the knowledge and experiences of students and their families. In Chapter 8, Abreu and Cline further contribute to this line of research that focuses on students' home communities. They do so by clarifying that the issue at hand is not merely one of cultural differences between home and school, but also involves status and privileging inherent in broader social structures. In particular, they demonstrate that the relative value attributed to different forms of mathematical reasoning in school typically reflects the position that the groups with whom those forms of reasoning are associated occupy within hierarchical social structures. They conclude, on the basis of their analysis, that it is not possible to reduce inequities in students' access to significant mathematical ideas unless active steps are taken to combat this differential treatment of out-of-school mathematical practices.

In Chapter 9, Nasir argues for the utility of focusing on students' co-developing goals and identities in order to understand the nature of their learning as it is situated in cultural activity. She grounds her perspective by analyzing students' mathematical learning as they come to participate in the practice of basketball in increasingly substantial ways in inner-city schools. Martin also employs the construct of identity as, in Chapter 10, he focuses on two realms of experience: being African American and becoming a doer of mathematics. His investigation of possible tensions between these two realms serves to situate the doing of mathematics within the larger context of being African American while simultaneously emphasizing that one does not shed his or her identity as an African American even in the relatively narrow context of doing mathematics. Finally, in Chapter 11, Cobb and Hodge propose an interpretive scheme for analyzing the identities that students develop in mathematics classrooms and that can inform instructional design and teaching. In doing so, Cobb and Hodge develop a perspective that frames issues of equity in terms of relations between communities of practice while simultaneously attending to how issues of power and authority shape mathematics learning as it occurs in the classroom.

Although the chapters vary both in specific focus and theoretical perspective, several overarching themes emerge as central. The contributors view equity as situated and relational and as being informed both by local schooling practices and by practices and ideologies that transcend school. The contributors also share a concern with mathematics education as a political process—they explore how issues of power play out both inside and outside math classrooms. In conceptualizing equity in this way, the authors grapple with the challenge of simultaneously bringing both issues of classroom interaction and broader sociopolitical structures to the fore. The general approach they take of employing the concepts of identity and Discourse as theoretical tools enables them to embed social, cultural, and political realities in daily practices both in and out of school.

EQUITY AS SITUATED AND RELATIONAL

One of the core themes that runs through the majority of the chapters in this volume is the reframing of what constitutes "equity" and "diversity." The authors move the discussion of equity beyond treatments limited to achievement scores and course-taking patterns among racial groups, women, and language minorities by considering the social and cultural processes by which equity (or the lack thereof) is defined, created, and maintained. For instance, Cobb and Hodge argue that equity does not merely involve helping minority students reach higher standards set by the mainstream, but is instead a matter of understanding diversity as a relation between the community of practice established in the math classroom and the other communities of practice of which a student is a part. Similarly, Nasir views equity as being constructed as students are afforded access to identities within particular cultural practices. Abreu and Cline, for their part, argue that an important focus is how the cultural practices of home and school are differentially valued, and these differences are rooted in the relative positions of groups in societies. The authors of these three chapters view equity as a situated process rather than a static outcome— as an artifact of cultural settings and the relations between them, rather than a property of individuals.

The idea that equity and diversity are an attribute neither of individual students nor of particular racial groups, women, or language-minority students is also prominent in the chapters by Gutiérrez, Davis et al., Boaler, and Lubienski. Gutiérrez supports the idea that "equity" and "inequity" are the product of a relation between people, mathematics, and global issues of power and social structure. Similarly, Davis et al. view equity as a social issue and see access to mathematics as essential to dealing with issues of equity on a societal level. Boaler and Lubienski argue for a sociocultural perspective that views equity as an interaction between people and cultural contexts, critiquing prior research on social class (Lubienski) and gender (Boaler) that has located the source of inequity within students. Additionally, Moschkovich focuses on the nature of mathematical communication to address how issues of language, both national and social (Bakhtin, 1981), are relevant to access and equity in bilingual classrooms.

Power and Authority in Math Classrooms

The view of equity as situated in social contexts and as involving relations between various communities of practice leads to a focus on how broader issues of power and authority are implicated in the regeneration of inequities. This theme plays out in almost all the chapters at varying levels of explicitness. Lubienski questions the relation of power implicit in the assumption that what is good for some students is good for all students, especially given her recent data on the differential effects of reform teaching in different communities. Cobb and Hodge as well as Abreu and Cline contend that power and access to the cultural capital of the mathe-

matics classroom play a significant part both in whose learning is valued as legiti-
mately mathematical and in how students come to see themselves as mathematical thinkers and as members of mathematics communities. Gutstein elaborates these
themes by describing a pedagogy of questioning that constitutes one way to work
toward a redistribution of power and authority. As he clarifies, students are encouraged to challenge authority and to question existing power relations, using
mathematics as a tool to do so.

This concern with authority, as it is distributed within cultural practices, also
underlies Nasir's chapter. She describes successful mathematics learning outside
school and highlights the importance of access to identities for students as doers
and learners of mathematics, and the increased levels of authority such learners
take for their own learning. In her chapter, Gutiérrez expresses a concern not only
with how culture, race, language, and gender come to affect classroom learning,
but also with how an equity approach to mathematics education can have implications more broadly in students' lives and in society. Martin as well as Davis and
colleagues share this concern for the relation between mathematics learning and
the regeneration of power and authority more broadly.

Equity as Informed by Practices and Ideology That Both Transcend and Are Reconstructed Within School

The challenge of finding a point of balance in the tension between equity as situated and relational, on the one hand, and equity as involving global issues of power
and race, on the other, is a delicate matter. For the chapter authors, understanding
equity requires a focus both on inequitable social structures and the ideologies they
give rise to, and on how such realities play out in day-to-day activity in classrooms
and other local settings.

Researchers who focus on culture and learning at the micro level of social
interaction typically identify cultural differences between teachers and students as
a primary source of inequities. These analyses tend to point out how children of
racial-, ethnic-, and linguistic-minority cultures; poor students; and girls can have
experiences in classrooms that somehow clash with their home cultures. Boaler,
Lubienski, Martin, and Moschovich all appropriate aspects of cultural-difference
models as a way to talk about inequity in many math classrooms. But their analyses do not end there. By employing concepts from sociology, linguistics, anthropology, and mathematics education, these authors as well as Martin, Cobb and
Hodge, and Davis and colleagues argue that social contexts are far from neutral
and have to be related to broader social class, gender, and racial dynamics in society. As they demonstrate, these "differences" have real-world consequences for
some students in terms of both future access and their developing sense of themselves. For instance, the authors in this volume draw on social-reproduction theory
and resistance theory to explore how cultural values, ideology, and practices get
played out in the context of mathematics instruction in ways that can have serious

implications for achievement and understanding. In doing so, however, the authors attribute agency to students as they construct identities that afford or delimit access to particular mathematical ways of knowing in particular educational settings. Additionally, Abreu and Cline as well as Civil tie these mathematical ways of knowing to experiences across home and school contexts, and Civil explores the pedagogical power of these home-school connections as a resource that can be used to support mathematics learning.

IDENTITIES AND DISCOURSES

In their attempts to understand the link between broad societal structures and equity at the micro level of classroom interaction, the authors have turned to the constructs of Discourse and identity as useful for exploring the local production of culture and equity in classrooms. The concern with classroom talk appears centrally in the work of Moschkovich, who illustrates how Discourse offers a way to capture both the linguistic processes in the bilingual classroom and the social, cultural, and political implications of that language use. Such a perspective expands our view of what counts as mathematical competence and avoids deficiency model traps, focusing instead on the resources that bilingual students use to communicate mathematically. Cobb and Hodge also draw on Discourse as the site of local production of culture, achievement, and equity. This use of Discourse incorporates a concern for not only language in a literal sense, but also for the cultural values and norms that the use of language entails, thereby grounding a focus on broad issues of language and power squarely in the everyday practices of mathematics classrooms.

As we have indicated, the chapter authors also explore the relations between identity on the one hand and culture, power, and mathematics learning on the other. In doing so, most of the authors depart from a traditional psychological perspective on identity and turn instead to theorists such as Wenger (1998) to conceptualize identity as fundamentally tied to both cultural practices and the ideologies inherent in them. From this perspective, equity depends in part on how students' identities as learners are enabled as they participate in classroom mathematical practices (through social interaction and participation structures) vis-à-vis their identities as "doers" of other practices. This is evident in the chapter by Abreu and Cline. Also along these lines, both Martin and Nasir argue that identity plays a significant role in learning and examine the relation between learning and identity as one potentially fruitful approach for understanding culture, diversity, and mathematics learning.

In sum, the contributors to this volume take the social and cultural worlds in which mathematics is learned to be central to our understandings of the dynamics of equity. To that end, constructs from multiple fields that include sociology, anthropology, linguistics, and education are employed. It should be clear that the issues raised in the chapters do not in any way constitute the final word on diversity and equity as they play out in mathematics classrooms. However, it is our sincere hope that our understandings of equity, diversity, and mathematical learning continue to evolve and that this volume will serve to spark thought, controversy, debate, and further research on this critically important topic.

NOTE

The development of the chapters for this book was supported by the National Science Foundation under Grant No. 9902982. The views expressed by the authors do not necessarily reflect the position of the foundation.

1

Research, Reform, and Equity in U.S. Mathematics Education

SARAH THEULE LUBIENSKI

In this chapter I discuss research in relation to two issues of particular importance at this time in mathematics education: equity and reform. I argue that, although researchers and reformers give attention to equity, such work tends to ignore relevant social and cultural issues. This limited focus affects ways in which current reforms have been conceptualized and studied. I begin the chapter by summarizing, in broad strokes, the attention given to equity in recent mainstream mathematics education research. I then discuss the implications of this limited research base for current mathematics education reforms in the United States. Drawing on a study of social-class differences in students' experiences in one reform-oriented classroom, I go on to consider both the difficulties and the potential contributions of sociocultural approaches to research on equity in mathematics education.

A BIRD'S-EYE VIEW OF EQUITY-RELATED RESEARCH: THE MAINSTREAM, THE MARGINALIZED, AND THE MISSING

Just a few decades ago, equity-related research in mathematics education was extremely scarce. For example, Fennema and Hart (1994) report that virtually no mathematics education research on gender was published before 1974. Since that time, gender research has gained acceptance and respect in mathematics education research communities in the United States and elsewhere. Evidence of this acceptance is provided by Lubienski and Bowen's (2000) survey of 3,011 mathematics education research articles. This survey encompassed articles published in 48 educational research journals between 1982 and 1998.[1] Of the 3,011 articles surveyed, 323 (more than 10%) pertained to gender.

Many researchers reasonably caution that gender needs continued attention, and perhaps a different type of attention from what it has received thus far. For example, some authors argue that research on gender must give more focus to earlier grades (Fennema, Carpenter, Jacobs, Franke, & Levi, 1998), should avoid viewing girls from deficit perspectives (Boaler, 1997b; 2002c; Rogers & Kaiser, 1995; Walkerdine, 1998a), and requires even further acceptance among some mathematics education research communities (e.g., the International Group for the Psychology of Mathematics Education; see Leder, 2001). Despite these valid concerns, gender-related research appears to have been successful in terms of gaining attention and respect from many mathematics education researchers.

In spite of the apparent successes of gender-related research, scholars continue to raise concerns about the lack of attention given to other equity issues in mathematics education. Reyes and Stanic (1988) and Secada (1992) assert that mathematics education researchers have virtually ignored issues of poverty and social class. Campbell (1991) notes that researchers rarely consider interactions between gender, ethnicity, and social class. Additionally, Tate (1997) argues that mathematics education research has tended to be narrowly focused, drawing primarily on the disciplines of mathematics and psychology—an orientation that Jacob (1998) describes as "cognition without context or culture" (p. 23).

Lubienski and Bowen's (2000) "bird's-eye" review of mathematics education research articles supports these claims. Of the 3,011 articles surveyed, more than 400 pertained to gender, ethnicity, *or* socioeconomic class. In contrast to the 323 articles on gender, only 112 discussed ethnicity, and 52 discussed class. Only 3 articles considered ethnicity, class, and gender together. Although fewer than half of the 3,011 articles were from journals not specific to mathematics education, more than two thirds of the equity-related articles appeared in those journals. Additionally, the percentage of mathematics education articles relating to gender was roughly double the gender-related percentage for the entire ERIC database; however, the situation was reversed for ethnicity and class. The relative lack of attention to ethnicity and class is particularly striking in light of the fact that U.S. mathematics achievement gaps related to race and socioeconomic status (SES) are roughly 10 times the size of gender gaps (Lubienski, McGraw, & Strutchens, 2004).

The articles were also categorized according to a variety of general topics, again based on the articles' descriptors. This analysis revealed that almost half (49%) of the 3,011 articles pertained to cognition, but only about 25% of ethnicity-, class-, and gender-related articles pertained to cognition. In contrast, although fewer than one fourth of the 3,011 articles related to achievement outcomes, more than two thirds of the articles on ethnicity or class related to achievement outcomes. Overall, relatively little attention (about 4%) was given to educational environments and students' roles in classrooms.

These findings suggest that mainstream mathematics education research gives considerable, yet spotty, attention to equity issues. Although these trends might be changing, the results support claims by Tate (1997) and Jacob (1998) about mathematics education research focusing primarily on cognition with little attention to social or cultural issues. In the following section I discuss the implications of this limited research base in the context of current mathematics education reforms as promoted by the National Council of Teachers of Mathematics (NCTM).

MATHEMATICS EDUCATION REFORMS AND EQUITY

Since 1989, NCTM has been working toward the goal of "mathematical power for all students," including those students previously underrepresented in mathematics-based careers (NCTM, 1989, 1991, 1995, 2000). Despite this worthy goal, NCTM's original *Standards* documents (1989, 1991) were criticized for merely mentioning equity and giving the impression that the needs of all students would be satisfied through high expectations and a single pedagogy (e.g., Meyer, 1991; Secada, 1991a; Stanic, 1991).

The newest *Standards* document (NCTM, 2000) gives greater prominence to equity. For example, the current document names equity as one of its guiding principles and states, "Equity does not mean that every student should receive identical instruction; instead, it demands that reasonable and appropriate accommodations be made as needed to promote access and attainment for all students" (p. 12). NCTM (2000) also specifically notes that teachers need to understand and attend to students' cultural differences.

However, NCTM is calling for a particular type of classroom environment, and any change in classroom culture could privilege those possessing "cultural capital" (Bourdieu, 1973, p. 71) in new, unanticipated ways. It might seem reasonable to think that open discussions, in which a variety of methods and ideas are considered, and open-ended problems that can be solved in a variety of ways (including drawing from one's own experiences), would communicate to all students that their ways of thinking and communicating are valued. But could the very nature of a classroom culture that expects students to share, puzzle over, and judge opposing ideas conflict with the beliefs or preferred practices of some groups of students? Might some students enter the mathematics classroom better positioned than others to learn in the ways envisioned in the *Standards*? Amid the movement to embrace and implement the *Standards*, the U.S. mathematics education community has given little attention to such questions. Instead, the struggles encountered by teachers attempting to implement the *Standards* with diverse students tend to be attributed to teachers' low expectations of students, lack of pedagogical skill or mathematical knowledge, or poor administrative support. The complexities of social class, ethnicity, and gender, as they combine to shape classroom processes, tend to be overlooked.

A sociocultural approach to studying mathematics instruction can help make the necessary links between micro- and macro-level issues, giving attention to both classroom practices and their relation to the beliefs and practices of various groups in society (Cobb & Yackel, 1996; De Abreu, 2000; Forman, 2003).[2] Although examinations of social and cultural components of learning are central to most sociocultural studies in education, such studies vary widely, with many giving no attention to issues of power and equity (Nasir & Cobb, 2002). However, a critical sociocultural lens in mathematics classrooms—one that considers instructional practices in relation to the beliefs and practices of both privileged and marginalized societal groups—can uncover culturally laden instructional methods that can help or hinder underserved students' mathematics learning.

DIFFICULTIES OF SOCIOCULTURAL STUDIES OF EQUITY IN MATHEMATICS CLASSROOMS

There are several obstacles facing any researcher who wishes to examine equity issues in mathematics education through a sociocultural lens. This work is situated at the intersection of several areas of inquiry, including those involving culture and power, ethnicity and social class, and mathematics teaching and learning (see Gutiérrez, this volume; Nasir, this volume). This complexity poses two major difficulties.

First, because of the specialized nature of academic fields, most mathematics education researchers tend to be unfamiliar with current research and theories relating to culture and power. A researcher wishing to conduct sociocultural studies of mathematics classrooms needs to be grounded not only in mathematics education research, but also in research from other relevant fields, such as anthropology and sociology. This is particularly difficult because the perspectives guiding studies of culture in these fields have been both highly contested and shifting.

Roughly a century ago, scholars embraced the concept of *culture* as a preferable alternative to the idea that racial differences were biological and fixed. González (1999) writes, "The idea that something external to the human organism, something called 'culture,' could contribute to perceived human diversity was at the time a pivotal shift in paradigm" (p. 431). However, a corresponding shift occurred, from genetic deficit theory to cultural deficit theory, both of which attribute the perpetuation of unequal academic and occupational outcomes to the "deficiencies" of disadvantaged groups. In reaction against cultural-deficit theory, scholars promoted a "cultural difference" model in which the language and practices of underserved students and their schools were viewed as simply "mismatched," and educators were called upon to bridge the gap.

However, cultural-difference theory has been critiqued in recent years for two reasons. First, the focus on classroom-level interactions tends to ignore larger, structural, power-related issues underlying inequities. Second, efforts to develop culturally responsive pedagogies run the risk of "essentializing," or portraying people in terms of fixed cultural traits instilled by a single cultural reference group (González, 1999). Conceptions of culture have evolved to include a greater recognition of people's multiple group memberships, the permeability of boundaries separating groups, and the interactive construction of languages and practices (as opposed to inherited, fixed "cultural norms"). Anthropologists, sociologists, and linguists continue to debate the extent to which the concept of culture itself is a helpful or harmful construct (see, e.g., González, 1999; Mannheim & Tedlock, 1995).

These shifts in theories of culture make discussion of group differences prone to accusations of essentialization and deficit views. Although discussion of students' culture-based strengths is often welcomed, researchers risk criticism when identifying any struggle a group of students might have with particular classroom norms. This is particularly true in the case of discussions of social class, which is itself a hotly debated construct. Although other dimensions of diversity, such as differing ethnic traditions, can be viewed in strictly positive terms, it is hard to deny the existence of negative aspects of large disparities of wealth and power, particularly for those who lack both (this is argued more fully in Lubienski, 2003).

Amid these foreign, shifting sands, it is easy to see why mathematics education researchers avoid discussing culture and power in relation to student learning. Additionally, the current climate of reform poses a second major difficulty. Many mathematics educators fervently espouse constructivist theories of learning and equate them with a particular method of teaching (Cobb, 1994). They consider all other teaching methods "nonconstructivist" and view them in opposition to "good teaching." Given this widely accepted dichotomy, when an author publishes findings that raise questions about any single aspect of "good teaching," some readers are quick to conclude that the author is promoting "bad teaching" (i.e., rote drill and practice) as the solution.

Having recently entered this rocky research terrain, I have experienced each of these difficulties firsthand. I struggled to become familiar with a variety of literatures and continue to do so. I faced criticism, much of it valid, from those who disagreed with my treatment of social class, culture, and reform-oriented teaching. But I am convinced that researchers must be willing to tread this terrain in order to better understand and address the enormous gaps between the mathematics achievement of White, middle-class students and their less-advantaged peers.

In order to illustrate both the potential benefits and difficulties of research on sociocultural factors in relation to mathematics classroom processes, I draw from a study I conducted on social class and gender in one *Standards*-based classroom. As the details of this study are reported elsewhere (Lubienski, 2000a; 2000b) I will summarize them only briefly here. I begin by describing several findings from the study in order to highlight the potential importance of this line of research. I then discuss some of the difficulties of conducting research of this type.

ONE EXAMPLE: A STUDY OF SOCIAL CLASS, GENDER, AND MATHEMATICS TEACHING AND LEARNING

For 3 years, I participated in the development of a National Science Foundation–funded middle school mathematics curriculum designed to implement the NCTM *Standards*. I helped write and pilot drafts of the materials in various classrooms. Although I was enthusiastic about the curriculum's goals and its impact on many students, I became concerned about disparities between the reform rhetoric and some students' reactions to the curriculum and my pedagogy. Having come from a working-class background and having experienced the socioeconomic mobility that high mathematics achievement can provide, I was particularly concerned about issues of socioeconomic equity in mathematics education.

In my 3rd year with this project, I worked as a teacher-researcher, piloting draft materials throughout the school year in one socioeconomically diverse (yet primarily Caucasian) seventh-grade classroom. In this qualitative study, I compared lower- and higher-SES students' experiences with many different aspects of instruction. Although there clearly was much diversity within each SES group, I identified some patterns that aligned consistently with SES.

I had assumed that I would find SES differences in parental support and familiarity with the contexts used in the problems. But this did not prove to be the case. Instead, I found SES differences in students' experiences with whole-class discussions and open-ended mathematics problems, both of which were central to the pedagogy and curriculum. Here I briefly describe the differences I found, giving particular focus to the experiences of the six girls I studied most closely.[3]

Whole-Class Discussions

My mathematics lessons followed a "launch-explore-summarize" structure, in which I introduced a problem from the curriculum, students worked on the problem in groups, and then we had a summarizing discussion in which I intended to "pull out" and highlight key mathematical ideas. As the teacher, I guided our whole-class conversations through questioning, occasionally inserting necessary information.

The lower- and higher-SES students seemed to view the purpose of these discussions differently. Whereas most higher-SES students said that discussions exposed them to different mathematical ideas, and that part of their role was to analyze those ideas, most lower-SES students talked about their role in discussions as obtaining or giving right answers. This distinction was strong in the multiple forms of data (three interviews, several surveys) gathered from students and is exemplified by the six girls' responses to the final survey given.

LOWER SES:

Rose: Yes, if I know what I'm talking about. But if I'm confused I just listen.
Sue: Sometimes—only if I know I've got the right answer.
Dawn: No, because I don't like to be wrong in front of a whole group.

HIGHER SES:

Guinevere: Yes, because I need to get my point across.
Samantha: Yes, because I want other people to understand my ideas. I like arguing.
Rebecca: Yes, because I do.

Differences in the two groups of students' conceptions of their own and the teacher's role seemed to relate, in part, to differences in their confidence in both contributing to, and analyzing, the ideas shared in our discussions. Rose and Sue said they only contributed to discussions if they were confident in what they had to say. Dawn said she was so afraid of being wrong that she did not participate. These patterns were consistent with those from the larger pool of 20 participating students. The higher-SES students rarely voiced the fear of being wrong.

There are undoubtedly a variety of factors that affected these seventh graders' confidence. One factor for Sue was the boys' treatment of her both inside and outside our mathematics class. When Sue was brave enough to ask questions during whole-class discussions, some of the boys would call her a "dumb blonde" in the hallway after class. Although I did my best to create a culture of "niceness" during class, I was not able to restrict ways in which sexism, classism, and other factors shaped students' experiences outside the classroom.[4]

The issue of confidence recurred in the data in relation not only to how students participated, but also in their own perceived ability to make sense of discussions. More lower-SES students consistently said that having a variety of ideas proposed in discussions confused them. In general, the confusion centered around feeling unable to discern which of the various ideas proposed in a discussion were sensible, or as Dawn put it, "I get confused, 'cause you don't know if this is right or this is right 'cause they don't agree." Most lower-SES students said they preferred more teacher direction—they wished I would just "show how to do it" or "tell the answer." For example, Sue explained:

> I learn more from just the teacher, because when everyone is there [in whole-class discussions], they give their opinions and stuff, and it may not be right, and I mix those two up, and it just confuses me. . . . I understand more without all the people.

In contrast, more higher-SES students said they could sort out which ideas were sensible and which were not. Six of the seven students who consistently said that the discussions were helpful to them were higher SES. Rebecca's response was fairly typical of higher-SES students:

> *Sarah Theule Lubienski:* Did you learn from our [whole-class] discussions?
> *Rebecca:* Yeah, I think it helps me learn more things. Instead of just, like, doing it on your own, I can know everybody's opinions and take it into consideration.
> *STL:* Do you find it confusing when you have all those different opinions out?
> *Rebecca:* Not really . . . some of 'em aren't true, and some of 'em are, and I can figure out which ones are true and which ones aren't and stuff.

Given the confusion that some students expressed, I probed their understanding of what happened when people could not agree on an idea. Students' responses revealed differences in their view of my intentions as the teacher. For example, Dawn believed that I did not directly say which statements were right or wrong because I did not want to hurt students' feelings. Although Dawn was correct in that I struggled with how to help students feel comfortable about being wrong in front of the whole class, more higher-SES students, such as Guinevere, seemed to understand my primary intentions:

STL: How do we figure out which ways are right and wrong?
Guinevere: Hints.
STL: What do you mean?
Guinevere: You say, "Well, I don't know if that would work."
STL: Why do you think I do that?
Guinevere: So we don't learn the wrong thing and think it's right.
STL: Why don't I just tell you, "She's right and he's wrong"?
Guinevere: So we can figure it out.

Guinevere understood my intentions as a facilitator of mathematical discussion: I wanted to help students figure things out for themselves, but I did not want them to flounder too much and end up learning "the wrong thing." After several higher-SES but no lower-SES students spoke in interviews about my use of "hints" or "clues," I began to wonder if they way I inserted information into the discussions might have been more helpful to the higher-SES students, who seemed more attuned to my conception of, and rationale for, our roles.

Contextualized Problems

Thus far, I have focused on just one aspect of instruction in our classroom, the whole-class discussions. Another key aspect of instruction that lower- and higher-SES students encountered differently was the open, contextualized mathematics problems in the curriculum. In brief, more of the lower-SES students, especially the females, complained about feeling overwhelmingly frustrated by the ambiguity of the problems in our textbooks. Sue and Rose spoke fondly about previous years when they felt they understood their mathematics exercises and were able to get high scores. In contrast, Rebecca said, "Before, we just sat there with hundreds of problems on a page. . . . I wasn't good at it and I'm good at this." Guinevere explained that problem-centered mathematics was easier for her because "I guess our family's just—we are word-problem kind of people." On the various surveys and interviews, lower-SES students tended to say they became frustrated and gave up when stuck, whereas more of the higher-SES students said they "thought harder" about the problem or interpreted it in a sensible way and moved on.

Given these responses, I need to clarify that many problems in the curriculum engaged the lower-SES students, who tended to consider a complex variety of real-world variables in solving the problems. Yet in the process, these students sometimes approached the problems in ways that allowed them to miss the generalized mathematical point intended by me and by the text. The higher-SES students were more likely to approach the problems with an eye toward the intended, overarching mathematical ideas.

As an illustration, in a pizza-sharing problem designed to help students learn about fractions, Sue and other lower-SES students expressed concerns about who might arrive late to the restaurant and talked about sharing pizza in terms of getting "firsts" and "seconds." These students were sophisticated in their consideration of multiple, real-world variables but did not encounter the intended ideas about fractions on their solution paths.

Two Themes

Students' reactions to whole-class discussions and the open, contextualized mathematics problems point toward two themes. First, while the higher-SES students expressed confidence in their abilities to make sense of the mathematical discussions and problems, the lower-SES students tended to say they were "confused" by conflicting ideas in the discussions and the open nature of the problems—they desired more specific direction from the teacher and texts. More of the lower-SES students said they were unsure of what they were supposed to be learning, and many said they wished that I as the teacher would just tell them "the rules" so they could have more time to practice.

Second, whereas the higher-SES students seemed to approach the problems and discussions with an eye toward the overarching mathematical ideas I intended to teach, the lower-SES students more often became deeply engaged in the context of the problem at hand and missed the intended mathematical point. This difference could be seen in the way in which the higher-SES students talked about discussions as focusing on ideas, as opposed to the lower-SES students' focus on right or wrong answers to specific problems. This difference was even more apparent in students' approaches to some of the "real world" problems in the curriculum. Whereas more higher-SES students complained about seeing the same mathematical ideas repeatedly with different story lines attached, more lower-SES students complained that they did not know what mathematics they were supposed to be learning.

In general, the higher-SES students seemed to enter my classroom with more of the beliefs and discursive skills that were assumed and rewarded by the pedagogy and curriculum. More lower-SES students expressed confusion about our roles in this discussion-intensive, problem-centered classroom. Although some differences were likely attributable to students' prior mathematics achievement, this was not a complete explanation.

SEARCHING FOR EXPLANATIONS

To try to make sense of the data, I went to literature from other fields, such as sociology and anthropology. Some of this research is heavily contested and has been criticized for promoting overly simplistic dichotomies and stereotypes. Also, as stated earlier, discussing differences in class cultures puts one at risk of being considered classist or a deficit theorist in this time of emphasizing strictly positive aspects of diversity (Lubienski, 2003). However, avoiding the subject is detrimental for lower-class students, whose strengths and needs are then ignored. The distinctions to be discussed are, of course, generalizations, in that one cannot assume that any particular individual will exhibit the characteristics said to be associated with his or her class. All people have multiple group affiliations such as those relating to ethnicity, gender, and geographic region, as well as social class. As my focus here is on social class, I emphasize social class distinctions alone in the following paragraphs.[5]

Some studies suggest that differences in the nature of work and societal position play a part in creating differences in social-class cultures. Although working-class jobs often require obedience and conformity to rigid routines, middle-class occupations allow more creativity, autonomy, and intellectual work (Kohn, 1963, 1983). Similarly, scholars have found working-class parents to be more overtly directive when instructing their children, whereas middle-class parents tend to use questioning, discussion, reasoning, and playfulness in child rearing (Duberman, 1976; Hart & Risley, 1995; Lareau, 2002; Walkerdine, 1998). More middle-class parents have been found to guide their children's problem-solving efforts by asking questions that help children focus on the structure of the problem, whereas working-class parents have been found to focus more directly on solving immediate problems as they arise in specific contexts (Bruner, 1975; Duberman, 1976; Heath, 1983; Hess & Shipman, 1965). Research also suggests a relationship between class and perceived locus of control, with more middle-class people believing that they have control over their futures than do working-class people, who are more likely to believe that outside forces (e.g., luck or authority figures) determine their fate (Banks 1988; Lareau, 2002).

Bernstein (1975) argued that because members of lower-status classes depend more on immediate friends and family and distrust mainstream authority figures, lower-status families tend to use language with implicit and context-dependent meanings. This language makes sense in contexts in which common knowledge is assumed to be shared. Bernstein maintained that the language and meanings of middle-class families tend to be more context-independent. Bernstein's theory has been criticized for promoting this dichotomy, on the grounds that it ignores variations within class groups as well across different languages (Hymes, 1996). However, as Hymes notes, such dichotomies can also be useful as "symptoms of recognition of an issue; first approximations in addressing it" (p. 55).

In her attempt to understand how Bernstein's theory might apply to children's thinking, Holland (1981) found that middle-class children tended to categorize pictures in terms of transsituational properties (e.g., grouping foods made from milk), whereas working-class children tended to use more personalized, context-dependent meanings (e.g., grouping foods they eat at Grandma's house). It is important to note that neither Bernstein nor Holland imply that children *could* not speak or think differently. Their point is that children tend to be raised with a particular orientation.

Although most work on the interplay between class cultures and learning has occurred outside of mathematics education, some British researchers have used a class-cultural lens when analyzing children's mathematical thinking. Two such studies offer further evidence of a correlation between social class and students' interpretations of "real world" mathematics problems. Cooper and Dunne (2000) found that class disparities were larger on "realistic" items than on "esoteric" items on the national assessment in England and Wales. On several of the realistic test items, lower-SES students tended to take the contexts more seriously than the test authors intended. Walkerdine (1990) also suggests ways in which class could affect children's orientation toward contextualized, "real world" mathematics problems. She argues that the wealthy have the luxury of performing calculations as a theoretical exercise (e.g., considering how much money would be left if a particular item was purchased), whereas such calculation problems are more real for the poor. Similar to the case described above, she observed working-class children becoming engrossed in mathematical contexts used in school (such as shopping) but not gaining the intended mathematical knowledge.

I readily acknowledge that much of the literature cited above tends to rely on dichotomous categories and ignores many relevant factors in addition to social class. Despite these important limitations, the data from my classroom and the literature discussed above provide a useful tool with which to uncover culture-related assumptions embedded in some instructional approaches. For example, the following quotes from the NCTM *Standards* can be viewed as laden with assumptions about how students will experience open-ended problems and whole-class discussions:

> Listening to others' explanations gives students opportunities to develop their own understandings. Conversations in which mathematical ideas are explored from multiple perspectives help the participants sharpen their thinking and make connections. (NCTM, 2000, p. 60)

> When challenged with appropriately chosen tasks, students become confident in their ability to tackle difficult problems, eager to figure things out on their own, flexible in exploring mathematical ideas and trying alternative solution paths, and willing to persevere. (NCTM, 2000, p. 21)

Clearly, the lower-SES students in my study did not experience the feelings of empowerment from whole-class discussions and open-ended problems that reformers, and I, had hoped for. However, the conclusion to be drawn is not that lower-SES children *could* not experience such feelings if such methods had been introduced years earlier or were better adapted to meet students' strengths and needs. Nor is the conclusion that we should revert to drill-oriented teaching for lower-SES students while giving other students access to higher-level mathematical skills, as has occurred in the past (Anyon, 1981; Means & Knapp, 1991). In fact, from the literature discussed above, one could argue that lower-SES students have the *most* to gain from mathematics classrooms that explicitly include problem solving and mathematical communication as part of the curriculum. Indeed, some studies have suggested that reform-minded practices are particularly beneficial for lower-SES children (e.g., Boaler, 2002a; Newmann & Wehlage, 1995; Silver, Smith, & Nelson, 1995). Certainly, the past decades of drill-and-practice pedagogies have not produced equitable results, and the current reformers' goal of high expectations and critical mathematical literacy skills for all students is a marked improvement over past initiatives geared toward developing talent in only some students or toward promoting only computational skills.

The larger point of this analysis is that the sociocultural lens I used in this study can help us see hidden assumptions in particular instructional approaches. Reformers are calling for substantial changes in classroom cultures; and in order to most effectively and equitably implement new pedagogies intended to empower all students, educators need help in understanding how particular changes can privilege some students while creating difficulties for others.

Holding high expectations for all students is necessary but not sufficient to produce equitable instructional practices. Researchers and educators should not assume that learning mathematics through problem solving and discussion is equally "natural" for all students. Instead, we need to uncover the cultural assumptions of these particular discourses. Only then can we identify and seek to address the difficulties that some underserved children could face in reform-oriented classrooms. For example, the lenses I developed in the above study enable me to recognize specific adaptations that experienced teachers make in low-SES classrooms in ways I could not have seen before (see, e.g., Lubienski & Stilwell, 2003).

However, when we understand ways in which a particular discourse differs from students' more familiar discourses, we must be prepared to grapple with dilemmas about whether the discourse we are promoting is inherently valuable as an end in itself, or is simply an arbitrary, value-laden means (perhaps a relatively White, middle-class means) to an end. In mathematics education, for example, this could mean that we must consider whether whole-class discussion of students' conflicting mathematical conjectures is simply one possible means to understanding mathematics, or if it is an important mathematical process in its own right. If it is an important end in itself, then efforts should be made to both help students understand the norms and roles assumed by such an approach, as well as to adapt the approach to students' needs and strengths.

Overall, the study in my classroom raised many more questions than it answered. I offer it, not as a flawless model of how to conduct such research, but to illustrate some of the challenges and dilemmas inherent in such research, as well as to provide a glimpse of the potential significance of such studies.

CONCLUSIONS

This is an important time for mathematics educators to take stock of their knowledge of, and commitment to, equity. Strides have been made toward achieving equity, but much work remains. Reformers are calling for teachers to attend to students' cultural differences when implementing new instructional methods, yet they provide few specifics regarding how to do so. Research indicates that some teachers have successfully implemented problem-centered mathematics approaches with lower-SES and minority boys and girls. However, these success stories do not negate the concerns raised above about the difficulties teachers and students can face in attending to issues of culture and class.

Making further strides toward equity in mathematics classrooms requires moving beyond the dichotomy of "traditional" versus "reformed" teaching. In identifying particular instructional aspects that conflict with the beliefs and practices that some students bring to the classroom, researchers must disentangle the many aspects of the instructional vision being promoted by current reformers. As a specific example, the study described above raised concerns about two particular aspects of instruction—the use of open, contextualized problems and whole-class discussions. It identified no correlation between social class and students' experiences with numerous other aspects of instruction that are also aligned with current reforms (and were used in this classroom), such as the use of graphing calculators, "hands-on" activities, heterogeneous-group work, or teaching with an emphasis on the meaning of mathematical concepts.

As I have attempted to illustrate, the goal of sociocultural studies on equity and instruction should not be to conclude that large-scale reforms "work" or "do not work" for underserved students. Instead, the goal is to understand and address the complexities of implementing meaningful instructional methods equitably. Such studies could help identify specific practices (e.g., specific forms of collaborative group work) that appear promising for particular groups of students. These studies could also identify ways in which other practices might be problematic for some students (such as particular uses of "real-world" problems), as well as the adaptations that successful teachers make to address such difficulties.

When one considers the sheer number of groups that exist in the intersections of different ethnic, class, and gender categories, this task can appear overwhelming. However, what is learned about cultural assumptions underlying particular reformed practices in one community can inform efforts to make practices more equitable for other groups. Additionally, we do not start with a blank slate in terms of research on cultural practices.

Although it is difficult, the mathematics education community would benefit from integrating *existing* research on equity and culture into the conversation about mathematics education and reform. This research includes both work in mathematics education that tends to appear in places other than mainstream journals, as well as work from fields outside of mathematics education, such as anthropology, sociology, and literacy education. With U.S. reformers promoting classroom cultures centered around whole-class discussions and other forms of discourse, it is particularly important to integrate existing research regarding culture and language into mathematics education reform efforts.

Sociocultural studies of equity in mathematics classrooms, along with theoretical analyses designed to integrate research from other fields into mathematics education, hold promise for informing our efforts to empower all students. This work can address some of the current shortcomings of mainstream mathematics education research and educational reforms, both of which have given limited attention to cultural factors in mathematics learning.

NOTES

The author would like to thank Jo Boaler, Marta Civil, Paul Cobb, Ellice Forman, Chris Lubienski, Na'ilah Nasir, and Beth Warren for their helpful comments on various drafts of this chapter.

1. The ERIC database, containing more than 500,000 abstracts for education-related books, papers, and articles, was the data source for this study. For more information about this study, see Lubienski & Bowen, 2000.

2. This chapter is not arguing for *all* mathematics education research to be conducted from a sociocultural perspective. For a discussion of the strengths and limits of such an approach, see Cobb & Yackel (1996).

3. Focusing on a subset of students enables a deeper examination of students' experiences in this limited space. Additionally, the major studies of social class and education thus far give more attention to males (Weis, 1988).

4. Lensmire's (1993) study of the ways in which "whole language" instruction played out in one classroom reveals how culture and power differences among students can come to the fore when educators "open up" classrooms and give students a stronger voice.

5. Gender interactions are outside the present scope but are discussed in more detail by Lubienski (2000b).

2

Paying the Price for "Sugar and Spice": Shifting the Analytical Lens in Equity Research

Jo Boaler

What are little girls made of?
Sugar and Spice and all things nice

INTRODUCTION

Nursery rhymes and limericks of old are not known for their sensitive or accurate portrayal of social relations, and the sugar-and-spice characterization above may appear simply foolish or humorous from a modern-day perspective. But I will argue in this chapter that the essentialism captured by this and other nursery rhymes has been a characteristic of many gender analyses and that these may have served to sustain, rather than eradicate, inequities in schools. I will also suggest that as mathematics educators move from a long tradition of gender research to an emerging focus upon the relationships between culture, ethnicity, and mathematics achievement, we may learn from the precarious path walked by our predecessors in equity research. In this chapter I will present some data and prior scholarship on gender and mathematics in order to consider the ways in which *gender*, as a construct, has been located and framed, and the implications of such framing for equity analyses more broadly. This will uncover a fundamental tension in equity research, as scholars walk a fine and precarious line between lack of concern, on the one hand, and essentialism, on the other. I will argue that negotiating that tension may be the most critical role for equity researchers as we move into the future. Further, I will propose that reflexive discussions of the ways in which inequalities are located and framed need to be central to any analyses of equity.

In the 1970s and 1980s, a great deal of interest was given to the issue of women's and girls' underachievement in mathematics. This prompted numerous different research projects that investigated the extent and nature of the differences between girls' and boys' achievement and offered reasons why such disparities occurred. But many of the analyses that were produced positioned girls in essentialist ways, attributing anxiety and underachievement as stable characteristics that are as potentially damaging as the "sugar and spice" labels of old. Thus, researchers searched for the origins of girls' underachievement, but even when these were linked to pedagogies or environments, they were generally presented as characteristics of girls, rather than coproductions of people, society, and environment (Bateson, 2000; Butler, 1993; Geertz, 2000).

Carol Dweck (1986), for example, has produced a number of influential analyses in which she concludes that girls, particularly those she terms "bright," have maladaptive motivational patterns that include avoiding high-risk learning situations and preferring situations in which they are sure to succeed. She claims that students with maladaptive patterns seek situations that will lead to correct answers, rather than those that are challenging and provide opportunity for learning. This characterization captures the essentializing to which I refer. Dweck offers "maladaptive" tendencies as a reason for the lower mathematical performance of some girls particularly at advanced levels, but she treats these motivational patterns as inherent characteristics of girls that exist outside the settings in which girls are taught. This argument seems to be fundamentally flawed, as motivations are surely highly situated. If we *were to* consider the tendencies Dweck noticed among "bright girls," outside their setting, we might conclude that the tendencies were indeed "maladaptive" in the sense that they were unproductive. But if we consider the system in which students were learning, we may view the tendencies of girls as highly adaptive. The majority of "bright" girls are taught mathematics in high-ability groups in which the attainment of correct answers, at a fast pace, is what is valued. In such an environment, choosing to seek situations that will lead to correct answers seems sensible and highly *adaptive*. The notion of adaptivity—central to theories of natural selection—rests upon environmental responsiveness, and the idea that "girls" have maladaptive tendencies contravenes that basic premise. A different analysis would consider the constraints and affordances (Gibson, 1986; Greeno & MMAP, 1998) that are provided by the environments in which girls work and that lead to such responses.

The two approaches I have mentioned, one that considers the girls as maladaptive and the other that focuses on the teaching environments that produce such tendencies, differ in their implications. The first leads to recommendations to change the girls, whereas the second points toward changing the teaching environments in which students are working—environments that produce motivational patterns that are unproductive for learning. Indeed, Dweck's proposed solution is to design "appropriate motivational interventions" (1986, p. 1045) for girls, placing the burden for change upon them (Rogers & Kaiser, 1995).

The tendency to attribute certain characteristics and attributes to girls and women reflects a wider societal regard to gender. Even those people who believe that males and females have equal intellectual potential, and vary in the extent to which they conform to stereotypes, generally regard gender as a characteristic of the different sexes, rather than a response to a particular set of conditions. Researchers have traditionally proposed, implicitly or explicitly, that women *have* a gender, which comprises a set of characteristics shared by the wide group of people in the world who are female. But as Butler (1993) has argued, gender is a *response* that emerges in certain situations, and its analytical home should not be people, but the discourse and interactions that emerge in practice. Culture is also a co-construction, as Cobb and Hodge (2002) and Gutiérrez (2002) both argue. It emerges in different forms in the home, the school, and the workplace, and it is constantly negotiated and renegotiated through everyday interactions. Yet culture, like gender, is generally conferred upon people and groups as a static and immoveable set of competencies, attitudes, and dispositions. When the National Council of Teachers of Mathematics (NCTM) in the United States released books offering perspectives on "African Americans," "Latinos" and "Asians," they communicated a number of good teaching approaches and a concern for equity, but they also essentialized these groups, suggesting that African American or Latino students possessed preferences for particular learning styles or teaching approaches, by virtue of their ethnicity or culture.

Cohen (1999) has given an important historical perspective on the tendency of researchers to locate underachievement within certain groups of students. She analyzed the furor in the United Kingdom that was prompted by national examination data showing that girls are now ahead of boys in almost all subjects. In doing so, she pointed out that female underachievement has always been partially accepted as a corollary of being female, whereas the idea of male underachievement has prompted recent, widespread investigations into the *external* culprits:

> Boys' achievement has been attributed to something within—the nature of their intellect—but their failure has been attributed to something external—a pedagogy, methods, texts, teachers. The full significance of this becomes clear when the subject of the discourse is girls, for in their case it is their failure which is attributed to something within—usually the nature of their intellect—and their success to something external: methods, teachers or particular conditions. (Cohen, 1999, p. 20)

The application of internal rather than external reasons for the underachievement of students is evident within many strands of equity research. Cohen traces this trend through English history to show its origination in the 17th century and its astonishing resilience in the intervening 300 years. At that time scholars went to enormous lengths to explain away the achievement of girls and the working classes, as it was boys, specifically upper-class boys, who were believed to possess true intellect. This required the construction of the idea that any quickness and superior verbal competence noted among girls or working-class students was a sign of weakness:

> The English gentleman's reticent tongue and inarticulateness which had been unfavourably contrasted with the conversational fluency of English women and of the French for most of the eighteenth century now became evidence of the depth and strength of his mind. Conversely, women's conversational skills became evidence of the shallowness and weakness of their mind. (Cohen, 1999, p. 24)

In 1897, Bennett argued that boys appeared slow and dull because they were thoughtful and deep, and "gold sparkles less than tinsel." "Thus as the eighteenth century came to a close, girls' brightness, construed as inferiority, and boys' dullness construed as potential, were woven into the fabric of gender difference" (cited in Cohen, 1999, p. 25).

The ideas of Bennett and others may (hopefully) appear ridiculous now, but their vestiges are evident within current perceptions and discourse. Cohen relates these early ideas to the present-day beliefs of some boys that studiousness and scholarly interest are feminine traits and that "Real Englishmen" (Mac an Ghaill, 1994, p. 70) do not try hard in school. "Effortless achievement" is a key concept in the English aristocratic attitude to education and constructs not only the power of the English gentleman but also his "other," the "swot," whose hard work is the very evidence of his lack of "natural" intellect: the "scholarship boy," academic achievers such as the working-class boys in Mac an Ghaill's study, and *all females* (Cohen, 1999, p. 29, italics added).

Varenne and McDermott (1999) address the essentialism and inward tendencies that lurk within equity analyses by offering two metaphors for culture. In the first, culture is represented as the "habits we acquire" (p. 14) as we go through life. This view of culture is one that is traditionally found in analyses of school achievement, with many researchers proposing that a students' culture or class may be thought of as a set of habits or characteristics that are acquired (Bourdieu, 1982, 1986). This leads to the idea that students who are successful in school have been properly socialized into the dominant culture and those who are unsuccessful have not (Bourdieu, 1982, 1986; Delpit, 1988; Zevenbergen, 1996). In their second, preferred metaphor, Varenne and McDermott suggest that culture be represented as "the houses we inhabit" (1999, p. 14). This metaphor allows for the fact that being Black, working class, or a girl, for example, only matters in some places. When people are working among others of the same culture, class, or gender, such categories become invisible. Yet researchers who consider the sources of inequity for students of minority ethnic and cultural groups often fail to capture the shifting and relational nature of culture. Varenne and McDermott (1999) propose that school is a system that is "filled with instructions for coordinating the mutual construction of success and failure" and that categories such as "low achiever" or "learning disabled" are "positions in education that get filled by children" (p. 152). In doing so, they relocate the focus, away from categories of people and the inherent characteristics that are attributed to them, and toward a dynamic system that *produces* responses of achievement, underachievement, gender, culture, and class. This is an important repositioning and I will spend some time now considering what it may mean for equity analyses by examining the case of gender.

A BRIEF REVIEW OF MATHEMATICS GENDER RESEARCH

Gender differences in mathematics achievement have been documented and examined for more than a half century, and in many countries in the world (Burton, 1990; Delon, 1995; Habibullah, 1995; Kaur, 1995; Singh Kaeley, 1995; Sukthankar,

1995). For the purposes of this chapter, I will reduce the complexity of gender patterns in mathematics achievement to four facts that I regard as notable and current and to which I shall return in my analysis. The first fact is that gender differences in mathematics achievement are generally small (Hyde, 1993) and insignificant when considered alongside the overlap in males' and females' achievement. Janet Hyde produced a meta-analysis of gender differences in 1993, and even at that time—almost 10 years ago—she found a minimal difference. She drew from more than 100 studies involving 3 million subjects and derived an effect size of +0.15 standard deviations. Hyde demonstrated that gender differences were too small to be recognized as meaningful, and concluded that they have been overplayed and glamorized in the media, which has contributed to a discourse of difference that has itself been implicated in the creation of differences in the achievement of girls and boys.

The second fact is that achievement differences have vastly diminished over time. That fact alone gives us important information about their origins, casting further doubt on the idea that gender differences may be attributed to genetic sources (Rogers, 1999). The third fact is that the greatest differences in mathematics achievement and participation are found at the most advanced levels. The evidence for achievement differences at high levels predominantly consists of results from short, closed tests, such as the SAT in the United States and the international Olympiad tests. Such tests persistently prompt small gender differences in favor of boys (Campbell & Clewell, 1999; Friedman, 1989, 1995). The fourth fact is that gender differences have tended to occur on mathematics questions that assess spatial ability and problem solving (Friedman, 1989). The first two of these four facts are highly positive and rarely regarded in gender analyses; the second two have seriously negative implications and have been the subject of numerous analyses.

Consideration of the participation of women and girls in mathematics courses and occupations reveals varying degrees of inequality. In 1994, women made up 45% of those taking the advanced placement mathematics examinations in North American high schools and 47% of undergraduate degrees. However, only 24% of mathematics PhDs in the United States go to women, and in 1992 only 6% of tenured university mathematics faculty were women. In other English-speaking countries—such as Australia and England—the participation of women at degree and PhD level is lower. In the workplace, men vastly outnumber women in mathematically oriented occupations (Kenway, Willis, & Junor, 1994; Leder, 1990).

One of the most persistent explanations for the differences that prevail in mathematics achievement and participation has focused upon the learning styles of boys and girls. Despite the absence of data showing clear differences in learning-style preference or tendency between girls and boys (Adey, Fairbrother, Johnson, & Jones, 1995), a number of mathematics educators have offered the idea that girls employ learning styles that are fundamentally different (and inferior) from those of boys and that limit their potential mathematics achievement (Bohlin, 1994; Fennema & Carpenter, 1998; Walkerdine, 1989). I will consider some of these analyses in this chapter in order to raise a number of issues, not only about gender inequalities and learning styles, but also about the focus of research, the methods employed in various fields, and the influence of different analytical perspectives on the conclusions that may be drawn about equity.

GENDER AND TEACHING ENVIRONMENTS

A few years ago, I completed a detailed longitudinal study of the achievement and participation of approximately 300 students in two secondary schools in England. I will briefly summarize the gender-related results of that study here in order to illustrate a different interpretive approach in equity research that leads to immensely different implications. In that study (Boaler, 1997a), I monitored a cohort of students in each of the two schools over a 3-year period, from when they were 13 to when they were 16. The two schools taught mathematics in completely different ways. At 13, before the students embarked on their different mathematical pathways, there were no significant differences in mathematical attainment of the two cohorts and there were no recorded gender differences at either school. Three years later, the girls who attended the school that I have called Amber Hill, which followed a traditional, procedural approach, attained significantly lower mathematics grades on the national examination than those of the boys at their school. In the other school, which I have called Phoenix Park, where an open-ended, project-based approach was employed, there were no gender differences between girls and boys at any level and the students attained significantly higher grades than the students at the more procedural school. In questionnaires given to the students each year that asked them about their confidence and enjoyment, the boys at the two schools did not respond significantly differently. But the girls at the project-based school, Phoenix Park, were always significantly more positive and confident than the girls following a procedural approach at Amber Hill (Boaler, 1997a, 1997b, 1997c).

In that study, I observed approximately 100 one-hour lessons in each school over 3 years, and I conducted in-depth interviews with 80 students. Those methods, alongside the questionnaires and assessments that I gave the students, helped me to understand the source of the differences in the girls' responses to their different mathematics approaches. I will summarize this analysis by saying that many of the girls in the school employing a procedure-oriented mathematics approach (Amber Hill) became disaffected about mathematics when the pedagogy of the classroom became relatively traditional. Further, many more girls than boys at the school developed a preference that I have called a *quest for understanding*. At Amber Hill, the teachers presented abstract methods that students were required to practice every lesson. This was problematic for many of the girls, not because that they were incapable of attaining success in such an environment. They were able to take the methods they had been given and reproduce them in textbook exercises, but many of the girls wanted more. They wanted to locate the rules and methods that they were introduced to within a wider sphere of understanding. Thus they wanted to know *why* the methods worked, *where* they came from, and *how* they fitted into the broader mathematical domain. The boys at Amber Hill also preferred approaches that gave them access to a more relational understanding of connections within and across the mathematical domain. When I asked students to name their "best-ever mathematics lesson" in a questionnaire, 81% of girls and 80% of boys chose the open-ended projects that they worked on for 2 weeks of each year ($n = 160$). But in the absence of such opportunities in their day-to-day mathematics lessons, many of the boys turned mathematics into a kind of game, repositioning their goals by focusing on competition and *relative* success. Many of the girls would not reorient their goals in this way and instead continued to strive toward depth of understanding, which worked to their disadvantage within that particular classroom system.

Phoenix Park school, where I also monitored students for 3 years, offered the type of mathematics environment that the girls at Amber Hill appeared to yearn for. The students worked on open-ended projects, usually in groups, and they were given explicit encouragement to think about how, when, and why mathematical methods worked. At this school, there were no gender differences in achievement, at any level, and the students attained significantly higher examination grades than did the students at Amber Hill, even though there had been no significant differences in the students' attainment 3 years earlier, before they began their different mathematics approaches.

The differences that emerged from this study of teaching and learning appeared to challenge a number of the interpretations that had been offered for girls' underachievement in the past. For example, girls at both schools sought a deep, conceptual understanding of mathematics, and those who where taught by teachers who encouraged the exploration of mathematical ideas were able to achieve this goal. This finding stands in stark contrast to the conclusions of other gender researchers in mathematics education, who have decided, for example, that women prefer rote and algorithmic approaches (Walkerdine & Girls and Mathematics Unit, 1989) and that they are less likely to develop conceptual understanding in response to a reform-oriented curriculum (Fennema & Carpenter, 1998; Sowder, 1998). The researchers who drew such conclusions all noted that boys outperformed girls on some tests, but none of the researchers observed the students' teaching environments or interviewed the students about their learning. As a consequence, they did not have adequate data from which to draw conclusions about sources of inequality. In the absence of such data, they were left only to speculate that the girls were lacking in some ways. This argument also holds for a number of studies conducted in the 1970s and 1980s that reported that girls achieved less than boys in tests of problem solving. The inherent deficiencies attributed to girls on the basis of these results seem questionable when we note that the majority of students taking part in such studies were asked to solve problems in tests that stood in direct contrast to the teaching approaches they experienced in school. Thus the lower performance of girls in such instances may reflect their responsiveness to their teaching. If the Amber Hill students had taken such tests, similar gender differences would probably have resulted. But the beliefs and achievements of the girls at Phoenix Park show that girls do not have to underachieve or become disaffected in relation to school mathematics and that such responses may be more appropriately considered as *responses* to particular teaching environments. Gender inequities are coproduced, and the conclusions drawn from analyses that leave students' instructional experiences out of the equation (often because of methodological restrictions) may be extremely misleading.

There were a number of indications from my study that many of the girls at Amber Hill and the boys and girls at Phoenix Park had developed preferences for what Gilligan (1982) describes as a kind of "connected knowing." Thus they wanted to understand the connections between mathematical methods, and they also wanted to know why they worked. Many of the boys at Amber Hill did not express such preferences and seemed content to manipulate abstract methods without considering their connections or relations. The problem for many girls in the past may have arisen because traditional mathematics environments have not allowed a connected, relational understanding (Boaler, 2000b; Boaler & Greeno, 2000). This has not always stood in the way of girls' success, but it may have contributed significantly to their participation. Such preferences, while more prevalent among girls than boys, only became significant in certain teaching environments. This suggests that connected knowing may be less accurately represented as a characteristic of women, as it has been in Gilligan's work, than a response to certain learning situations. The data I collected appeared to indicate that such preferences are highly situated and that different approaches to school mathematics vary in the extent to which they encourage and satisfy such preferences.

Two years ago I gave a talk in England to a group of teacher education students about the possible gender-related preferences that students may develop in certain teaching environments. After the presentation, three young women approached me from the audience to talk about their experiences as undergraduate mathematics students. I conducted interviews with the women at a later stage. Surprisingly, in such a small group, all three had been extremely high-attaining mathematics students in school, winning prizes for their mathematics achievement and gaining the highest grades. They each went on to study mathematics at three of the United Kingdom's most elite universities. In England, students choose the subject focus of their undergraduate degree when they begin university. All three women started mathematics degrees but switched out of their programs after a relatively short time. They reported that the reason for doing so was because they wanted to understand the mathematics they were learning in the depth that had previously been available. In school they had been encouraged and enabled to understand the mathematics they met. But when they arrived at university they found they were expected to copy down endless formulas and procedures from chalkboards. They reported that the men in their classes seemed content to do so, but the women wanted more. The three women all described how their love of mathematics ended and the severe distress that this caused them—one spoke of her relationship with mathematics "spiralling out of control." Two of the three women describe their experiences below:

> It was horrible for me because I had always found maths so easy and suddenly sitting there and not having the slightest clue what they were talking about. It was so abstract. To me it was the most meaningless thing I had ever heard. It seemed utterly pointless, utterly meaningless and stupid—we just copied at very high speed, I just had these pages and pages that I copied down from the board. (Imogen, Oxford University student)

> I think it was my fault because I did want to understand every single step and I kind of wouldn't think about the final step if I hadn't understood an in-between step. . . . I couldn't really see why they, how they got to it. Sometimes you want to know, I actually wanted to know. (Julie, Cambridge University student)

The three women came from a very small and opportunist sample, but they gave important insights into the preferences they held for a certain way of knowing (Gilligan, 1982) that emerged *in response* to their university classes. These women, like many of the girls I interviewed at Amber Hill, talked about the importance of understanding, rather than simply following steps, and the harsh consequences of not understanding what they were doing. These students' accounts offer insights into the reasons why relatively low proportions of women continue with mathematics courses at university, despite their propensity to understand, insights that are entirely consistent with the views expressed by the students I have interviewed from a number of different high schools (Boaler, 2000b; Boaler & Greeno, 2000).

There are many societal differences in the ways that girls and boys are treated (Singh Kaeley, 1995; Sukthankar, 1995) that would be likely to give rise to the different preferences for connected understanding in some teaching environments. But for mathematics educators it may be less important to understand why these differences occur than to understand the nature of teaching environments that preclude the realization of such preferences and turn the preferences of girls into anxiety and disaffection. If some teaching environments produce inequitable attainment through the creation of conflict between the preferences that girls develop and the opportunities that prevail, then it is important to question whether nonconflicting environments can be produced that are productive for the learning of mathematics. Phoenix Park school is not the only example of an environment that encourages equitable attainment (Silver, Smith, & Nelson, 1995), but it is one site that may provide insights into the ways in which *teaching and learning practices* may promote equity (Boaler, 1997a, 1997b, 1997c, 2002a, 2002b).

As differential gender responses were produced within one of the two environments I studied, it seems fair to conclude that the underachievement and disaffection of girls from Amber Hill was a coproduction, with the mathematics environments playing a central role. Indeed, the vastly different responses and achievements of girls within the two different school environments would support the idea that environments rather than institutionalized categories, such as gender or culture, may be a more productive site for the location of equity analyses. This relational analysis, which locates gender as a response that emerges between people and environments, may seem obvious and noncontroversial, but it differs from traditional equity analyses in fundamental ways. In a recent sequence of six articles that appeared as part of a special issue of *Educational Researcher* (Fennema & Carpenter, 1998a)—one of the American Educational Research Association's leading journals—researchers from different fields offered their explanation for the gender differences that emerged from a study of 38 girls and 44 boys in Grades 1–3 (Fennema & Carpenter, 1998b). The students followed a reform curriculum for 3 years and were assessed on routine and nonroutine problems each year. The researchers found no gender differences in the students' ability to solve problems, except for some higher achievement patterns among boys on extension tests. However, they found differences in the problem-solving strategies that boys and girls used in all grades. Girls tended to use concrete solution strategies and traditional algorithms, whereas boys tended to use more abstract solution strategies that they had invented. This result is given considerable importance by the authors and the editors of the journal, who suggest that it may explain all the subsequent differences in mathematics achievement that occur between girls and boys.

In this collection of articles, Fennema and Carpenter invited the field to engage in the worthwhile activity of thinking through and understanding a case in which gender differences emerged. It is important to stress that Fennema and Carpenter were concerned to understand these gender differences and to explore their origin with scholars from different disciplines. However, their lack of attention to the teaching and learning environments seems problematic for two reasons. The first is that it underplays the importance of the particulars of teaching and learning (Chazan & Ball, 1999, Lampert, 1985)—the different scholars were told that the classes were following a "reform curriculum" and were presumed to know what that meant for classroom interactions. As the field of mathematics education has expanded to include analyses of different versions of "reform" teaching (Boaler, 1997a, 2002a; Chazan & Ball, 1999; Cobb & Bauersfeld, 1995; Gutiérrez, 1996, 1999b; Lubienski, 2000b) we have become aware of the vastly different environments that may be created through slight variations in the practices of teaching. This tells us that it is insufficient to know that a teacher was "reform oriented." My second concern for analyses that leave out the practices of teaching and learning is that researchers are inevitably left to draw conclusions about "girls" and to position gender as a characteristic of groups of people, rather than a situated response.

The tendency to focus analyses of underachievement upon categories of students, rather than the environments that coproduce differences, is not unusual in equity analyses. In mathematics education, researchers have variously discovered that girls lack confidence, develop anxiety, and attribute failure to themselves. These tendencies have generally been presented as properties of girls, rather than as responses that are coproduced by particular working environments. This has led educators to propose interventions aimed at changing the girls so that they become less anxious, more confident, and *essentially* more masculine. But the location of gendered responses *within* women and girls may be directly linked to the fact that early gender researchers worked within a positivist research paradigm, in which researchers were expected to control, rather than understand, variables such as teaching. These researchers analyzed test and questionnaire data and found gender-related attitudes and achievements, but they did not have access to the teaching and learning environments that would have allowed them to understand the gendered responses. Contemporary educational researchers have the resources to investigate and understand the interactions of teaching and learning, drawing from different methods in order to produce "thick descriptions" (Geertz, 2000, p. 3) of the ways in which environments contribute to differential responses. An important responsibility of gender researchers in the future will be to build upon our predecessors' work and search for explanations of the differences they found, not within the nature of girls, but within the interactions that produce gendered responses.

CONCLUSION

I have spent some time in this chapter arguing that gender, like culture, is a response rather than a characteristic. My preference for a situated, relational conception of gender and culture derives in large part from the implications that such conceptions carry for action and change and for the responsibility they endow upon educational organizations for making change. We have a long history of equity research that has drawn conclusions about groups of people and publicized these, at some cost. In my interviews with high school students, I frequently encountered stereotypes about the potential of students from different sexes and cultural groups. But it is particularly disturbing to know that the prevailing idea that girls are mathematically inferior often derives from the findings of equity researchers. In a recent interview with a group of high school students in California, I asked two girls about gender differences:

> *JB*: Do you think math is different for boys and girls or the same?
> *K*: Well, it's proved that boys are better in math than girls, but in this class, I don't know.
> *JB*: Mmm, where do you hear that boys are better than girls?

> K: That's everywhere—that guys are better in math and girls are like better in English.
>
> JB: Really?
>
> B: Yeh I watched it on *20/20* [a television current affairs program] saying girls are no good, and I thought—well if we're not good at it, then why are you making me learn it? (Kristina & Betsy, Apple school)

The girls refer to a television program that presented the results of research on the differences between the mathematical performance of girls and boys. This extract speaks clearly to the ways in which categories of students are essentialized by the media, which generally draws upon research findings and presents them in sensational ways. Headlines that have appeared in the media in recent years include one from the *New York Times*: "Numbers Don't Lie: Men Do Better than Women," with the subheading "S.A.T. Scores Accurately Reflect Male Superiority in Math." But this article, like many others, was based upon research results and analyses that constructed performance differences as a characteristic of women, rather than as a response by women to particular teaching and learning environments.

The girls' reflections above also speak clearly to the ways that such reporting may affect the motivation and confidence of students in schools—"If we're not good at it, then why are you making me learn it?" expresses a view that is shared by students of different sexes and cultures when they are subject to deficit stereotypes. The prevalent discourse that constructs girls and other categories of students as "not good" at mathematics is a particular language that must surely have played a part in the underrepresentation of girls and women in mathematical competitions, courses, and professions. We can only speculate about the ways the world would be different if researchers had focused on learning environments when they attempted to identify sources of inequalities. However, we can learn from the past and position research analyses in different ways. In 1981, Fennema raised this issue in an important article that sounded a cautionary note to equity researchers about the ways our work might be used and about the responsibility we bear for consideration of the ways it may be published. As a specific example, she considered the media reports claiming that girls are genetically inferior to boys in mathematics that were based on the research interpretations of Benbow and Stanley (1980). Fennema pointed to the ways in which Benbow and Stanley's interpretations of their data *constructed* the idea of genetic difference, an observation that is important in its own right. In addition, she raised a general question that continues to be important to consider:

> Am I and others who are deeply concerned with helping women achieve equity, as well as Julian Stanley, helping females to achieve true equity in mathematics education? Or are we helping to perpetuate the myth that there are large and non-changeable sex-related differences in mathematics? Are we indeed creating a new mythology of female inadequacy in the learning of mathematics? (1981, p. 384)

It is important for all researchers to ask such questions of their work, but equity researchers, in particular, bear an enormous responsibility for considering the ways in which they are interpreting and framing their data, as well as the "mythologies" of inadequacy that may be constructed. Varenne and McDermott (1999) advocate a refocusing of the equity lens away from individuals and categories of people, and onto the systems that coproduce difference. The refocusing that they suggest will involve departing from the essentialism of categories evident in claims that girls are "maladaptive" or conceptually lacking and will entail a commitment to careful explorations of the circumstances that produce differences between groups. If we are serious about eradicating underachievement—not only for girls, but also for students of different racial, ethnic, cultural, and socioeconomic groups—then it must surely be time for ideas of intrinsic inferiority to be displaced. This shift may be a simple but powerful analytic resource in this endeavor.

NOTE

I am deeply indebted to a number of people who gave help with this chapter. Jerry Lipka suggested some different ways to focus the analysis that were extremely generative. David Bloome, Paul Cobb, Sarah Lubienski, and Ellice Forman all provided very careful and helpful reviews of the chapter. Tom Carpenter and Elizabeth Fennema generously engaged in helpful discussions. Deborah Ball and Dylan Wiliam gave their usual careful and thoughtful advice.

3

(Re)Defining Equity:
The Importance of a Critical Perspective

ROCHELLE GUTIÉRREZ

Although traditionally ignored, issues of equity in mathematics education have garnered greater attention from policy makers, educators, and the general public in recent years. Diversity is becoming central both to funding agencies seeking to improve the mathematics teaching and learning of all students[1] and to teacher education programs seeking to prepare teachers. This spotlight on equity provides researchers a unique opportunity to offer guidance. However, they must be prepared with tightly developed arguments and fully supported theories, as a number of obstacles threaten their influence.

First, equity is threatened by the underlying belief that not *all* students can learn. That is, while there is a belief in other countries that differences in student achievement result from effort (Stevenson & Stigler, 1992), in the United States, there is a tendency to believe that achievement is more directly related to inherent mathematical ability. Such beliefs undermine efforts to develop support systems or improved teaching for students who historically have not performed well in mathematics.

A second obstacle in addressing equity issues is the underlying deficit theory that tends to be applied to students who have been marginalized in mathematics. Most researchers and educators have moved beyond thinking that it is mainly the fault of students themselves, their families, or their cultures for why they do not perform well in mathematics. Yet even equity proponents tend to frame their arguments in ways that suggest that benefits move from mathematics to persons and not the other way around. The assumption is that certain people will gain from having mathematics in their lives, as opposed to the idea that the field of mathematics will gain from having these people participate. In other words, most "equity" research currently assumes that the deficit lies within students who need mathematics rather than (or in addition to) that mathematics needs different people's participation. Such an approach implies that the people being served by the programs need to improve, but not mathematics.

Finally, and perhaps most important, we still operate under a very loosely structured and poorly articulated research agenda around issues of equity in mathematics education. Secada (1991b) summarizes the problem eloquently:

> [The] urgency [involving issues of equity] is often translated into a rush for answers and solutions, not only among policymakers and the larger community of

practitioners, but also among researchers and others who usually take the time to carefully define issues and concerns in all areas of scholarly inquiry. (p. 149)

A range of issues get clumped together under the "equity" umbrella in ways that make it almost impossible to address them all or to investigate any one of them in depth. For example, issues of cultural diversity and linguistic diversity play out differently from issues of gender or class. And all four issues interact in ways that may differ greatly from the mere accumulation of the disparate research findings. In many research programs, equity becomes an afterthought or a backdrop, not a central tenet. Moreover, even when researchers are concerned centrally with equity, the ideas embraced tend to reflect relatively parochial national concerns rather than global issues. For example, little has been written in mathematics education that addresses how mathematics might play a role in broader global politics or planet sustainability.

We generally agree that we want *greater* equity. The leading document for our professional organization, *Principles and Standards of School Mathematics*, highlights equity as one of five key principles (National Council of Teachers of Mathematics [NCTM], 2000). However, because *equity* is a value-laden term and requires human judgment, we have had fewer examples of what equity might mean empirically. That is, how might we know it if we saw it? In our race for solutions, we seem willing to work with a poorly defined goal. Perhaps the lack of a clear definition is what contributes to a general consensus that equity is worth striving for, everyone having his or her own vision of what it means. However, having a poorly defined target means we are only sure we are moving toward it when, in fact, we are very far away.

In this chapter, I propose a working definition of equity, illustrating with examples from an urban high school I studied. More specifically, I assert that we must coordinate (1) efforts to get marginalized students to identify with "dominant" mathematics with (2) efforts to develop a critical perspective among all students about knowledge and society in ways that ultimately address (3) a positive relationship between mathematics, people, and the globe.

WHAT SHOULD OUR THEORETICAL LENS BE?

Debates about equity have traditionally revolved around the idea that, as a nation, we cannot enable our highest-performing students to excel while simultaneously bringing our lower-performing students up to a higher level. The "excellence versus equity" debate implies that the two goals are inherently in conflict—that the strategies that would raise lower-performing students to a much higher standard (e.g., detracking, receiving higher-quality teachers and resources) would limit the opportunities for higher-performing students to excel. Although the excellence-versus-equity debate has not been completely resolved

(Lee, 2001; NCTM 2000), in its place has arisen the debate over "traditional versus reform" mathematics.

Most reform documents have been created not just to offer different content but to broaden the cross-section of society that can engage in meaningful mathematics. That is, the nature and function of basic algorithms change (Vithal & Skovsmose, 1997) when students are expected to use them to make important decisions about data or to analyze patterns. In redefining school mathematics, reform mathematics has the potential to encourage practices that resemble learning in out-of-school settings (Addington & Lipka, 2000; Civil, 2000; Cobb & Hodge, 2002; Lave, 1988; Nasir, 2002; Nunes, Schliemann, & Carraher, 1993).

However, reform mathematics in its current state does not position students to consider power issues in society, something that (for me) is at the core of equity. Students can learn to read the world using mathematics, but depending upon the goals of instruction, that world may remain politically neutral. For example, students might be encouraged to see geometrical shapes and spatial relationships in the buildings and artifacts in their town or city. Students may collect data and make inferences about how tall and large such buildings or artifacts are in relation to themselves, using concepts such as estimation, measurement, ratio, proportion, and volume. They may even redesign their own city to make better use of space or to reflect their unique desires, all while deepening their understanding of the relationships between shape and volume. In the process, (mainstream) students will have opportunities to develop mathematical skills by exploring their worlds, and this can be quite empowering. However, they may never be encouraged to question whose interests are served by the buildings and structures that surround them. By relating to one's world (and possibly broadening the base of people who are engaged in mathematics), reform mathematics brings us closer to addressing issues of equity than does traditional mathematics, which has emphasized memorizing facts and basic skills. But reform mathematics alone does not ensure that power issues in society are addressed.

As such, I suggest that the new tension that threatens progress is caused not by the paradigm of excellence versus equity or by that of traditional versus reform, but by one of *dominant* versus *critical*, mathematics education. What I mean by *dominant* mathematics is mathematics that reflects the status quo in society, that gets valued in high-stakes testing and credentialing, that privileges a static formalism in mathematics, and that is involved in making sense of a world that favors the views and perspectives of a relatively elite group. The practice of mathematics that is currently used in schools throughout the globe tends to reflect a Western (colonial) frame of reference (D'Ambrosio, 1985; Gutiérrez, 2000a; Powell & Frankenstein, 1997; Secada, 1994; Vithal & Skovsmose, 1997). The practice of such mathematics both in countries outside the West and with indigenous peoples in the West represents a kind of recolonization. In other words, whether students identify with the central ideas of school mathematics (with its emphasis on the dominant perspective)[2] is distinct from (and at times in conflict with) the issue of whether they create and use mathematical practices to critique the world (with an emphasis on nondominant perspectives).

What I mean by *critical* mathematics is mathematics that squarely acknowledges the positioning of students as members of a society rife with issues of power and domination. Critical mathematics takes students' cultural identities and builds mathematics around them in ways that address social and political issues in society, especially highlighting the perspectives of marginalized groups. This is a mathematics that challenges static notions of formalism, as embedded in a tradition that favors the West. For me, the distinction between *dominant* and *critical* is not one of acquisition and application, but rather one of aligning with society (and its embedded power relations) or exposing and challenging society and its power relations.

While there still exists great tension between reform and traditional mathematics, for my current purposes it is useful to collapse the two under the same umbrella (dominant mathematics). I do this because I see the distinction between dominant and critical mathematics education as having more serious implications for broader definitions of equity that I propose later in this chapter.

Although I highlight the tension between dominant and critical mathematics, for me it remains an empirical question whether we can coordinate them in ways that address broader issues of equity. In fact, I suggest that, at first, we should strive to achieve both. In fact, learning dominant mathematics may be necessary if students are to critically analyze the world; and being able to critically analyze the world with mathematics may be an entrance for students to engage in dominant mathematics. Therefore, my definition of equity has two central thrusts that reflect a common goal of broader equity in the globe.

DEFINING EQUITY

How we define equity has serious implications for how we seek to achieve or measure it. Equity has meant many things to many people over the years. Debates in the 1980s led researchers to emphasize such concepts as educational access (e.g., equal resources, quality teachers, opportunity to learn), paying slightly less attention to student outcomes. Today, more researchers are focusing upon students' mathematical literacy (e.g., ability to apply knowledge in new domains, ability to make sense of data) or identity.

Although *equity* means "justice" or "fairness," it is often blurred with *equality*, which means "sameness." For example, equality in a mathematics education setting might mean that all students are given the *same* access to powerful mathematics, the *same* quality of teachers, the *same* curricular materials, the *same* forms of teaching, and the *same* supports for learning. This sounds good, if learning is universal and occurs in a social, political, and historical vacuum. However, in order to redress past injustices and account for different home resources, student identities, and other contextual factors, students need different (not the same) resources and treatment in order to achieve "fairness." Beyond holding that school approaches be the same, equality might also mean that student outcomes (e.g., mathematical literacy) are the same—that students all end up in the same place. Yet having all students reach the same goals does not represent "justice" for students' own desires or identities. The distinction between equality and equity is, therefore, an important one to keep in mind.

I recognize heterogeneity within and between groups of students. For example, two Latina students cannot be expected to be any more alike (in previous achievement, lived histories, natural talents, or personal interests) than can any two White students (Nieto, 1996; Oboler, 1995). Consequently, the definition of equity that I propose assumes neither equal approaches (e.g., same treatment of students, same resources) nor equal outcomes (e.g., same achievement). Instead, both approaches and outcomes should be equitable, not equal. My argument rests on the assumption that there exists natural variation between people in terms of goals, strengths, and interests. Therefore, under a "just" system, we could expect to see students achieve in school and aspire to do a *variety* of things. That is, we would not expect *all* Latinas/Latinos to perform poorly or exceptionally in school mathematics. There would be natural variation within any given group—females, males, those in poverty, middle class, rich, First Nations, Anglos, Blacks, Chinese, and so on.

In the definition of equity that I propose in this chapter, I emphasize the goal of being unable to predict student patterns (e.g., achievement, participation, ability to critically analyze data/society) based solely upon characteristics such as race, class, ethnicity, gender, beliefs, and proficiency in the dominant language. Being unable to predict such patterns addresses issues of power. Rather than expecting that mathematics reform will lead to middle-class White men falling out of power only to be replaced by another group (e.g., students in poverty, Black females), an equitable situation is when *no* group oppresses another (Freire, 1970, 1998; Macedo, 2000).

Equity is not just an abstract goal; it is a process (Rodriguez, 1998). In order to make headway in that process, we must be willing to develop working definitions of the concept, assuming we will refine them at a later point. I see equity in mathematics as having three main parts, each of which has levels and time frames of its own. There are stages at which we might expect to see certain trends before others. Studying the trends systematically (via an indicator system) would be an important contribution to research. I borrow from D'Ambrosio's (1999) "trivium for a new millenium" in developing a working definition of equity. Using a sociocultural lens, I flesh out this definition with examples from a high school math department that was successful in advancing its Latina/o students to calculus without asking them to give up their cultural/linguistic identities.

1. *Being unable to predict* students' mathematics achievement and participation *based solely upon characteristics such as race, class, ethnicity, gender, beliefs, and proficiency in the dominant language.*[3]

I call for an *inability to predict* student outcomes based *solely* upon cultural markers. One might question whether establishing the grounds for such "inability to predict" leads to encouraging assimilation. In other words, does striving for a lack of significant variation between groups encourage students to all become the same? Allow me to clarify. I contend that only when there is sufficient variation *within* groups and no clear patterns associated with power or status in society *between* groups can we conclude that this aspect of equity is being addressed. I am less concerned with student patterns if they do not also relate to power. So it may be that students from a particular group show patterns of achievement or participation that cluster them together, but it may also be that these patterns do not confer on them particular status (high or low) in society. In other words, I do not mean that everyone will end up in the same place (equality of outcomes). I am not looking to erase cultural markers in the process of erasing power relations.

In principle, I am adamantly against viewing students as mere embodiments of cultural markers. My identity as a Chicana in a society that does not value brown-skinned people or Spanish speakers means I am constantly being reduced to a category. However, I do believe that there is a time and place for *strategic essentialism.*[4] I define strategic essentialism as the process of deliberately categorizing people based upon definable traits for the purpose of reaching higher (equity) goals. That is, I use characteristics such as race, class, ethnicity, gender, beliefs, and language because these characteristics are the very markers used in society to determine power. To ignore these characteristics would be to assume that power relations do not exist in society. If at some point we (as marginalized people) are not willing to use these very markers to assess progress, inequity will always be reduced to a degree of relativism.

What I mean by *achievement* is mainly scores on standardized mathematics exams that confer power on individuals. However, achievement could also include course grades and scores on nonstandardized exams, especially ones that measure students' conceptual understanding and ability to apply mathematics. Similarly, *participation* refers to advanced mathematics courses (course-taking patterns), mathematics-based college majors, and mathematics-based careers, but could also refer to individual students' participation in class discussions or activities. I liken this aspect of equity to D'Ambrosio's (1999) definition of *numeracy,* which includes the ability to understand graphs, tables, the condensed language of codes, and other ways of informing the individual. It is the ability to read data and communicate it. I also include aspects of D'Ambrosio's "matheracy" in this outcome measure. Specifically, we might also measure success by how well students can draw conclusions from data and from their own calculations, make inferences, and propose hypotheses. According to D'Ambrosio, matheracy is the first step in the students' development of an intellectual and critical posture.

Another strong measure of achievement might be the five interwoven strands of proficiency that were developed by the Mathematics Learning Study Committee (National Research Council, 2001). The committee suggests that students are proficient in mathematics when they have developed the following:

1. conceptual understanding—comprehension of mathematical concepts, operations, and relations
2. procedural fluency—skill in carrying out procedures flexibly, accurately, efficiently, and appropriately
3. strategic competence—ability to formulate, represent, and solve mathematical problems
4. adaptive reasoning—ability for logical thought, reflection, explanation, and justification
5. productive disposition—habitual inclination to see mathematics as sensible, useful, and worthwhile, coupled with a belief in diligence and one's own efficacy.

We might label D'Ambrosio's numeracy/matheracy and the Mathematics Learning Study Committee's five strands of proficiency as mastery of "dominant"[5] mathematics because it tends to reflect critical thinking within the confines of given mathematics in society, not on broader issues I attend to later in this chapter.

For me, equity in mathematics education can be measured at a number of different levels (e.g., classroom, teacher, school, district, state, nation) and at a number of different time frames (e.g., 4th grade, 8th grade, 12th grade, college, graduate school, mathematics-based positions in society). For instance, at the classroom level, evidence of equity might be that a given teacher could look at her class and be confident that an observer is not able to predict, based solely upon student characteristics, who will command center stage (e.g., time at the board, called upon for answers, relied upon for leadership or authority in the class). In order to address justice, a clear pattern of hegemony would not be observable over a period of time. Of course, what that time period ought to be is not clear. Teachers would have to use their own judgment, but a time frame of any given 3–4 years seems reasonable. As I have seen in my teaching experience, some students are just more outspoken, and in some years a cohort of students might become especially empowered as they move through the school system. However, I would expect teachers over the course of their careers to find ways to counter the ability of any single student or group of students to command power in the classroom. Teachers should be able to look at their classes and not see predictable patterns of achievement (e.g., on standardized tests, weekly exams, mastery of mathematical discourse) throughout a given year or across years. Again, these are ambitious goals and would not necessarily be achieved right away.

Let us consider the school level. Here, a principal should be able to look at her school and get a sense of whether students are disproportionately from a particular background in particular courses (an overrepresentation of African American, Latina/Latino, First Nations, or recent immigrants in courses such as prealgebra, extended algebra, algebra and an underrepresentation of the same students in such courses as trigonometry, precalculus, and calculus). Of course, equitable outcomes at a given school site would not necessarily be assessed on a yearly basis. A 3- to 4-year time frame seems more reasonable for assessing such patterns. Because of the history of underrepresentation of certain groups in advanced mathematics, it would initially be necessary to support an overrepresentation of those groups (African Americans, Latinas/Latinos, First Nations, students in poverty, females) in advanced mathematics classes in order to address equity. I provide these examples not as an exhaustive list of what teachers or principals can or should look for, but rather as a means to envision what *could* count as equitable.

Let me further explain what I mean by equity in dominant mathematics with examples from a high school math department I studied that serves low-income, primarily Latina/Latino students (Gutiérrez, 1999a, 2000b, 2003). The math teachers at Union High decided they wanted more for their students than mere mastery of reform curriculum. In line with Wenger's (1998) notion of "learning as becoming," they thought of teaching as offering students a new identity. Over a period of 10 years, teachers developed a tradition of meeting regularly, discussing curriculum and students, observing one another's classes, revising their teaching schedules, and teaching courses in a way that encouraged students to begin thinking of themselves as "legitimate participants" (Lave & Wenger, 1991; Wenger, 1998) in the mathematics community.

What was once a dead-end curriculum with lots of lower-level courses now has seven (instead of two) 3rd-year college-preparatory courses with three full calculus sections in senior year. At the time I was collecting data, nearly 40% of the senior class was taking calculus. Having so many students take calculus could be a by-product of ushering only the best students forward, possibly being overrepresented by Whites. Yet students who are Spanish dominant, failing other courses, females and males alike, are all active math participants in this school.

I attended the school on average 2 days a week every other week and sat with students in their groups, doing mathematics with them. Although I never administered a formal exam to measure student "understanding," I was impressed with their ability to tell me conceptually and algorithmically what they had been doing on the days since I last was there. Many could describe not only what they did, but also how that fit with what we were working on today. I could approach just about any student in class and elicit his or her perspective. The students also were not shy about arguing their perspectives on a given problem with others in class.

Interviews with students suggested that they were comfortable with mathematics and that they felt that they "belonged" in the calculus classroom. Given that only a small proportion of students in the United States make it to calculus in high school, I had expected these students would feel proud, special, elite to a certain extent. However, during interviews, most students downplayed the status of the class, saying such things as, "Nah, it ain't no big deal. I mean, it's just math. We're all just in there doing our thing." The fact that they saw a kind of "normality" in their participation signaled to me that they had incorporated aspects of this learning environment into their identities. An end-of-year survey found that approximately 80% of the calculus students planned to attend college (had acceptances or could name the college). In fact, eight of the students ended up attending the most prestigious research institution in the state, which gave me the opportunity to follow them after high school—something I will address later in this chapter.

As a kind of outward projection of their identity, students created T-shirts, developed annual potlucks with family members, and elected calculus representatives who went on to give presentations to middle schools. These calculus representatives organized the class and social events and met with teachers to help improve their teaching. Students seemed to own their experience in a way that reflects the notion of *learning as becoming* that teachers espoused. In this sense, teachers were addressing the first aspect of equity.

In the words of one teacher, a key measure of their success was not just that more students were taking more mathematics but also that the essence of being "smart" was not reducible to a particular student characteristic. When asked what students got out of calculus, he responded:

> Besides the academic benefits of possible college credit, the grades, I think they get, there's somewhat of an espirit de corps, like we are the smart kids, we are the cool kids, we are the kids who went together over the summer.
> . . . Union as an integrated school has this effect . . . kids from different cultures working together. . . . There's a kind of nice spirit of people working together at a high level seeing each other as achievers, as smart, you know, the smart kids are not of one race.

I consider this first aspect of equity to deal with dominant school mathematics— the mathematics that is overwhelmingly validated by society. Such mathematics includes both reform and traditional mathematics. While students who have mastered traditional mathematics are not always able to use it in their everyday lives (Boaler, 1997c), this is the mathematics of the college-preparatory system that allows for certain paths in life. In other words, this aspect of equity addresses the kinds of cultural capital that students need in order to fully participate (economically) in society.

However, gaining the cultural capital to participate in an unjust society does not address "fairness." Can we call it equity if students are expected to give up their cultural identities or political stances in order to participate? Mathematics education might also prepare students to analyze world data and to develop a critical eye toward knowledge and a proactive stance on justice. As such, I describe a second aspect of equity that I contend is essential.

2. *Being unable to predict students' ability to analyze, reason about, and especially critique knowledge and events in the world as a result of mathematical practice, based solely upon characteristics such as race, class, ethnicity, gender, beliefs, and proficiency in the dominant language.*

This aspect of equity borrows from D'Ambrosio's (1999) definition of matheracy ("concerned with more than utilitarianism," "emphasis on critical focus," "deals with the ability to be analytical"). It also reflects Powell and Frankenstein's (1997) vision of a liberatory mathematics. The emphasis on equity here is that students would be able to participate democratically (not just economically) in society and contribute to the field of mathematics. It acknowledges that not all persons desire to attend college or to take future course work in mathematics, yet also that everyone has a right to an education that is relevant and useful in life—one that supports their pursuits of happiness.

This aspect of the definition includes ethnomathematics—the diversity of mathematical knowledge that is created, transmitted, diffused, and institutionalized within different cultures, especially outside formal educational settings, and that challenges the notion that mathematics was discovered exclusively by Europeans. However, my concern is not just with the mathematics of other (often third world) cultures that relies upon Western mathematics as a basis for rationality. I also include mathematics inherent in the practices of peoples, regardless of its relation to what is normally considered formal mathematics. Following the work of Restivo (1994) and other sociologists of mathematics (e.g., Brown, 1994), mathematical ideas become communicable concepts only when they can be shared. Therefore, the current base of mathematics will continue to be limited as long as mathematics is defined solely by the practice of an elite group.

Evidence that this aspect of equity is being achieved is more difficult to measure, partly because the ability to be critical of data or mathematics in society has not been the focus of (mathematics) assessment materials. What might we expect to see if students were able to question mathematics and practice mathematics as a critique of society? Students' ability to analyze relationships between people in different positions in society and mathematics might constitute evidence of equity, as might the ability to develop insights into justice/injustice through the exploration of data (e.g., distributions of wealth). While the first aspect of equity dealt primarily with the achievement gap (between middle-class Whites and marginalized students) and conceptual understanding for *all* students, this aspect centers more upon whose mathematics gets created, whose mathematics is valued (Stevens, 2000), and how mathematics is represented and consumed (e.g., Apple, 1995a; Bloor, 1994; Restivo, 1994). It also includes naming the world with mathematics where all groups are respected and have a voice (e.g., Anderson, 1990; Burton, 1990; D'Ambrosio, 1985, 1990, 1999; Dowling, 1998; Gutstein, 2003, this volume; Powell & Frankenstein, 1997; Volmink, 1994; Zaslavsky, 1979, 1994, 1996).

As part of his analysis of the social context, Ernest (1994) raises questions about the values that are inherent in mathematics (pp. 205–206). I have borrowed from some of his questions and raised them as goals here. As such, additional evidence that students are engaging in mathematics from a critical perspective might be that they can recognize the relationship between mathematics and power, or that they are able to see how mathematics has reoriented the modern worldview so that *quality* is seen in terms of *quantity*. At some level, students should also be able to recognize both the origins of mathematical knowledge and how the Western tradition became the dominant one. Do students see whose interests mathematics serves and what its implications are for humankind? Do they recognize that mathematical knowledge (as an outgrowth of human interaction) always brings with it values?

At the classroom level, teachers might begin to witness a process in which marginalized students see a connection between mathematics and their lives. Students may bring up examples or raise questions about events or information from their personal worlds that they want to explore through mathematics. Students of all backgrounds may be able to develop mathematical practices that help them analyze data embedded in controversial issues in society. When encouraged to investigate topics of their own choosing, students of all backgrounds may choose issues that relate to equity either in their local community or in broader society (e.g., housing patterns, school funding, chemical dumping) and might make connections that indicate that they are seeing how mathematics plays out in their lives or the lives of others (e.g., recognizing the cultural capital gained by taking advanced placement courses). Students also ought to be able to investigate and question the knowledge base of mathematics. That is, they might come up with conjectures or see connections that are not part of the canon of mathematics today. Beginning with entirely different goals, they may start to ask questions that require the development of mathematics in unique ways (similar to the work of female scientists who changed the nature of science). Moreover, they should be able to recognize that mathematics can be a "persuasive influence in decisions that may affect them either positively or negatively" (Wagner, Roy, Ecatoiu, & Rousseau, 2000, p. 108).

Earlier I explained how Union High teachers clearly supported students' developing an identity with dominant mathematics that was not reducible to cultural markers such as race and class. What teachers did to address equity in this second aspect of the definition is more subtle. They set goals for themselves that recognized that not all students have desires to continue their mathematical studies beyond high school. However, unlike teachers who radically change the curriculum so that students can critically analyze the world, teachers in this school sought to encourage an identity whereby students could recognize the relationship between mathematics and power as well as become actors in society (hooks, 1994).

One teacher describes the philosophy of the math department:

> More than anything we provide a vision for kids . . . having them believe in themselves as a group, having them be able to do math as a group, having them believe they can go to college as a group . . . and then at a whole 'nother level, um, it's like a political level, um, this society as most others, um, have inequalities, injustices, um, the rich and wealthy, the suburban have more, have better schools. Um, have laws that protect them. And the students at Union for example, have the bottom end of everything

economically, psychologically, equivocally, etcetera, so . . . Organizing, I mean, I, I mean, at some level my way of teaching tries to organize them to be actors rather than acted upon.

While they may not have been provided with opportunities to question the history of mathematics or to explore mathematical data that showed injustices in society, Union students were expected to analyze the relationship between themselves and mathematics in ways that highlighted power issues. One sign that they recognized this relationship arose when they were challenged to "prove" themselves outside the mathematics classroom and outside their low-income and predominantly Latina/o and African American communities. For example, those who attended the state's prestigious research university talked about their first encounters with White students and higher-income students from the suburbs. When students who were middle class or White or both relied upon stereotypes of "who is good in mathematics" or questioned the inner-city students' right to attend a research institution, Union students articulated how "bringing out the calculus card" made a difference. That is, they understood the political consequences associated with course-taking patterns and used this knowledge to reposition themselves in more powerful ways. Their identity with calculus conferred on them more than just legitimate participation in the mathematics community. It offered cultural capital in a society rife with issues of power and domination.

3. *An erasure of inequities between people, mathematics, and the globe.*
    This aspect of equity addresses the fact that having equal access to cultural capital and critical stances to society are necessary but insufficient conditions for change. That is, just because students can problem-solve, reason about their surroundings, and identify inequities through mathematics does not ensure that they will choose (or be able) to act upon the findings of their critical analyses.
    This aspect of equity is likely the most difficult to comprehend and measure. In fact, a complete erasure of inequities between people, mathematics, and the globe is not likely to happen in my lifetime. However, if we do not have long-term goals in mathematics education reform, we risk the possibility of creating a ceiling on equity. Building upon the Universal Declaration of Human Rights, D'Ambrosio (1999) suggests that mathematics can play an important role in ensuring that all peoples are accorded freedom to develop themselves as they wish and to enjoy justice in broader society.

> It is an undeniable right of every human being to have access to all the natural and cultural goods needed for her or his material survival and intellectual enhancement . . . I see mathematics playing an important role in achieving the high humanitarian ideals of a new civilization with equity, justice, and dignity for the entire human species without distinction of race, gender, beliefs and creeds, nationalities, and cultures. (pp. 142–143)

Beyond evidence that there is more equitable distribution between the participation, achievement, and identity of students, we must look for changes outside school that affect broader society. Evidence that equity is being addressed in this area might include some of the following: There is shared distribution of wealth throughout the globe; mathematics is not being applied in ways that destroy the planet; mathematical fields are not aiding in the oppression of other countries; there is a raised awareness of ethnomathematics and the multicultural origins of mathematics without condemning any group of learners as "others" or "primitives"; there is a growing positive relationship between mathematics and a reduction of dominance; and forms of egalitarian and liberatory mathematics are increasingly developed.

A number of questions arise. Who would monitor what gets "counted" as mathematics (McDermott & Webber, 1998)? Would we require mathematicians to monitor the application of mathematics? Would we expect applied mathematicians to include a focus on the ethical uses of mathematics? Would we expect PhD programs to include a kind of mathematical ethics development in course work, research appointments, and fellowships? Would mathematicians strive for awards that showed mathematics was aiding in peace? Would an environmentally friendly movement develop that mathematicians embraced?[6]

It might be the case that the first two aspects of equity must be addressed before we would see any changes in this third aspect. That is, students who gain both (1) dominant and (2) critical mathematics identities will lead to different kinds of mathematicians in the academy, thereby changing what counts as mathematics as well as how it is evaluated. The important thing to consider in this (admittedly simplistic) model is that neither the first nor the second aspects of equity are sufficient to redress injustices in the world. Students need to be able to do both—be able to play the game of mathematics that is currently associated with power and intellectual potential, and be able to change the game of mathematics to serve a better society.

NOTES

An earlier version of this chapter was presented at the conference "Diversity and Equity in Mathematics Education," Northwestern University, Chicago, September 2000. The author wishes to thank Deborah Ball, Paul Cobb, Juan Guerra, Carol Malloy, and the editors of this volume for their helpful comments on an earlier draft. In addition, the ideas for this article were influenced by interaction with other members of the RAND Mathematics Study Panel. The views expressed in the article are solely those of the author.

1. See, e.g., the National Study Panel created and supported by RAND Corporation and the Office of Educational Research and Improvement.

2. *Dominant perspective* here refers to the fact that in the United States (and elsewhere), Whites, males, and middle-class/wealthy individuals are automatically in a position of power because the views and perspectives that are portrayed in society tend to be

in line with their own beliefs and interests. These very beliefs and interests are so embedded in our society that most people are not consciously aware of them. See, e.g., McIntosh's (1989) article or Lipsitz's book (1998) on Whiteness or Ladson-Billings and Tate's (1995) article on Critical Race Theory. The dominant perspective also refers to the fact that the aforementioned beliefs and interests tend to be supported by formal institutions in society (e.g., law, education, marriage) *to the exclusion* of other beliefs and interests.

3. Although the dominant language in the United States is English, I use the term *dominant language* to highlight the fact that there are other countries where English is not the dominant language. Moreover, at some later point in time, English may not be the dominant language of the United States.

4. I borrow and adapt this term from my colleague Mary "Fong" Hermes at the University of Minnesota, Duluth.

5. I use the term *dominant mathematics* to suggest that the knowledge base currently used in schools throughout the world reflects a Western (colonial) frame of reference (D'Ambrosio, 1985, 1990; Powell & Frankenstein, 1997; Secada, 1994; Gutierrez, 2000b). The use of such mathematics knowledge in countries outside the West and with indigenous peoples in the West represents a kind of recolonization.

6. I liken this movement to that which has occurred in the investment world (to a modest extent) where "green funds" are now seen as socially desirable.

4

"So One Question Leads to Another": Using Mathematics to Develop a Pedagogy of Questioning

ERIC GUTSTEIN

So one question leads to another question, and then you have to answer four more, and those four questions lead to eight more questions. So I think that [racial disparity in mortgage lending] is not racism, but that leads me to the conclusion that if it was not racism, then why do they pay more money to whites? Is that racism?

> —Vanessa,[1] Grade 7, December 2002, written for a mathematics project titled Mortgage Loans—Is Racism a Factor?

INTRODUCTION: SETTING THE STAGE

In September 2002, I began, once again, teaching a seventh-grade mathematics class at Rivera Elementary School, where Vanessa was my student. Rivera is in a large, working-class, Mexican-immigrant community in Chicago. My journal, recorded right after the first class, reads:

> I told them what we'd be doing this year, that we'd be studying algebra, geometry, number, and probability/statistics, but that we'd also be studying about the world. . . . I told them that . . . we'd be using mathematics to understand a lot of real-world issues. I told them that what they'd be doing would be to learn how to question, that if they left my class with more questions than they walked in with, I'd be happy and would feel that I'd done my job. I told them that I wanted them to question what I told them, what other teachers told them (I was careful to not include questioning their parents), to question their texts. (September 6, 2002)

The following week, I gave my students a mathematics project titled Cost of the B-2 Bomber—Where Do Our Tax Dollars Go? The essence of the project was for students to compare the cost of one B-2 bomber (about $2.1 billion) to a

4-year scholarship (including room, board, and books) at the University of Wisconsin–Madison and to find out how many years the money for one bomber would pay for four-year scholarships for the whole graduating class of 250 students (79 years!).

This was the first of several *real-world* projects in which students used mathematics as a principal analytical tool to investigate social-justice issues. These projects often emerged from students' own questions. I developed this project after a class discussion with a couple of students about why one's older brother was in the navy rather than in college (lack of money). But *that* discussion emerged because another student had a question for me: Would I go to fight in a war against Iraq? And the impetus of this question for me was that 2 days earlier I taken 30 minutes of class time for students to raise *their* questions about the World Trade Center bombing. Thus the chain of events, set into motion by creating the space for students' questions about September 11, eventually led to the B-2 bomber project.

From the first day of the class, I tried to make clear to students that we would develop a *problem-posing* environment together (Freire, 1970/1998) in which they would learn and use mathematics as a way to question, understand, challenge, and critique the world. This environment, which I refer to as a *pedagogy of questioning*, is an aspect of teaching for social justice. In this chapter, I examine these concepts in depth and provide a detailed example in order to make explicit what teaching mathematics for social justice means in theory and practice.

ADDRESSING THE PURPOSES OF THIS BOOK

This volume poses two basic questions: Why are there dramatic inequities in mathematics achievement between students of color and Whites, and between students of different socioeconomic classes? Given that the inequities exist, what can be done? Obviously, the questions are inextricably related, and how one understands the first largely determines how one addresses the second.

With respect to the first question, there is a complex set of explanations on which the mathematics education community has some semblance of agreement, among them resource gaps (Secada, 1992), insufficient opportunity to learn (Oakes, 1985, 1990), the *savage inequalities* facing urban education (Kozol, 1992), and the lack of building on students' cultural/linguistic knowledge and lived experiences (e.g., Ladson-Billings, 1995; Moll & González, 2004). These have general currency and are within the broad purview of what the National Council of Teachers of Mathematics (NCTM) (2000) designates as its first principle in the *Principles and Standards for School Mathematics*—the *equity* principle.

Other analyses about the undereducation of students of color and low-income students are more controversial. These views explicitly name inequitable and unjust relations of power and analyze the interconnections of oppressive societal structures such as capitalist economic relations (Darder, 2002), globalization (Lipman, 2004), market-driven accountability regimes (Apple, 2001), imperial domination (McLaren, 1998), and racism and systems of White supremacy (King, 1991; Watkins, 2001; Woodson, 1933/1990). Although not all of the above theorists draw direct connections between unjust social forces and the underachievement of specific groups of students in U.S. society, all their analyses examine the relationships between inequitable power distribution in society and the education experienced by marginalized students.

Paulo Freire's work exemplifies this latter trend (1970/1998, 1994; Freire & Faundez, 1992; Freire & Macedo, 1987). Consistent in his work over 35 years are some basic themes: Education needs to hasten the end of domination and the (re)emergence of humanization; the oppressed play a fundamental role in the struggles for their own liberation; and teachers, students, and communities need to join together as genuine partners in emancipatory social movements, both inside and outside education arenas. A particular contribution Freire (1970/1998) made to understanding the education of marginalized students is the elaboration of the concept of *banking* education, in which he used a metaphor of teachers dispensing *deposits* into passive *recipients* (students) to be filed, stored, and retrieved on demand.

One should not equate banking with didactic direct instruction, however, as in Freire's (1970/1998) view, the former is far more insidious and disempowering:

> The more students work at storing the deposits entrusted to them, the less they develop the critical consciousness which would result from their intervention in the world as transformers of that world. The more completely they accept the passive role imposed on them, the more they tend simply to adapt to the world as it is and to the fragmented view of reality deposited in them. The capability of banking education to minimize or annul the students' creative power and to stimulate their credulity serves the interests of the oppressors, who care neither to have the world revealed nor to see it transformed. (p. 54)

The concept of banking education, as Freire sees it, "is well suited to the purposes of the oppressors, whose tranquility rests on how well the people fit the world the oppressors have created, and *how little they question it*" (p. 57; emphasis added).

Freire (1970/1998) juxtaposed banking education to problem-posing education. He wrote that students in a problem-posing environment "are now critical co-investigators in dialogue with the teacher. . . . [P]roblem-posing education involves a constant unveiling of reality . . . [and] strives for the *emergence* of consciousness and *critical intervention* in reality" (pp. 61–62).

The second purpose of the present volume is to address what to do about the deplorable (mathematics) miseducation of low-income students and students of color in the United States. Clearly, interventions exist, among them the Algebra Project (Moses & Cobb, 2001), designed to create the conditions for youth (especially African American youth) to demand mathematical literacy and economic access as part of a larger struggle for political rights. An underexamined perspective is Frankenstein's (1987) *critical mathematics education,* which "can develop critical understanding and lead to critical action" (p. 192). Frankenstein's framework makes strong use of Freire's work and challenges mathematics educators to reconsider their teaching in ways that contribute to the processes of human emancipation. Her adult mathematics students, over the past 20-plus years, have mathematized social practices to reveal their political nature, for example, by analyzing how the U.S. government decides who is, and who is not, counted in calculating unemployment statistics (1998, p. 306). She employs a Freirean framework to aid students' development of critical consciousness. I adapted many of her ideas in teaching middle school students to address this volume's second question—what to do about the inequities. I advocate that students need to be prepared through their mathematics education to critique injustice and challenge, in words and actions, oppressive structures and acts. Like Frankenstein, I contend that mathematics education can serve the larger struggles for emancipation. I also argue that teachers need to envision their own roles as part of larger social movements and explicitly attempt to create conditions in which young people can become active participants in changing society (hooks, 1994).

One term for describing this type of pedagogy is *teaching for social justice.* In mathematics, I see such a pedagogy as having four main components (Gutstein, 2003, 2005): to develop (1) academic success (i.e., both mathematical power and what is needed to pass gatekeeping tests, attend college, and obtain access to advanced mathematics courses and related careers if desired); (2) sociopolitical consciousness; (3) a sense of social agency; and (4) positive cultural and social identities. But while this may name constituent parts, it does not adequately describe the classroom *culture* and *norms; relationships* between student and teacher or *dispositions* toward knowledge, teacher, text, and "truth." These aspects of the classroom environment, which I collectively refer to as a *pedagogy of questioning,* are more than pedagogy in a narrow sense but rather embody a larger set of sociocultural phenomena that exist within any classroom. Their development is my focus here. The three key questions I address are (1) What is a pedagogy of questioning? (2) How does one create such a pedagogy? and (3) What is the role of mathematics in such a pedagogy?

CONTEXT AND STUDY

Rivera is a K–8 school of 800 students, 99% of whom are Latino/a (the vast majority Mexican) and 98% low-income. Students are mainly first- or second-generation immigrants, and almost all speak Spanish, although to differing degrees. Rivera has three programs: a monolingual English program, a bilingual program, and an honors bilingual program whose students are demographically indistinguishable from regular-track students (I taught in all three programs). In Grades 6–8, classes are departmentalized, and standardized-test scores are a major concern for both the school and individual students, who cannot go on to high school in Chicago without a sufficiently high score. Most Rivera graduates attend the neighborhood high school, which has a drop-out rate of around 50%.

This was a practitioner-research investigation (Anderson, Herr, & Nihlen, 1994). I used semi-ethnographic methods, including participant observation, open-ended surveys, and textual analysis of documents (Hammersley & Atkinson, 1983). My data include standardized-test scores, unit tests, in-depth mathematics projects (including the real-world projects), samples of class and homework, and the field notes of a research assistant. I also maintained a practitioner journal in which I regularly recorded reflections and observations on classroom climate and culture, students' mathematical work and dispositions, my interactions with them and their families, and classroom discussions. I collected weekly journal assignments containing students' reflections on their mathematical learning and thoughts about issues we were studying or discussing.

The seventh-grade class I discuss here had 30 students and was in the bilingual honors program. I taught the class from September 2002 until the end of January 2003. An important part of the story was that I used the *Mathematics in Context* [MiC] curriculum (National Center for Research in Mathematic Sciences Education & Freudenthal Institute [NCRMSE & FI], 1997–1998) approximately 75–80% of the time and the real-world projects and other miscellaneous mathematics activities the rest of the time. I consider the role of MiC briefly later in this article.

Over the 10 years I have worked with Rivera I have learned much Spanish and spent much time in the community. Nonetheless, as a White male professional, I am in many ways an outsider to Rivera's culture, community, and language. Clearly, there are issues and dilemmas with "teaching other people's children" (Delpit, 1988), and these may be even more complicated when teaching for social justice. Although I do not have space here to discuss these issues, they are central to my research. I discuss them (and others I mention briefly here) in depth elsewhere (Gutstein, 2005).

WHAT IS A PEDAGOGY OF QUESTIONING?

A pedagogy of questioning is a classroom environment with several characteristics that are co-created by students and teacher. First, it is a space in which students have opportunities to pose their own real, meaningful questions. Of course, given that most public schools do not provide these opportunities, teachers may have to seed the process, as I needed to do in providing space for students to raise their questions about September 11. Second, students must have the opportunity to *name* (i.e., understand deeply, in sociopolitical context, with the capacity to shape) their own realities. This naming by students must be collaboratively done with teachers, who are themselves genuine questioners and learners in a pedagogy of questioning (Freire, 1970/1998, p. 159).

Third, it is a setting in which "one question leads to another question, and then you have to answer four more, and those four questions lead to eight more questions," as noted by Vanessa, the student quoted at the beginning of this chapter. Answers and "truth" are provisional and relational, and students and teacher keep this in mind as they strive to unravel complex social phenomena—such as racism—and understand their interconnections and root causes. Fourth, these interrelationships and complexities are explicitly on the table for all to analyze. Fifth, students engage and analyze multiple perspectives, not as a way to debate or artificially pretend to take someone else's view, but to build on one another's knowledge and understand that all positions reflect a particular perspective on the world. Sixth, when possible, questions are tied to actions and social movements. Finally, questions are integrated and ubiquitous and are not just posed when a teacher thinks of it. As Freire (Freire & Faundez, 1992) noted, "It is not simply a matter of introducing a question-and-answer session into the curriculum between nine and ten, for example" (p. 40). Students should feel that they can ask their teacher, at any time, if he or she will support or join a war effort against Iraq.

HOW DOES ONE CREATE A PEDAGOGY OF QUESTIONING?

I do not mean to prescribe a "method" in any sense here, or to suggest that all the conditions described above existed equally at all times in my classroom, or to propose that they necessarily need to in any particular classroom. Rather, I address this question by examining how we co-created a particular environment and draw out possible implications. In October 2002, I read a *Chicago Tribune* article about a report done by ACORN, a national community-organizing group, that analyzed mortgage-rejection rates, by race, in 68 metropolitan areas, including Chicago (Manor, 2002). In December, I gave my students the project Mortgage Loans—Is Racism a Factor? The article had many statistics and presented alternate perspectives. A quote attributed to an ACORN spokesperson read, "'Institutional racism' is to blame for the difficulty blacks and Latinos encounter in getting mortgages." The article also quoted a bank-loan officer who said it was "unlikely" that racism was to blame; rather, "lenders are in the business of making loans. We want to make loans." This was an opportunity for students to sift through text and data and try to judge whether racism was indeed a factor—and if so, how.

But was it the students' own question? On the surface, no, since I initiated the question. However, we starting discussing whose families owned their own homes and whose wanted to, and several students recounted their families' efforts and difficulties in getting a mortgage. An important aspect of the story is that rental housing in the communities where Rivera students live is often substandard, and overcrowding is common. So not only did students have experience with the issue, but owning a home—and understanding why some families had been unsuccessful—were both concrete and important. Thus, it quickly *was* their question as well.

However, the project was not just about the mathematics of home ownership. One could easily do a project about whether a 15- or 30-year mortgage was preferable, and so on. But this project was qualitatively different because I asked students to address whether and how racism was implicated. Freire (1994) wrote:

> And let it not be said that, if I am a biology [or mathematics] teacher, I must not "go off into other considerations"—that I must *only* teach biology, as if the phenomenon of life could be understood apart from its historico-social, cultural, and political framework. . . . If I am a biology teacher, obviously I must teach biology. But in doing so, I must not cut it off from the framework of the whole. (p. 78; emphasis in the original)

To discuss mortgages without contextualizing that Latinos/as were almost three times as likely as Whites to be denied a mortgage in Chicago would be to cut off "securing a mortgage" from the framework of the whole.

Freire was also clear that dialogue in which both teacher and students had real questions and listened to—and learned from—each other is essential in a problem-posing pedagogy. Dialogue transpired in our class through students' writings on their projects and journals and my responses to them. For example, question number 9 was

> Write a *good* essay answering the following question (you *must* use data from the article or the quote above to make your argument): Is racism a factor in getting mortgages in the Chicago area?

I made virtually every student rewrite her or his essay, some twice, for various reasons. But I responded to each student, sometimes extensively. My responses generally challenged students, raised further questions, gave them feedback, and responded to *their* questions.

Below, I provide one interchange between Nilda, a student, and me and then examine it in some detail. Although among the longest, it was otherwise unexceptional. What follows is her journal entry near the project's end and my response. I reproduce these to show the dialogical nature and explicitly political character of the exchange.

> Mr. Rico,[2]
>
> Was this project to confuse us and really make us think? Because that's what it did. After our last discussion on Friday, everyone was talking about what we had discussed.
>
> In my first article I said that I thought racism was not a factor, after our second discussion I thought racism was a factor, but I think that we don't really know. Even though the rate for Blacks was 5Xs higher than

whites in being rejected, that does not necessarily mean it is racism. It could be because of their debt, income, or maybe it could be racism. But Mr. Rico, how do we know how the people at the bank think, and isn't it illegal for any business to deny service to their customers? And if someone were to be denied wouldn't the bank give them a reason why?

. . . Now I am positive that we cannot tell if racism is a factor using the data and information we have unless we got into the minds of the people at the bank, but we can't, we can only assume. But that's not so great either, because we could assume wrong. So now I think that we can never really know. So in my next journal, can you please answer my questions, thanks!

Nilda

And my response:

Nilda,

I mean it, you are really deep. That is really great! You have taken this project and *really* tried to understand all the very complicated issues (and there are *many!!*). First of all, the project certainly was to make you all think. I believe that you are *very* able to think about a lot of complicated, deep things in the world, and the sooner you start, the better. And, of course, it is a very good way to learn mathematics, not only to learn mathematics, but to learn how important mathematics can be in understanding the world. . . .

Yes, you are right, it is illegal to deny service or to discriminate against people because of their race, language, gender (male or female), sexuality (if they are gay or straight), etc. And you make a very excellent point, that we cannot know what is in the minds of individual people to be able to tell whether or not they are racist. That is why I tried to make clear what the difference is between *individual* racism (e.g., I don't treat you well because you're Mexican) and *institutional* racism (there is a whole system that exists, that has a history and has been around for years and years that affects whole groups of people—as we see here with the racism in the mortgages). The fact that the *disparity ratio*[3] exists, and people of color have such a hard time compared to Whites in getting a mortgage, to me, is a clear example of institutional racism. To the bank spokesperson who says, "We want to loan money to everyone," I say, "The data shows that you *don't!*" And the reason, beyond individual racism (which is there, no doubt, but is not the main thing), is that there is the whole system that has kept African Americans and Latinos from having the *wealth* to really be able to afford mortgages. Just take a good look at the table I will give you about wealth and race in the U.S. If we understand what that table really tells us, the evidence is pretty clear, and if we were to read the whole book where that table comes from, we would understand much better the whole history of racism in the U.S. Nilda, just think about this. . . . For hundreds of years, millions of African Americans worked as slaves. . . . All that time, the White slaveowners (*not* poor Whites, just a few *rich* Whites) kept all their wages. When African Americans finally got their freedom, they were still kept down, not allowed into good jobs, kept out of good schools, kept in ghettos and poor communities. . . . It's no wonder at all that they have so little wealth. Racism is as much a part of this country as the U.S. flag. . . . This country was built on racism, from the stolen lands of the Native Americans to the stolen wages of African slaves.

These are my views. I am not asking for you to accept them; in fact, I want you to question my views as much as you question any others. Just think about them, and keep thinking about them, as I see you doing.

Mr. Rico

In responding to Nilda, I tried to reinforce aspects of classroom discussions, particularly the distinctions between institutional and individual racism. I tried to help her understand a key conceptual issue I raised at the end of the project: Historically, the *income* difference between African Americans and Whites has been tiny compared to their *wealth* difference (Oliver & Shapiro, 1997). Those data were relevant in understanding the disparities in the rejection rates, because banks give loans based not just on income, but also on assets and liabilities (i.e., wealth). However, this point was difficult to grasp, and I planned to return to it later in the year.

Furthermore, I often explained my analyses to students, although not in the initial parts of the projects, and always tried to give students the space in which to develop their own. I put forward my thoughts because I accept Freire's (1994) proposition that education cannot be "neutral." However, I was quite conscious of the difficulty of walking the line between expressing my views and defining my analyses while simultaneously creating opportunities for students (especially younger ones) to develop their own. I continue to struggle with this dialectic. (For parents' views on this issue, see Gutstein, 2005, in press.) Freire (1994) addressed this complicated subject:

> Inasmuch as education of its very nature is directive and political, I must, without ever denying my dream or my utopia before the educands, respect them. To defend a thesis, a position, a preference, with earnestness, defend it rigorously, but passionately, as well, and at the same time to stimulate the contrary discourse, and respect the right to utter that discourse, is the best way to teach, first, the right to have our own ideas, even our duty to "quarrel" for them, for our dreams . . . and second, mutual respect (p. 78)

There is always the risk of unduly influencing students. But I subscribe to Freire's view on risks: "Is there a risk of influencing the students? It is impossible to live, let alone exist, without risks. The important thing is to prepare ourselves to be able to run them well" (p. 79).

The exchange with Nilda shows the character of my interactions with students. I tried to build relationships with students both in and out of class that supported these intense interchanges, for example, by socializing with students and families when appropriate, talking to students about their concerns, and responding to their journals (which were confidential). But the distinction between these types of relationships, which many teachers build with students, and those such as the dialogue with Nilda are about establishing "political" relationships (for lack of a better term) with students. This was essential in creating a pedagogy of questioning.

Dialogue was also present in other ways. To end the project, students sat in a circle for two periods and read aloud their essays if they chose to. I prefaced the readings by emphasizing that we were not "debating," with "winners" and "losers," but rather were "discussing," to find common understandings, including agreeing to disagree. As an indication of how some students approached the discussion, Ivan journaled after the first period, "Even though we discussed it, the whole class has not yet solved the problem [whether racism is a factor]. On Monday, for sure, we will solve the problem."

Engaging students in examining issues from multiple perspectives—versus debating—is yet another component of a pedagogy of questioning. Question number 6 was

> The Bank One representative argues that racism is not a factor because banks "want to make loans." *Using data from the article/chart*, list *two* questions you would ask him that would challenge that position.

And question number 7 was

> Pretend, for a moment, that your group members are representatives of Bank One. Write what you think you would or could say to defend the statement in the article, that it was "unlikely that racism was causing lenders to refuse loans to Black and Latinos here [in Chicago]." In other words, see if you can come up with some *other* explanations, besides racism, to explain why there is a *disparity ratio* in the Chicago area.

Thus, students had to understand different viewpoints. Many students changed their minds (some several times) as they studied the issues, listened to others, responded to my questions, and rewrote their essays. Tita's response was typical, demonstrating that students heard and reconsidered their ideas:

> Well about the essay, I have changed my mind. Now I think that there really isn't a way to know if racism is or is not a factor. At first I had two arguments but they were not very good to support that racism was *not* a factor. During our discussion at class I heard many arguments from both sides of the story.

Another way to create a pedagogy of questioning is to pose difficult questions that are also real for teachers. This is part of the notion that "truth" is relative and provisional, a process of knowing, rather than an answer (Freire & Faundez, 1992). One of the project's most difficult aspects was for students to understand that the disparity ratio actually *worsened* as one went *up* the income ladder. That is, the disparity between upper-class African Americans/Latinos/as and upper-class Whites was greater than that between lower-class African Americans/Latinos/as and lower-class Whites. In fact, most students thought the opposite was true, because they knew, in general, that people of color are poorer than whites. This data initially confounded me also, and thus this question was real to me.

Creating a pedagogy of questioning should also ensure that questions reverberate beyond school. Several students wrote comments like Aida's, "Me and some of the girls have been talking about the conversation," and Nilda's, "After our last discussion on Friday, everyone was talking about what we had discussed." Although I am not completely clear why, and unfortunately did not ask systematically, this project deeply engaged students. I believe that it was because it tied into their aspirations, experiences, community issues, and sense of justice. Students talked about their lives, wrote that they had been discussing the project with friends, and connected to stereotypes about themselves as Mexicans.[4] These together suggest that the questions and issues went beyond the classroom, were personally meaningful, and became their own. Leandro wrote:

> This project was very interesting because it has happened to one of my uncles. He was looking for a house and found one. But in the end, he was turned down. This really is important to me because I will like to buy a house when I grow up, not only for me, but for my cousin and my sister.

Additionally, creating a pedagogy of questioning should ensure that questions and ideas flow freely in the classroom yet lead to deeper analysis. Students raised excellent and provocative questions on their own in their writing and discussions. Manny asked: "Is racism also in job applications?" Moises wrote: "This project made me think that maybe they weren't being discriminated for loans, but does that also mean that they are not being discriminated when they apply for a job?" Tita wrote: "If they [the banks] want to make loans then why is there a drastic difference between the percentage of rejection for African Americans 31.66, Latinos 16.2 percent and whites 6.3?" Garbina wrote: "If machines choose who gets a mortgage [i.e., if there is a computer program that does not ask race], then how can we explain the data that we have?" and "If lenders want to make loans then why doesn't everyone get one? Is it lack of money or racism?" Vanessa wrote: "But then why do whites get paid more and is that racism and if so why are they racist?"

Students became quite used to both my questions and to asking their own. When I asked former students, whom I taught for almost 2 years (when they were in seventh and eighth grades, from 1997–1999), to write a hypothetical letter to a seventh grader entering my class, Rosa (then entering eleventh grade) wrote: "What would I write to a seventh grader in Rivera, mmm . . . Well that you ask a lot of questions, and that you ask a lot of questions, and by the way, you ask a lot of questions!" Rosa also wrote, in describing our class when she was a high school senior:

> While taking Mr. Rico's class, I myself was skeptical of his teaching methods. Nonetheless, I have realized that through his teachings I learned of racism and discrimination and its effects on not only our Latino community but other communities through out the United States and the world. . . . Mr. Rico's method of teaching always encouraged us to ask questions and to find answers through our own analysis. . . . Like I said before I myself always questioned him, over and over, but it was that questioning, that ability to even question the teacher that made me grow academically.

Her view was the norm for my students. Marisol, also a senior, wrote:

> By no means [did he] expect us to believe everything he said. In fact, we were always encouraged to speak up in class whenever we disagreed with him. He never pushed us to believe certain things but instead challenged us to question *everything*. And we did. We not only questioned things going on in our very own neighborhood and in the world as a whole, but we also questioned Mr. Rico and debated ferociously with *him* about his own opinions. That is what he taught us, to question everything around us and not just to take "somebody's word" on an issue, even if it meant not taking his.

WHAT IS THE ROLE OF MATHEMATICS IN CREATING A PEDAGOGY OF QUESTIONING?

My argument here is that mathematics can play a role in creating a pedagogy of questioning—under certain conditions. The central condition is that students regularly use mathematics as a tool to *read the world* (Freire & Macedo, 1987), that is, develop a sociopolitical, historical understanding of one's own life conditions and broader society. However, to read the world on this project was particularly difficult, unlike, for example, on the B-2 bomber project. In that project, students used mathematics to uncover what the money for one bomber would mean for the college education for Latino/a students like themselves. I call that reading the world with mathematics because students used mathematics to investigate and calculate the various costs for different ways to use public money; put their mathematical analyses into sociopolitical, historical context; and built community and a dramatically different orientation toward mathematics and its use in understanding reality.

However, the mortgage project was much more complex. Thus, one has to understand that reading the world can happen in different contexts. The article was difficult to disentangle, and the data were confusing. Students had to pick their way through, and compare and contrast, data about mortgage rejection rates for Whites, African Americans, and Latinos/as, in Chicago and nationally, as well as examine data across various years for these different groups. The culminating essay, "Is Racism a Factor?" was preceded by many other questions. Throughout, students needed to understand data and how they related to the questions. I asked students to generate explanations for why the disparity ratio worsened as incomes increased, and questions number 6 and 7 above show how students had to use mathematics from different perspectives to justify or criticize lending practices. Students also answered algebraic questions for which they did not know the algorithms, such as the following:

> (3) We do not know how many Latinos or Whites were denied loans in the Chicago area in 2001. But suppose 1,500 Latinos were *denied* loans in the Chicago area. Using that estimate, and data from the article, find how many Latinos *did* get home loans last year in the Chicago area. *Explain your mathematics!*

In this situation, reading the world with mathematics has to be seen as a complex process of sifting one's way through a murky field of numbers and words to develop tentative conclusions and justifications, addressing myriad questions along the way. It is not a simple matter of examining some straightforward numbers and proclaiming that an injustice has occurred, as one might do in choosing whether to fund education or war preparation (e.g., on the B-2 bomber project). Yes, the disparity ratio shows us that in Chicago, African Americans are rejected five times more often than Whites, and Latinos/as almost three times more often—but that does not say whether racism is a factor, and if so, why or how. More analysis is needed, and that is precisely the lesson that virtually all students took away from the project. The world is complicated, and although mathematics is a powerful tool with which to disentangle some of the complexities, open questions will remain. Consider Jesse's essay, in which he argued that the data suggested racism but also that one needed to account for alternative perspectives:

> I think that it is inconclusive whether or not racism is a factor when it comes to getting a mortgage loan in the Chicago area.
> It is a factor because white applicants no matter what their income was they were always denied less times than African Americans and Latinos. And it also is a factor because the ratio of applicants denied between African Americans and whites is 5:1 and between Latinos and whites is 3:1. That data shows that racism is a factor.
> There are always two sides to a story. Racism is not a factor because we do not know whether or not those people had bad credit or if they were

unemployed. It could be possible that a lot of those people could have been in debt. Even though the banks want to make loans they also want to make sure that they get paid.

So with the data provided it is very hard to conclude whether or not racism is a factor when it comes to obtaining a mortgage loan in the Chicago area.

A sociocultural analysis suggests that as individuals are enculturated into community norms and practices, even as they participate in their development, they take on the habits of mind and dispositions of that community. This is essentially what my data show, from an earlier class I taught for almost 2 years (their seventh and eighth grades, 1997–99; see Gutstein, 2003, 2005). That class completed 17 real-world projects in which we used mathematics to explore racism, the growth of Latino/a populations, wealth inequality, neighborhood gentrification, and other sociopolitical issues related to their lives. At the end of eighth grade, I gave students an open-ended survey[5] with the question: "Do you feel now you are better able to understand the world using math? Examples?" Of the 23 responders, 20 said yes, 2 said no, and 1 said "sort of." Even the two students who reported disliking math more after my class said that they understood the world better using math. Paulina wrote:

> Yes, I think I'm able to understand the world with math. All the math problems, projects, discussions about drug testing, Chicano history, etc., have made me understand because knowing about those issues and the discussions that we did made me think of what math might be involved. The math that we did helped me even more. (quoted in Gutstein, 2003, p. 61)

Although I did not ask the same question of the class that completed the mortgage project, my analysis suggests that they also believed mathematics was part of understanding the world because that was how they used mathematics. Students wrote unsolicited responses, for example:

> Oh! And Mr. Rico I wanted to tell you that it was a really good project cause we are learning about the world using math. This would be like doing two subjects or learning about it in math. And don't think that I just wrote this to make you feel good cause it is the truth.

The evidence, from this project and others, suggests that this class also was beginning to see how mathematics was connected to understanding complex social phenomenon.

This complicated, engaging real-world project included proportional reasoning (ratios, percentages, decimals, and fractions), algebraic reasoning, medians, data analysis, and graphing. Doing the mathematics, *with* conceptual understanding, was essential to answering whether racism was a factor—and there were still limitations even if one had this grasp, as I discuss below. Thus mathematics became both a means with which to investigate this matter and an entry point into more involved conversations about historically embedded racism. These deeper discussions do, in fact, require further mathematical learning and analysis. It is precisely in that dialectical relationship—between doing mathematics and reading the world—that the role of mathematics in creating a pedagogy of questioning is played out.

Furthermore, there is an important relationship between one's formal curriculum and a problem-posing environment. The MiC curriculum places students in the position of arbitrating knowledge, examining multiple perspectives, and making sense of reality with mathematics, even if the reality may seem contrived and not their own (Gutstein, 1998). MiC helps develop dispositions in students toward knowledge that support a pedagogy of questioning and are therefore important. But there is no reason to expect that by itself, MiC (or any "reform" or "standards-based" curriculum) would create such a pedagogy, or that "thinking critically" about mathematics (à la NCTM, 2000) translates into thinking critically about the world.

The distinction between students becoming "critical thinkers" in mathematics and students reading the world with mathematics is significant. Many teachers and various curricula help students develop mathematical power and think critically about mathematics. That is important to my work, albeit not by itself my paramount goal. On the mortgage project, students' difficulty with certain mathematical ideas limited their grasp of some political ones. For example, some students' difficulty in understanding the disparity ratio made it hard for them to understand that it worsened as one got richer, and this in turn made it harder to understand *why* this occurs. And one group of students consistently argued that African Americans were rejected more often because they applied more, misunderstanding the concept of *rate*. It was clear that students needed a certain level of sophistication with mathematics to use it as a tool to analyze injustice.

CONCLUSION

I now consider three dilemmas that confronted me at Rivera and that manifested themselves in this project—and then address one last question. First, when teachers attempt to engender in students the disposition to "question all your answers," as Tita wrote, there is a potential danger of relativism, that nothing is knowable and no truth exists. That is, there is a dialectic between needing to keep probing and problematizing what we think we know, and coming to accept that after much research we can have a decent, if provisional, understanding of a situation. My data showed this possibility. Of course, we want students to learn how to defend a position while keeping open minds. Two thirds of the class (20 of 30) argued that racism either was or was not a factor, and most of the rest argued that more data were needed. A typical comment was Abril's: "I think that I cannot make a deci-sion if racism is or is not a factor. There are many possibilities, and there is much more information needed." But others had another view, expressed, for example, by Garbina: "With all of the arguments brought up in class I have reached to a con-clusion that there really isn't a way to show if racism is one of the major factors or not." That is, a few students seemed to feel we could *never* know. These views led me to appreciate the complexity of the question, How can we promote ceaseless critique while concurrently encouraging students to hold firmly to their own be-liefs? In raising this dilemma, however, I do not wish to blur an essential point—these students actively and consistently raised their own questions throughout this project. This is a major step in learning to read the world.

The second tension is between teachers expressing their analyses while si-multaneously creating space in which students can develop their own. I referred earlier to the risk of unduly influencing students to accept our views. But how, precisely, do we do that? I know that exhorting students to question, critique, and challenge my positions is definitely necessary, as is creating a climate in which all views are respected while being subject to question. But then I have the weighty responsibility to be honest in return, for I cannot ask students to question my views and then not openly provide them. So creating a pedagogy of questioning demands that teachers be more open than we are generally used to being. And the more open we are, the more there is the potential to influence students to accept our posi-tions, as well as possibly to cause our positions to clash with those of the students' families, of the school administration, and of the students themselves. Resolving these potential conflicts so that all are learners in a Freirean dialogical setting is a considerable—and open—challenge in teaching for social justice.

The final issue is the limitation of using mathematics by itself to answer com-plex sociohistorical questions. In this project, even with bringing to bear deep mathematical understanding, the issues were sufficiently complex that one needed substantial background knowledge to know whether racism was a factor. Thus mathematics was a necessary but insufficient tool to address the question. From my point of view, the project's main weakness was that I was unable to have stu-dents fully grasp the complicated sociohistorical reasons for the disparities. Carmen actually touched on the ideas in her essay, but despite my probes (I am the "some-body" she refers to below), she maintained that though there was *historical* dis-crimination, racism was not a factor in *current* disparities:

> Racism is totally not a factor in mortgages. . . . the reason why a lot of
> Black[s] and Latinos are being rejected is because they have less collat-
> eral. . . . Somebody asked me why whites had more collateral and I said
> because they have been here . . . longer. Then that person asked me why
> didn't Blacks have more collateral if they've been here longer, and to that
> . . . I would say that since long time ago whites owned lots of things and
> Blacks were not able because they were slaves. Even in the 1970's blacks

were being discriminated. So I have to say that Blacks had the shortest amount of time to get to own stuff.

While mathematics may initially demonstrate that something is amiss (e.g., African Americans get rejected five times more often than Whites), it cannot tell us why. Mathematics may be necessary in interpreting further data (e.g., in 1988, the median net worth of African Americans was only 8% of that of Whites; see Oliver & Shapiro, 1997), but the orientation to look deeper for that data is a component of a problem-posing pedagogy—and not, I would argue, necessarily a part of mathematics. Thus teachers must provide students with the necessary historical knowledge, the disposition to continue to probe, *and* specific mathematical tools if they are to actualize a pedagogy of questioning in a mathematics classroom. Doing all these within one classroom is a considerable challenge and raises implications for the preparation of teachers as well (Gutstein, 2005).

Clearly, creating such a pedagogy takes more than one project, but I have tried to show pieces of what it looks like and how mathematics relates. The question that remains unanswered is, Why one would want to create a pedagogy of questioning in the first place? For those who see themselves as equity and justice advocates/activists in education (and society), one purpose is to create opportunities for youth to develop into people who will struggle to change the world. In the context of high-stakes "accountability" regimes that create more inequity for urban youth (Lipman, 2004) and increasing world wealth and quality-of-life polarization, it is not idle chatter to say that "the youth are our future." We can prepare them in many ways, including using tools such as mathematics to analyze injustices, while developing the necessary mathematical power to support them in passing gatekeeping tests. They need to both dominate the "dominant curriculum" (Freire & Macedo, 1987) and develop sociopolitical consciousness, social agency, and positive identities so they become strong, confident people who will work to create a more just and equitable society. This is why Freire (Freire & Faundez, 1992) referred to "learning to question" as a "pedagogy of liberation," and an anathema to dominant regimes: "Problem-posing education does not and cannot serve the interests of the oppressor. No oppressive order could permit the oppressed to begin to question: Why?" (Freire, 1970/1998, p. 67). As Antonio Faundez, a Chilean collaborator of Freire, stated, "I think that it is a profoundly democratic thing to begin to learn to ask questions" (Freire & Faundez, 1992, p. 34).

NOTES

1. A pseudonym, like all proper names in this article.
2. My classroom name is Mr. Rico. I have had the nickname "Rico" for 30-plus years because my mother, who taught Spanish at my neighborhood junior high school, sometimes

called me Erico, and "Rico" came from that. When I first started working with Rivera in 1994, a Colombian teacher called me Mr. Rico, explaining that it was customary in Colombia to address teachers by the title *Mr.* or *Ms.* and their first name.

3. The *disparity ratio* was defined in the article as the ratio of the rejection rates. So, e.g., in Chicago, African Americans were rejected 31.66% of the time in 2001, Whites were rejected 6.32% of the time, and the disparity ratio was 31.66 ÷ 6.32, which is 5.01.

4. Two students wrote that banks denied African Americans mortgages because they did not keep up their houses. This unleashed much commentary about negative stereotypes of Mexicans.

5. It was almost the last day of class, right before graduation, and I no longer had any institutional power over students at that time. Also, the survey was anonymous. Thus I believe that their answers were truthful, and my other data also supported their responses.

5

Transactions of Mathematical Knowledge in the Algebra Project

Frank E. Davis, Mary Maxwell West, James G. Greeno, Melissa S. Gresalfi & H. Taylor Martin (with Robert Moses & Marian Currell)

INTRODUCTION

The Algebra Project was founded by Robert Moses and colleagues in the mid-1980s to increase the proportion of African American and other students of color who enter and succeed in college-preparatory mathematics courses. As a project in which the members of the community who are experiencing inequity have themselves designed and worked toward solutions over many years, it offers an opportunity for researchers to examine how community members define and address the problem. In this chapter, we present Moses's analysis of the problem, and our observations from Moses's Grade 9 Algebra I classroom in Jackson, Mississippi, and from Marian Currell's Grade 6 classroom in San Francisco.

Our observations are part of a study of three Algebra Project schools whose students met the project's fundamental goal. In these schools, Algebra Project students went on to college-preparatory mathematics courses in Grades 9 and 10 at about twice the rate of non–Algebra Project peers in the same districts (Davis & West, 2000; West, Davis, Lynch, & Atlas, 1998).[1] Half or more of the teachers became involved in the project's activities, which included after-school and community initiatives as well as the work in classrooms, and the mathematics programs changed significantly.

We studied Moses and Currell intensively because they have been "prime movers" of the project in their areas (Moses first in Cambridge, then in one neighborhood of Jackson; and Currell in the Bayview/Hunters Point area of San Francisco). Moses and Currell also qualify at the highest level of the Algebra Project's own internal standard for excellence in teaching and in developing teachers (defined in the project's trainer program).

Davis and West visited the classrooms of Moses and Currell every 1 or 2 months throughout one academic year (during 2000–2001 in San Francisco, and 2001–2002 in Jackson), observing and usually videotaping the same class for 3 or 4 days in a row, attending teacher meetings, interviewing teachers, meeting with the principal, and attending school and parent events. Greeno and Gresalfi visited and videotaped classes conducted by Currell and other teachers, as well as teacher meetings in San Francisco during 2001–2002, and Greeno visited Moses's classes in Jackson twice. All of us reviewed selected videotapes of these classrooms.

MOSES'S ANALYSIS AND STRATEGIES

Moses's analysis of the problem is reflected in his description of Chad:

> Chad, a young Black seventh grader, recently looked up from reading a page in the first chapter of a traditional algebra text and said to his mother, "It's all just words." For too many youngsters, mathematics is a game of signs they cannot play. They must be helped to understand what those signs really mean, and construct for themselves a basis of evidence for mathematics. (Moses, Kamii, Swap, & Howard, 1989, p. 37)

He and his colleagues note a particular set of historical and political conditions in our society linked to individuals' civil and economic rights (see, e.g., Moses and Cobb, 2001, pp. 23–87). In the first half of the 20th century, education offered African Americans little more than elementary literacy, reflecting at that time the need for field workers to be available in abundance and at the right times and the need to stabilize an existing social order. As industrialization gradually made such labor unnecessary, the vocational purposes of these schools became irrelevant, while the need to maintain the social order remained strongly in force. Moses refers to this type of education as "serf" or "sharecropper education," which was transferred out of the South to various parts of the country as African Americans moved to America's cities to find work.

> Sharecropper education, the hidden subtext of the struggle to reform the nation's system of public education, is now the main institutional force perpetuating the country's caste system, tying menial education to menial work, and mis-education to criminalization (Moses, 2004).

The Algebra Project also notes that shifts toward computer technologies now require placing mathematics literacy on a par with reading and writing literacy and that such literacy is required not only for specific jobs but also for participation as informed citizens (Moses, 1994). The project's current goal is to demonstrate how high school instruction can establish a "floor" for mathematics literacy for all students, whose performance criteria are passing the mathematics tests necessary for graduation, performing adequately on the mathematics portion of college admissions tests, and placing out of remedial mathematics courses in college so that mathematics is not an obstacle to the career of their choice.

WHAT MATH SHOULD BE TAUGHT, AND HOW?

The Algebra Project answers these questions with reference to two bodies of literature—experiential learning on the one hand, and the history of the philosophy of mathematics as articulated by W. V. O. Quine, on the other. Quine's work constitutes a summary of the work of philosophers who sought to delineate an evidentiary basis of mathematics during the first 30 years of the 20th century, producing a "new sort of mathematical philosophy" (Benacerraf & Putnam, 1983). Moses believes that one of Quine's insights has particular relevance to school math.

> Quine insisted that elementary arithmetic, elementary logic, and elementary set theory get started by what he called the "regimentation of ordinary discourse, mathematization in situ." To which list we should now add elementary algebra. Scientists, Quine said, put a straitjacket on natural languages. (Moses & Cobb, 2001, pp. 197–198)

Moses integrated ideas from the philosophy of mathematics with ideas about experiential learning, particularly from the work of John Dewey and Kurt Lewin:

> Experiential learning theory is grounded in the countless cyclical experiences in which people try something, then think about what they did, then make improvements, then practice their improvements. It would seem that we learn most of what we know, from language to cooking to building shelters to live in, by applications of this process. (Moses & Cobb, 2001, p. 198)

When Moses began to work with teachers, he explained how math could be taught as a "five-step curricular process" in which students should (1) engage in a physical experience, which they could then (2) represent in their own words and pictures, then in structured language, including (3) everyday language ("people talk"), (4) "feature talk," and (5) conventional mathematical notation. For example, in everyday language ("people talk"), we say: *Shakeela is taller than Marcus.* The same statement in "feature talk" is *The height of Shakeela is greater than the height of Marcus.* This phrase can easily be translated into the symbolic representations used in algebra.

Moses also notes that mathematical understandings emerge as the result of a social process:

> In academic language, this process can also be described as the "social construction of mathematics." Students learn that math is the creation of people—people working together and depending on one another. Interaction, cooperation, and group communication, therefore, are key components of this process. (Moses & Cobb, 2001, p. 120)

ORGANIZING

A large component of the Algebra Project involves engaging students, parents, and educators in understanding schooling in a sociocultural and historical framework, and in understanding how changes in social and economic conditions frame what schools ought to do. The issue for the project is *how to facilitate change*, or how to facilitate and sustain a "movement," defined as groups of individuals who see themselves working together toward a shared goal.

This feature of the project draws on the legacy of organizing Black sharecroppers in the Delta of Mississippi to demand the right to vote. According to Moses, that effort became possible because of an "opening" that was provided when the federal government no longer allowed the right to vote to be denied on the basis of race. Civil rights activists, sharecroppers, and others began to meet to explore how to achieve various goals. Moses argues that an analogous opening exists today for work on mathematics literacy. This opening also involves policies at the federal level, based on the core value that no student who can learn should be denied the opportunity for education.

The work needed to actualize this vision is complex and must take place at both national and local levels. Again Moses draws lessons from the civil rights movement. For an organizer, the tasks involve assisting others to develop their understanding of the social context (either in the past, the social context surrounding registering to vote and voting, or in the present, the social context of school mathematics and learning how to do mathematics) and then helping them to organize themselves to achieve goals they have defined. Moses notes:

> Effective organizing in the 1960s in Mississippi meant an organizer had to utilize the everyday issues of the community and frame them for the maximum benefit of the community. Staking out some area of consensus was necessary, but an organizer could not create consensus, an organizer had to find it. . . . Then, if the organizer found it, the question of how to tap into this consensus, how to energize it and use it for mobilization and organization, remained. Organizers—civil rights organizers in the 1960s, math literacy organizers now—work to flesh out consensus. (Moses & Cobb, 2001, p. 85)

Facilitating the study of the local and broader social and legal contexts in which voting rights were being contested, structuring environments where the knowledge necessary for achieving the right to vote could be generated and shared, and where sharecroppers and others could take on and evolve identities as advocates for their own rights, were critical organizing tasks.

Part of the Algebra Project effort is to demonstrate to the public that students can learn important mathematics ideas under the right circumstances:

> In my view, many people will see our vision as impossible. There's a sense in which most people are not going to believe or accept any of this agenda until they are con-

fronted with the products of such an effort: students who come out of schools and class-rooms armed with a new understanding of the mathematics and with a new under-standing of themselves as leaders, participants and learners. (Moses, 1994, p. 110)

HISTORICAL CONTEXT OF MOSES'S
AND CURRELL'S CLASSROOMS

Robert Moses began designing instructional materials with several teachers in the mid-1980s when his own children were in middle school in Cambridge, Massa-chusetts. That work resulted in the Transition Curriculum, intended to enable stu-dents in Grades 5–7 to bridge from arithmetic thinking to algebraic thinking (Moses et al, 1989; appendix to Moses & Cobb, 2001). Later he assisted sixth-grade teachers at Brinkley Middle School in Jackson, Mississippi, in 1993, and in 1996 followed a cohort of Brinkley graduates to Lanier High School, where he now teaches full-time. This school has been the lowest performing of Jackson's nine high schools. Under the program that he developed there, enrollment in the college-track math courses in Grade 9 increased from 13% in 1996 to 89% in 2002, and in Grade 10 from 32% to 82%.

Marian Currell was trained in San Francisco as the Algebra Project spread in the early 1990s. Later she was hired to teach Grade 6 at the Dr. Martin Luther King, Jr., Academic Middle School, where two other teachers had also been trained. Here, from 60–70% of the 550 students qualify for free or reduced-cost lunch per year, 15% are English Language Learners, and 20% receive special education. About one third of students are African American, one third Latino/a, and one third Asian.

The mathematics teachers at King, mostly African American women, revised the Grade 6–8 curriculum so that all students could take Algebra I in Grade 8. From 1996 to the present, no other mathematics course has been offered for Grade 8.[2] Data on high school course enrollment of seven cohorts of graduates show that since 1996, King graduates have been enrolling in college-preparatory courses at about twice the rate of similar students from other middle schools in San Francisco.

FINDINGS

We have viewed Algebra Project classrooms using three lenses, ranging from "wide angle" to "close up." The first view draws on West's 11 years of ethnographic ob-servations in the Algebra Project and focuses on how students are motivated in Moses's and Currell's classrooms. The second draws on Davis's 14 years of observ-ing the project and focuses on how mathematics is presented, through an exami-nation of the epistemological dimension of Moses's teaching. The third draws on Greeno's and colleagues' analysis of videos of classroom activity, using standard methods of cognitive science, including interactional analysis, and analysis of conversational interactions and the structures of information generated in activity. These methods are used to examine how students are positioned in the teaching and learning of mathematics and how new curricula are used in classrooms.

Observing Algebra Project Classrooms Through an Ethnographic Framework [Editors' note: Prepared by Mary Maxwell West]

What do exemplary Algebra Project teachers define as key issues in classroom implementation, and how do they address them? We will answer this question through examination of the project's recommendations for the classroom and through our own observations.

First, the project's recommendations for classroom work in high schools now include small class sizes, 90-minute mathematics classes (block schedule) every day for 4 years, and common periods for teachers to plan and debrief among themselves and across sites. These requirements convey the projects' value on "time on task" for students, as well as the need to create a learning community for teachers in which their mathematical and pedagogical knowledge can grow. The project is also working now toward, and has succeeded in, bringing university mathematicians into the materials-development and teacher-training work, reflecting its value in the mathematical knowledge itself.

Second, the Algebra Project practices an experience-based pedagogy designed to lead students through several steps from a shared experience to competent use of the conventional mathematical representations and procedures and the conceptual understandings shared in the discipline and discourse of mathematics (Moses & Cobb, 2001; and see the section by Frank Davis, this chapter). This process is found in the project classroom materials as well as in work with teachers and teacher trainers. The project's materials are intended to provide students with what Moses calls "evidence for mathematics"—observables that students can agree upon as true or not true, and a process by which their *own* observations about events, and their natural language about events, can be transformed into the key concepts and representations of mathematics.

Third, Moses notes the task of getting students' attention. In addition, the initial step of the five-step process, the "physical experience," usually includes activities in which students walk or travel through space and time, which easily engages their attention. For example, in the Flagway game and Road Coloring unit, students walk paths on the floor that represent mathematical structures. In the Trip unit, which appears in the Transition Curriculum and Algebra I materials, students take an actual trip within the school or in their community. Students then "regiment" their everyday language in additional steps of the curricular process, delineating key features that can later be represented and operated on using conventional mathematical representations. These latter steps can be observably "hard work" for students at all the grade levels, yet are critical to the project's intended "learning trajectories" (such as those described by Gravemeijer,

Cobb, Bowers, and Whitenack, 2000, and Lesh and Doerr, 2000). In some units, extensive work with laptop or handheld computers is present, which helps to sustain students' attention; but these steps can be challenging for teachers and students alike.

The challenge is especially strong in the kinds of high schools that the project is currently seeking to improve. Our observations reveal that in the classrooms of less effective teachers, students talk to one another about their personal lives, joke, and chat when the teacher's back is turned and either do not work efficiently or do not work at all. As others have noted (for example, Gutierrez, Rymes, & Larson, 1995), there appears to be an agenda of "peer work" that competes with the teacher's agenda of "school work" in these classrooms.

One way that Moses handles the divergence of students' attention is to speak directly to them about the task. He speaks of "building a culture to do knowledge work," which may require "sitting with a problem" for a long time, and that it's OK, and often necessary, to "struggle" while learning. As he told his ninth graders one day, we need to "work on how we work." Below I will describe some additional ways that Moses and Currell motivate students to persist through the more tedious learning tasks.

Currell has articulated the importance of teaching that does not result in students being "too dependent" (we were discussing an incident in which a student did not begin his worksheets without repeated scaffolding from the teacher). Currell's concern for independence, and Moses's concern for students to change their notions of learning, are consistent with a key long-term goal of the Algebra Project—to develop students' capacity to be autonomous learners.

My observations of Moses's and Currell's classrooms indicate that the following are important features of their work:

- They develop a sense of group safety, equity, and co-responsibility for mathematics learning
- They attend to students' language and questions and develop evidence that will ground students' understanding of key concepts
- They make math important and develop students' confidence as learners by allying math with the importance that already resides in recognizable social roles or performances that command attention and embody expertise
- They establish their authority as teachers, while also cultivating students' abilities to teach and learn

Algebra Project teachers and trainers strive to create an environment that is "safe" for expression of ideas. Although the notion of safety is not voiced explicitly by either Moses or Currell, most new and experienced Algebra Project teachers see creating a safe environment as a distinguishing feature of the project (in comparison with other math programs). For example, a Grade 5 teacher in rural South Carolina noted:

The low-achieving students are not intimidated because they know their answer is just as acceptable as yours, and "I am accepted" in this environment. . . . [In other math programs], the connection is just not there, and the encouragement to just go out on your own and come to your own conclusions . . . that there are many ways to achieve this goal and we are *all* going to end up at the same place. . . . It brings everybody so much together. (WL, Interview, April 29, 2004)

Teachers and trainers use certain social-interaction routines to encourage participation. A routine modeled in teacher workshops, and common in elementary and middle school classes, goes like this:

Teacher: Who has an idea about this?
Student 1: [offers idea]
Teacher: Oh so your idea was to [repeats idea and may ask for clarification]. OK, any other ideas?
Student 2: [presents an idea]

If some students are not speaking up, the teacher may address them: "Marcus, what was your idea?" Another student speaks. And so on.

Algebra Project trainers, who facilitate all project workshops and meetings, routinely encourage wide participation and avoid situations that might cause participants to "shut down." They avoid labeling participants' responses immediately as right or wrong and solicit varying ideas. Trainers value participation and extended discussion so much that they allow discussions to take precedence over covering all units of the instructional materials in teacher workshops.

Another routine used in Algebra Project classrooms, teacher workshops, and project and community meetings is small-group work followed by "reporting out." The groups are reminded to work as a team and may be encouraged to assign roles such as "facilitator" or "recorder." When groups have finished (confirmed by an answer to the question, Does anyone need more time?), each group reports its conclusions and responds to questions. This routine creates equity in participation (every group reports out), allows individuals the flexibility to take comfortable roles (recorder, etc.), gives practice in collaboration, develops communication and presentation skills, and gives mathematics importance by embedding it in a kind of performance. Moses and Currell often coach students with such comments as, "Wait until everyone is paying attention," "Speak loudly," "Face this way," and so on.

Moses and Currell also prepare individuals and small groups to take "leading roles," including teaching. Observations in Currell's class throughout 2000–2001 show that she began to cultivate co-responsibility for teaching in her Grade 6, Period 3, class from the very first day of school. Standing at the door as students entered, she first established her authority through statements giving permission and questioning: "You can sit anywhere. Where are you guys coming from? PE?" Next, she established a role for students as co-responsible for the business of the class-room. Looking at her class list, she asked, "Who's counting to see if there are 24?" Minutes later, her first assignment to students conveyed both an expectation that students wanted to learn, and that her job was to assist them: "Write about what you most want to learn in math before you leave Grade 6, and why. My job is to be sure that you learn that one thing." The following day, Currell continued to de-velop co-responsibility by framing her request for Antoine to explain his idea as a highly desirable teaching role. After asking him to present his idea to the class, she commented, "Every day someone will get a chance. Everyone is a teacher and every-one is a learner." One month later, students were able to lead class themselves. Currell came to class with laryngitis, and she asked in a whisper for volunteers to "first, go over the homework and, second, continue the work you were doing about the years, so we can finish and present, and, third, present homework for tomor-row. Volunteers?" Hands shot up, and students took turn leading the class.

Moses provides opportunity for young people to take leading roles whenever possible. When invited to give a talk, he often brings with him young people who engage adult, professional audiences in mathematics activities.

Finally, lessons in the project's instructional materials for algebra and geom-etry take the form of a dialogue between a male and female student. The dialogues contain all the teaching; students are depicted as the source of mathematics and enact the mathematics when they read their parts.

Discussion

These observations suggest that students can be motivated through activities and social routines that hinge on the power of performance to engage an audience and to demonstrate expertise. Taking leading roles in which students are publicly seen to display mathematical competence makes mathematics worthy of everyone's attention and also assists students to see themselves as competent in mathematics. Through such demonstrations, participants and audiences see that "we can do it," which helps to create the "minimum common conceptual cohesion" needed for organizing (Moses & Cobb (2001, p. 92). The importance of these public demon-strations is consistent with Theresa Perry's (2003) finding that schools that pro-duce high-achieving African American students engage in *public* demonstrations that communicate and celebrate high achievement.

Scholars of African American traditions have identified cultural features that can serve as classroom resources (e.g., Delpit, 2002; Gay, 2000; Ladson-Billings, 1994, 2001; Lee, 2001; Lee, Spencer, & Harpalani, 2003; Murrell, 2002; Perry, 2003). Some studies have also linked use of culturally familiar activities or problem fea-tures to increased students achievement (e.g. Hilliard, 2003; Lipka & Adams, 2004; Tate, 2002). The classroom participation routines, and use of performance, that we observed may be an example of a reference to something that is culturally familiar to African Americans and therefore has particular meanings for these students. However, elements of these forms also resonate with features of "Western" theories that speak of learning through modeling, imitation, apprenticeship, and "action psychology" (see, e.g., van Oers, 2000). The use of modeling and imitation in Algebra Project classrooms, enhanced through performances, may be an example of the "coordinated functioning of multifaceted cultural practices in human development" as described by Rogoff and Angelillo (2002).

While these forms are apparent in observations of classrooms, we note also the importance that the project places on small class size, time on task, and teachers' mathematics knowledge and community through its requirements for high school implementation.

Observing the Algebra Project Through an Epistemological Framework [Editor's note: Prepared by Frank Davis]

Moses's view that successful teaching involves both experiential learning and a transformation and structuring of language about mathematics (mathematics in situ) gives rise to the questions that I sought to address: What are the features of the mathematical knowledge that emerge in classroom experiences that are being transacted in students' discourse as well as in the discourse of mathematics, and how are they linked to successful teaching and to success in school mathematics? In posing these questions, I use Gee's (2001) notion of Discourse to refer to a language generated by a particular community of practice, in this case composed of mathematicians and mathematics educators who have a long social and cultural history of practice that shapes their conversations about mathematics as well as the goals of school mathematics (Cobb & Hodge, 2002). I interpret Moses as arguing that successful teaching involves first engaging students in mathematical activities that they can obtain access to and reflect on in their own language, and then assisting them in constructing mathematical knowledge that is reflected in the Discourse of mathematics. Indeed, the Algebra Project's "five-step curricular process," which supports translation of ordinary discourse into more structured meanings, is designed to set in motion classroom interactions in which multiple interpretations of experiences, and of the features and structure of mathematics, are explicitly recognized as necessary and important in comprehending the Discourse.

A framework that can capture both what might be considered fundamental features of mathematics and their links to experience and language is required to do justice to the Algebra Project's ideas about mathematics learning. I have chosen to use an analytic scheme developed by the philosopher Stephen Pepper (1942) for this purpose. Pepper was concerned with debates about metaphysics—debates that sought to define the underlying structure of reality and knowledge. He argued that underlying knowledge is a process of knowing that seeks to establish beliefs on the basis of criticized evidence. This criticism involves a structuring of knowledge using metaphors, such that "facts" tend to corroborate other "facts" and such that individuals can agree with one another that a "fact" is a "fact." Pepper clarified that this process is not intended to imply that a "fact" can ever actually be identified. Rather, he contended that knowledge that appears to have a factual basis relies on the construct of ever-larger agreed-upon structural webs of evidence that have increasing precision and scope. Pepper identified four such structures, which he collectively called "world hypotheses," and which he named "formism," "mechanism," "contextualism," and "organicism," respectively.

I have discussed the relevance of Pepper's framework to contemporary ideas about cognition, the sociology of knowledge, and mathematics and science learning elsewhere (Davis, 1990, 1998, 2003). Figure 5.1 summarizes a set of interpretative frames for analyzing mathematical knowledge and learning based on these world hypotheses and what Pepper called their "basic root metaphors." It is important to see these frames as providing different ways to structure mathematical knowledge that are not reducible or equivalent to one another.

Pepper's work gives a comprehensive framework for analyzing knowledge or a Discourse (e.g., the Discourse of mathematics), and the process of acquiring such knowledge (e.g., the process of learning and teaching mathematics in classrooms, or what we have referred to as transactions of mathematical meaning). I have used this framework to analyze segments of an Algebra I class taught by Moses.[3] What follows includes a sampling of the analysis (Davis, 2003).

Taking a Prescription Drug—A Study of Change That Leads to a Steady State

Moses began work with a problem about the amount of a prescribed drug remaining in a human body over time. There was discussion about why drugs are given in doses over time and about students' experiences with prescriptions. This discussion sets a context for a problem that will take several days to solve. It produced some intuitive ideas about a common experience shared by almost all students. Students were drawn into the work from a *contextualist* point of view. The mathematics has some type of functional and practical meaning.

Work was guided by a series of worksheets that asked students to first think about the event in "people talk." For example, the statement "From 6 a.m. to 10 a.m. the amount of the initial dosage in the body decreases by 25% before another dosage is given" guides calculations with various initial dosages. Students were than drawn to features in the statement that could then be symbolized, such as the amount of the drug in the body at 6 a.m., the amount eliminated, the amount of a new dosage given at 10 a.m., and the appropriate mathematical relations between quantities. Moses noted that his intent was for students to relate a set of experientially grounded notions about the decrease and increase of an amount of drug in the body (people talk), to a set of symbolic expressions ("feature talk") and a symbolic

FIGURE 5.1. A framework for mathematics and mathematics learning based on Pepper's "world hypotheses"

Formism	Mechanism	Organicism	Contextualism
(Root Metaphor: Idea of similar forms defined by qualities and relationships between qualities.)	*(Root metaphor: Idea of cosmic machine in which everything is reducible to the parts and mechanisms of the machine.)*	*(Root metaphor: Idea of the living organism whose development leads to more coherent and cohesive structures.)*	*(Root metaphor: Idea of an historic event that has a social context that gives it a particular texture and quality.)*
Learning mathematics requires abstract conceptualization. Mathematical knowledge is drawn from a correspondence of mathematical forms to regularities in experience, reflecting a logical structure of qualities and relations.	Learning mathematics requires generalizing from concrete experiencing. Mathematical knowledge is drawn from a correlation of mathematical qualities to experience and an underlying mechanism.	Mathematics learning is a process of reflective abstraction. Mathematical knowledge is drawn from a sense of developing coherence in thought.	Mathematics learning reflects human problem solving, intention, and experimentation. Mathematical knowledge is a matter of operational achievements.
Example: (The study of Euclidean geometry involves deductive reasoning on a given set of definitions or axioms about geometric qualities.)	*Example:* (Numbers and operation on numbers correlate with physical objects, forces, motions, and models of their interconnections)	*Example:* (The ability to apply an inverse operation to solve an algebraic equation, such as subtracting 2 to reverse the effect of adding 2, reflects an developmental organization of cognitive processes and structures that are reversible.)	*Example:* (Mathematical entities emerge from functional needs. The human need to measure, keep records, engineer, etc., structure mathematics.)

representation. A *mechanist* process was embodied in classroom work, which offered an explicit scaffold linking people talk to feature talk to symbolic representations. As students calculated dosages in the body at successive time intervals, the similarity of the process (its recursiveness) was emphasized through the pattern of the calculation (*a formist perspective*), and eventually a symbolic representation that described the calculation for any interval.

From the perspective of students, these engagements in constructing mathematics sometimes looked quite different. For example, in the beginning several students had difficulty understanding how a decrease by 25% was equivalent to 75% remaining in the body. Moses could be heard in several conversations asking students to think about corresponding forms. "What is 25% of a dollar? What part of a dollar is a quarter?" These difficulties continued when students tried to follow the symbolic expressions and their transformation (a *formist* strategy), with an "easier" experiential sequence of calculation (this is in the body, and then this goes away) that also produced the correct result (a *mechanist* strategy).

The analysis over several days displayed interplay between a *formist* sense of meaning and a *mechanist* perspective. From time to time the intent of the problem was restated ("Can we understand what will happen over time—over any amount of time?"), suggesting that remembering the context of classroom work was critical to understanding the mathematics (*contextualism*). Later in the episode, there were also instances of students struggling with unexpected results. For example, many looked for errors in their work when they observed the amount of the drug in the body reaching a steady state. At this junction, mathematical meaning seemed thwarted by previous conceptions, requiring an inner restructuring of knowledge to include different notions about change (an *organicist* perspective).

From the perspective of world hypotheses, the classroom work was extremely rich and varied in drawing students into structuring mathematics directly upon experience (mechanism), through the search for forms (formism), through intention and purpose (contextualism), and through a search for coherence of knowledge (organicism). This process was also driven by conflicts within the ongoing discourse about how to mathematize the problem. For example, it was not uncommon for students to experience difficulty constructing and understanding the mathematics within a particular frame (illustrated above in examples where the underlying mechanism of drug intake and dissipation could not easily be attached to a symbolic form that was recursive). They frequently persisted until their approach seemed to be "incoherent" or "different" from others. Sometimes the instructor and students appeared to talk "past each other." Richness of classroom work is also measured in the degree of seemingly conflicting interpretations that are exposed and entertained. What is easily missed in the brief excerpt above was the instructor's capacity to listen patiently to students, to draw out students' ideas, and to craft responses intended to help students link rather than discard their ideas and language about mathematics to the Discourse.

Discussion

World hypotheses provide a vehicle for understanding the richness and complexity of the Discourse of mathematics and for understanding the discourse of classroom work and its relationship to those aspects of the Discourse that we expect students to learn. Moses's classroom may be a good illustration of how teaching and learning looks when careful thought has been given to how to the Discourse of mathematics can unfold within the discourse of classroom work. It is important to emphasize that Moses's classroom is not representative of all Algebra Project classrooms. Indeed, a major effort of the project is to enable teachers to create these types of learning environment for students, both through the design of instructional materials and through the improvement of teaching practice.

The use of world hypotheses to analyze the classroom work of Moses reveals the multiple processes involved in students' construction and transaction of mathematical knowledge and their discourse about it. This approach suggests that effective mathematics education involves "building" or "unpacking" or "making transparent" (see the section by Greeno, Gresalfi, and Martin, below) such aspects of the Discourse of mathematics. The analysis indicates that effective teaching involves the capacity to guide students through a series of activities in which they can connect their own mathematical discourse to the Discourse of mathematics.

Observing Transparency, Competence, Authority, and Accountability in Classroom Interactions [Editors' note: Prepared by James Greeno, Melissa Gresalfi, and H. Taylor Martin]

The question that organized our research activity in this project was the following: How do teachers and students interact in order to achieve the Algebra Project's educational aims? In other words, what are some characteristics of activity—things that teachers and students do together in classrooms—that are consistent with the aims of the Algebra Project and may contribute to the achievement of those aims? This question comes from our goal of contributing to better understanding of how learning mathematical concepts and methods occurs through students' participation in the organized social activities of the classroom (Gresalfi, 2004; Schwartz & Martin, 2004; Stenning, Greeno, Hall, Sommerfeld, & Wiebe, 2002).

The Algebra Project is committed to providing more students with access to the mathematics they need to participate as full citizens. The tradition of organizing, which focuses on achieving consensus on shared goals and assisting people in achieving goals they have defined for themselves, requires that students are positioned to contribute to their learning as active participants, with conceptual agency in

Pickering's (1995) sense. For students to be positioned with conceptual agency, the mathematics that students are asked to learn has to make sense to them, and they need to be positioned with agency for understanding and taking intellectual initiative. If students are to participate meaningfully in determining goals of their learning, the contents of what they learn need to be coherent both conceptually and with their experience. We present results of our analyses of two episodes, one from Moses's high school algebra class, the other from Currell's sixth-grade mathematics class. These episodes illustrate four aspects of interaction that we hypothesize as supporting the aims of the Algebra Project. Three of these aspects—competence, authority, and accountability—involve students' participation with the teacher, with other students, and with the domain of mathematical concepts and principles.[4] The fourth aspect—transparency—involves the extent to which the teachers expect students to understand the meanings and significance of mathematical symbols, operations, and technologies, rather than only learning to use and apply them correctly.

Authority, Accountability, Competency, and Transparency in a Sixth-Grade Mathematics Class

Our discussion of positioning with authority, accountability, and competence follows earlier work in our group (Engle & Conant, 2002; Greeno, 2001; Gresalfi, Martin, Hand, & Greeno, in preparation). We consider these characteristics as achievements of interactions, led by teachers, in which teachers and students co-construct productive situations for learning with positive agency.

Our first episode occurred in the classroom of Marian Currell. In the following excerpt, the students were working on developing a *trip line*, a key activity in the Algebra Project Transition Curriculum that includes work on the nature of symbolic representation (Moses & Cobb, 2001). The class was in the stage of feature talk, in which an abstract concept of a *trip* was developed, defining this concept as having four features, including the trip's direction. The students needed to represent a collection of trips in a way that specified all four features of each trip they included. Each student had constructed representations of several trips (the assigned number was 10), and the task for each student was to collect a set of three trips from every student in the class.

The interaction presented here followed a complaint by one of the students, Callie, that she was unable to determine the directions of the trips that she had collected from another student's, James's, list of trips. Currell called James and expressed her own lack of understanding James's symbols.

> *Currell:* James, come here. I'm just going to ask this question because I don't understand it. This symbol three represents all this, right?
> (*gesturing to his page*)
> *James:* I was heading north.
> *Currell:* How would I know that?

James: I don't know. . . .

Currell: This means that that is where you finished. This means that is
    where you started, so I need to know, this symbol means direction? I
    don't know direction; how would I know which direction?

James: I'll change it. Darn you, Callie.

Currell: She just wants you—why? 'Cause she just wants you to think a
    little bit?

Currell and her students were engaging with mathematics in ways that were
consistent with the goals of the Algebra Project in that the students were active participants in their own learning, engaging in discussions with one another by exercis-
ing conceptual agency. The distribution of authority included students' creation of
symbols and use of their own knowledge to determine whether these symbols were
mathematically sufficient. Students had been the *authors* of the symbols that were at
issue and were, therefore, the authorities for their interpretation. At the same time,
the students were accountable for constructing symbols that could be interpreted by
others to refer to all four of the prescribed features of trips. They were positioned as
being competent to interpret the representations themselves and to evaluate the
meaningfulness of those representations independently. This accomplishment is illustrated in the questions that Currell asked throughout the interaction, giving James
the space to respond, rather than defend. By using a form that placed the problem
with herself—"*I* don't understand"—she displaced her authority and suggested that
they were working on a goal (of sense-making) together.

Transparency, Competence, and Accountability in an Algebra Class

Our discussion of transparency followed Lave and Wenger (1991), who include
opening up the "black box" of any technology, in effect transforming it into a "glass
box," as well as providing access to its significance as part of cultural practice.

Both aspects of transparency are illustrated in the previous episode in Currell's
classroom. Students got legitimate peripheral access to authentic mathematical
activity by becoming responsible for holding one another accountable for making
their representations make sense (i.e., opening the black box of representation).
And the cultural significance of symbolic representations, which includes their function of conveying information from one person to another and the design requirements for fulfilling this function, were at issue in the incident.

Our other episode is from Moses's teaching. Moses was interacting with his
students around mathematics, creating an opportunity for students to obtain access to the understanding of a representational practice. He engaged the students
in practicing the talk and practices of mathematics, and he illustrated and unpacked
how mathematics works as a representational tool.

Moses was working with a group of three students on an activity that depended
on the distinction between a number and a representation in the base-10 place-

value system. The activity focused on what the curriculum called the algebraic representation of a four-digit number. A discussion about the difference between numbers and digits was raised when one student asked, "What do we mean, a four-digit number?" The difference between digits and numbers was then taken up as the topic of the subsequent discussion between Moses and the group of students. At the beginning of their conversation, the discussion focused mainly on the concept of a digit as a *representation* of a particular number. This is an example of the first aspect of transparency—opening the black box about numbers versus digits:

> *Student 1:* What do we mean by *four-digit number*?
> *Student 2:* Like four . . . two thousand three hundered and fifty-eight?
> *Moses:* Fifty-eight, yeah. In other words these numbers here have how many digits?
> *Student 1:* Four.
> *Moses:* Four. Yeah. One, two, three, four. So these are all four-digit numbers. But if I say a hundred and thirty-seven, that has how many digits?
> *Student 2:* Three.
> *Moses:* Three. Not three numbers. One number, three digits.

The discussion made the representation of numbers more of a glass box by distinguishing explicitly between the whole representation and its parts, its digits. In addition to opening up the concept of representation, Moses took on a second aspect of transparency—making the mathematical significance of the tool clear to its users. In this example, Moses and the students discussed the workings of a representational tool (place value) in terms of its use and meaning. Moses continued:

> *Moses:* Well, I'm not thinking of . . . yes, I'm not thinking of the one as a number 'cause in the number one hundred thirty-seven the one doesn't represent one. It represents what?
> *Student 1:* Three.
> *Moses:* No, in one hundred thirty-seven, the one represents?
> *Student 2:* One.
> *Moses:* No, in one hundred thirty seven, the one represents?
> *Student 3:* Is it in front of the . . .
> *Moses:* A hundred.
> *Student 2:* Oh, I see.
> *Moses:* A hundred. And three represents—three tens, and three tens represents what number? Thirty. And the three represents what number?

In these interactions, Moses and his students constructed the students' positioning with significant competence and entitlement for understanding the mathematical content of numerical representation. The students were positioned as competent to understand how the representational system works, not just to follow procedures for manipulating symbols, and Moses did not simplify the nature of the mathematical information that they were presented with. His presentation of content was quite directive, with him directing the discussion and providing much of the information and doing most of the work to evaluate the accuracy of students' responses. Along with this authority, Moses was accountable to the students for presenting the mathematical analysis that was needed. He was also accountable for reaching mutual understanding with the students of the way that referential significance of the symbols is composed of the meanings of their constituents.

Discussion

The brief episodes above illustrate aspects of interaction that we believe are relevant to the question of how the educational aims of the Algebra Project are achieved in classroom activities. We have focused on four features of interaction, three of which refer to positioning of students in participation structures and the other to a way in which mathematical subject matter content is treated.

In working toward its aim of providing African American youth with the mathematics they need to participate fully in contemporary America, the Algebra Project organizes students' learning so that they can participate meaningfully in authentic mathematical knowing and thinking. The five-step curricular process is designed to provide students with a basis for participating in the construction of mathematical meaning and the use of mathematics for understanding significant aspects of their experience. The learning environments of Algebra Project classes are intended to entitle students to participate in decisions about mathematical representations and their meanings.

For students to participate meaningfully in these ways, discourse practices need to be organized to support students' participation with conceptual agency regarding one another and regarding the subject matter of mathematics. Activity systems in which students have competence, authority, and accountability regarding mathematics, and in which the conceptual structures of mathematics are made transparent to the students, are consistent with the educational aims of the Algebra Project, and we have illustrated some of the ways that they occurred in the classroom activities that we observed.

CONCLUSIONS

Using different lenses, we have examined social interactions in Algebra Project classrooms and found examples that are consistent with the project's view of mathematics education as a literacy effort that must address not only the learning of mathematical content but also how students are positioned in relation to their learning of this subject. We found participation structures that involved collaboration and social negotiation, an epistemology suggesting multiple ways of constructing mathematical knowledge, and the positioning of students in relation to the subject matter that requires critical thinking and sharing of authority, which, we believe, are significant learning aims in their own right and provide these students better access to learning the conventional mathematics. This kind of access actively integrates the development of learning identities, attitudes about learning, and classroom social and sociomathematical norms into the teaching and learning of mathematics as an activity. West looked at how students were motivated to learn mathematics and found that lessons and social routines imbued mathematics with importance, placed a value on students' thinking, and created co-responsibility for learning and teaching. Davis looked at how mathematical knowledge was presented by Moses in an Algebra I class and found that it reflected the full epistemological complexity that occurs in the "Discourse" of mathematicians/math educators, rather than a narrow view of mathematics that focuses only on procedures and algorithms. Greeno, Gresalfi, and Martin examined mathematical discourse and noted how students were positioned with competence, authority, and accountability regarding mathematics and how the conceptual structures of mathematics were made transparent to the students.

There is strong convergence across our analyses in certain areas: West's and Greeno et al.'s analyses both indicate that students are accorded some degree of authority and competence as learners. Davis and Greeno et al.'s analyses converge in that "opening" the mathematical black box (seen as a process of making transparent, or through various world hypotheses) is an important aspect of mathematics teaching. All of us noted how Moses and Currell "unpacked" mathematical representations, reflecting an assumption that students can learn the fundamentals of the Discourse (not just its superficial features; see Gee, 2001) and conveying that this Discourse is a sociocultural product. The complexity of mathematics, and its social construction, was apparent in how these teachers and their students examined representations and in how students were expected to use them in communication.

We, like other education researchers, would like to conduct research that can be used to improve education outcomes for students who are not being reached by current approaches. Research that serves this aim needs to track students' educational outcomes over the long term and describe how students' learning was supported, or not supported, in the multiple communities in which the students participate. At a school, research is needed to detail the resources that are being provided at different levels, how mathematics learning is structured and supported in school and after-school opportunities, how the teacher team functions and relates to the school and community, and the role of any university mathematics specialists such as teaching fellows.

Providing, documenting, and analyzing existence proofs also fits with Burkhardt and Schoenfeld's (2003) ideas about design experiments, or research that resembles a process of engineering, that may be a more adequate means of addressing fundamental problems of schools. We would like to follow up this exploratory study with more clinical-experimental approaches to studying the development of student thinking on specific concepts. Closer attention to individual students, and how they describe specific activities that they have engaged in, would further illuminate some of the ideas we presented here. This kind of research is also needed in order to break down the monotonic notions of culture that have occupied past work (as called for, for example, by Lee (2003a, 2003b) and other authors in the special theme issue of *Educational Researcher*, Reconceptualizing Race and Ethnicity in Educational Research, June/July 2003).

Research on the Algebra Project as a movement may entail a different set of questions (see Davis, 2003), such as How do educators and teachers engage in developing whole-school reform linked to long-term goals, in the face of short-term objectives such as performance on standardized tests? In this context, a question could be posed about education research: Can educational researchers produce work that is useful to an educational reform movement?

We hope that the beginning work reported in this chapter is an indication that this question can be answered affirmatively. We believe that an important condition of achieving this usefulness is that the research be done in close collaboration with those who work and learn in schools. The kind of research needed cannot be conducted on short visits, or through analyses of test scores and questionnaires alone. It requires spending time in schools and with teachers and students. We have also learned in our work that research can be significantly informed by applying the tools of different disciplines to jointly observed phenomena—particularly when the phenomena are as compelling and necessary as the work of the Algebra Project.

NOTES

This chapter is a condensed version of a longer article that can be obtained from the Algebra Project, Inc. (www.algebra.org).

1. This study was supported by NSF Grant No. 0087664; the earlier evaluation work was supported by National Science Foundation (NSF) Grant No. ESI9630116 and several private foundations. The opinions and findings expressed in this chapter are those of the authors and do not necessarily reflect the views of the NSF or other funders.

2. Even though the Transition Curriculum can no longer be used in Grade 6, because it is not on the list of district-recommended texts, this school continues to fulfill the Algebra Project's fundamental goal for middle school students.

3. This episode represents the Algebra Project's ideal for teaching, particularly in anchoring the teaching and learning process in students' discourse, and in delineating important aspects of the Discourse that students need to learn. It is not representative of all Algebra Project teachers or classrooms that we have observed.

4. Analyses focused on competence were initially suggested by Marian Currell, in a conversation about alternative issues that we could address. Currell suggested that it would be particularly valuable to learn more about what it means to be a mathematically competent learner.

6

Bilingual Mathematics Learners:
How Views of Language, Bilingual Learners,
and Mathematical Communication
Affect Instruction

JUDIT MOSCHKOVICH

Understanding the relationship between language and mathematics learning is crucial to designing mathematics instruction for students who are English learners (ELs) and/or bilingual.[1] Before we can address questions about instruction for this population, we need to examine views of bilingual mathematics learners and how they use language to communicate mathematically. In this chapter I consider how our conceptions of bilingual mathematics learners influence instruction for this population. In particular, I examine how views of the relationship between mathematics and language constrain instruction. I describe three views of bilingual mathematics learners; examine how these views affect instruction; and critique the views, using a sociocultural perspective.

Understanding bilingual mathematics learners and developing principled instruction is a pressing practical issue, particularly for Latino students. An increasing number of school-age children in the United States are Latinos; Latino students constitute the majority of many major of urban school districts in the country (Young, 2002). By 2050 there will be approximately 100 million Latinos in the United States. In the future, most public school teachers in cities, suburbs, and rural areas will be teaching Latino children. Mathematics achievement scores for Latinos on tests such as NAEP (National Assessment of Educational Progress) fall below those of Anglo-American and African American students, and the gap between 1990 and 2003 NAEP scores for Whites and Latinos did not change significantly (National Center for Educational Statistics [NCES], 2004). These are all good reasons to examine how views of bilingual mathematics learners (Latinos in particular) affect instruction.

Early studies of bilingual students learning mathematics focused on word problems, especially translating word problems from English to mathematical symbols. Most of these studies characterized the challenges that bilingual students faced while acquiring vocabulary or struggling with the mathematics register. Recommendations for instruction for English learners that emphasize vocabulary and reading comprehension skills reflect this focus. In contrast, current research on mathematics learning emphasizes how students construct multiple meanings, negotiate meanings through interactions with peers and teachers, and participate in mathematical communication. Although research has explored mathematical communication as a central aspect of learning mathematics in monolingual class-rooms, few studies have addressed mathematical communication in bilingual class-rooms (for examples, see Adler, 1998; Brenner, 1994; Khisty, 1995; Khisty, McLeod, & Bertilson, 1990; Moschkovich, 1999).

The increased emphasis on mathematical communication in reform class-rooms could result in several scenarios. On the one hand, this emphasis could cre-ate additional obstacles for bilingual learners. On the other hand, it might provide additional opportunities for bilingual learners to flourish. And last, it might create a combination of these two scenarios, depending on the classroom context. With-out empirical studies that explore these hypothetical scenarios and examine mathe-matical communication in classrooms with bilingual students, it is impossible to reach conclusions regarding the impact of reform on bilingual learners. When carrying out these studies or designing instruction, we need to first consider how we conceptualize language, bilingual learners, and mathematical communication. As researchers, designers, or teachers we can only see what our conceptual frame-works allow us to see. Our views will have great impact on our conclusions and recommendations.

The aim of this chapter is to describe three views of bilingual mathematics learners and explore how these views influence instruction and equity for this population. I examine three perspectives on bilingual mathematics learners, de-scribe how the first two constrain research and instruction, and consider how a sociocultural perspective can inform our understanding of the processes underly-ing learning mathematics when learning English. The first perspective emphasizes acquiring vocabulary, the second emphasizes multiple meanings, and the third emphasizes participation in mathematical Discourse practices. The third perspec-tive is a situated and sociocultural[2] view of language and mathematics learning that uses the concepts of registers (Halliday, 1978) and Discourses (Gee, 1996, 1999).

I question the efficacy of the first two perspectives for understanding bilin-gual mathematics learners and designing instruction for this population. These first two views can create inequities in the classroom because they emphasize what learn-ers don't know or can't do. In contrast, a sociocultural perspective shifts away from deficiency models of bilingual learners and instead focuses on describing the re-sources bilingual students use to communicate mathematically. Without this shift we will have a limited view of these learners and we will design instruction that neglects the competencies they bring to mathematics classrooms. If all we see are students who don't speak English, mispronounce English words, or don't know vocabulary, instruction will focus on these deficiencies. If, instead, we learn to rec-ognize the mathematical ideas these students express in spite of their accents, code switching, or missing vocabulary, then instruction can build on students' compe-tencies and resources.

Below I describe three perspectives of bilingual mathematics learners: acquir-ing vocabulary, constructing multiple meanings, and participating in Discourse practices.[3] I argue that the third view, a sociocultural perspective, enriches our views of the relationship between language and learning mathematics, expands what counts as competence in mathematical communication, and provides a basis for designing equitable instruction. To make this case, I first compare and contrast the three perspectives and then present two examples to substantiate my claims regarding the contributions of a sociocultural perspective.

ACQUIRING VOCABULARY

One view of bilingual mathematics learners is that their main challenge is acquiring vocabulary. This first perspective defines learning mathematics as learning to carry out computations or solve traditional word problems and emphasizes vocabulary as the central issue for English learners as they learn mathematics. This view is reflected in early research on bilingual mathematics learners that focused primarily on how students understood individual vocabulary terms or translated traditional word problems from English to mathematical symbols (for examples, see Cuevas, 1983; Cuevas, Mann, & McClung, 1986; Mestre, 1981, 1988; Spanos & Crandall, 1990; Spanos, Rhodes, Dale, & Crandall, 1988). Recommendations for mathematics instruction for English learners have also emphasized vocabulary and reading comprehension (Dale & Cuevas, 1987; MacGregor & Moore, 1992; Olivares, 1996; Rubenstein, 1996).

Although an emphasis on vocabulary and reading comprehension may have been sufficient in the past, this emphasis does not match current views of mathematical proficiency or the activities in contemporary classrooms. In many mathematics classrooms today, the main activities are not carrying out arithmetic computations, solving traditional word problems, reading textbooks, or completing worksheets. Many students participate in a variety of oral and written practices such as explaining solution processes, describing conjectures, proving conclusions, and presenting arguments. As a consequence, reading and understanding mathematical texts or traditional word problems are no longer the best examples of how language and learning mathematics intersect.

Even in traditional classrooms where there may be little oral discussion, learning mathematical language involves more than learning vocabulary: Words have multiple meanings, meanings depend on situations, and learning to use mathematical language requires learning when to use different meanings. Vocabulary (along with decoding) is certainly an aspect of developing reading comprehension *at the word level*. However, vocabulary is not sufficient for becoming a competent reader. Reading comprehension involves skills beyond the word level, such as constructing meaning from text, using metacognitive strategies, and participating in academic language practices (Pressley, 2000).

An emphasis on vocabulary provides a narrow view of mathematical communication. This narrow view can have a negative impact on assessment and instruction for bilingual learners. English oral proficiency can affect how teachers assess a student's mathematical competence. For example, if we focus only on a student's failure to use the correct word, we can miss the student's competency in making conjectures, constructing arguments, addressing special cases, or dealing with contradictory evidence. If we conceive of "language" as only vocabulary, we are limiting the scope of communicative activities used to assess mathematical competence, and many students will appear less competent. Instruction focusing on low-level linguistic skills, such as vocabulary, neglects the more complex language skills necessary for learning and doing mathematics.

Further, this view perpetuates a deficiency model of bilingual learners that can have a negative impact on English learners' access to mathematical instruction. English learners may have a smaller or less accurate mathematical vocabulary in English than that of native English speakers. We can see this as a deficiency or we can notice this difference while also noticing other competencies for communicating mathematically. "Vocabulary" need not be construed as a deficiency, a reason for remedial instruction, or a prerequisite that bilingual learners must achieve before they can participate in more conceptual or advanced mathematics instruction. English learners can learn vocabulary at the same time that they participate in many types of lessons, including conceptual mathematical activities.

CONSTRUCTING MULTIPLE MEANINGS

A second perspective on bilingual mathematics learners describes learning mathematics as constructing multiple meanings for words. Work in mathematics education from this perspective has used the notion of the mathematics register. Halliday (1978) defined *register* in the following way:

> A register is a set of meanings that is appropriate to a particular function of language, together with the words and structures which express these meanings. We can refer to the "mathematics register," in the sense of the meanings that belong to the language of mathematics (the mathematical use of natural language, that is: not mathematics itself), and that a language must express if it is being used for mathematical purposes. (p. 195)

A register is a language variety associated with a particular situation of use. Common examples of registers include legal talk and baby talk. The notion of register includes not only lexical items but also phonology, morphology, syntax, and semantics as well as nonlinguistic behavior. The notion of register thus involves aspects of the situation.[4] From this perspective, since there are multiple meanings for the same term, students who are learning mathematics are learning to use these different meanings appropriately in different situations. There are several examples of such multiple meanings: the phrase *any number* means "all numbers" in a math context (Pimm, 1987); *a quarter* can refer to a coin or to a fourth of a whole (Khisty, 1995); and in Spanish *un cuarto* can mean "a room" or "a fourth" (Khisty, 1995).

Multiple meanings can create obstacles in mathematical conversations because students often use colloquial meanings, while the teacher (or other students) may use mathematical meanings. For example, the word *prime* can have different meanings depending on whether it is used to refer to "prime number," "prime time," or "prime rib." In Spanish, *primo* can mean "cousin" or "prime number" as in the phrase *número primo*. Another example of multiple meanings is Walkerdine's (1998b) description of the differences between the meanings of *more* in the mathematics classroom and at home. While in a classroom situation *more* is usually understood to be the opposite of *less*, at home the opposite of *more* is usually associated with "no more" as in, for example, "I want more paper" and "There is no more paper."

The multiple-meanings perspective considers differences between the everyday and mathematical registers. This perspective has contributed to descriptions of how learning mathematics involves, in part, a shift from everyday to more mathematical and precise meanings. For example, studies have described how students' language use moves closer to the mathematics register by becoming more precise and reflecting deeper conceptual knowledge (Moschkovich, 1996, 1998; O'Connor, 1992).

Using two national languages, such as English and Spanish, may complicate moving across two registers. For example, distinguishing between the two uses of *más* (more) is crucial in a mathematics context:

hay cuatro más _____ que _____ (there are four more _____ than _____)
hay cuatro veces más _____ que _____ (there are four times as many _____ as _____)

These two sentences refer to two different mathematical situations and yet the word *más* (more) is used in both cases. The multiple-meanings perspective adds complexity to our view of the relationship between language and learning mathematics. Emphasizing multiple meanings shifts the focus from examining how students acquire vocabulary to examining how students negotiate the multiple meanings of mathematical terms, from acquiring words to developing meanings for those words, from learning words with single meanings to understanding multiple meanings, and from learning vocabulary to using language appropriately in different situations.

This perspective should not be interpreted to imply that the two registers are separate or that everyday meanings are necessarily obstacles. Forman (1996) offers evidence that the two registers do not function separately, but that students and teacher interweave the everyday and academic registers in classroom discussions. Although differences between the everyday and mathematical registers are sometimes obstacles for communicating in mathematically precise ways and everyday meanings can sometimes be ambiguous, everyday meanings are not always obstacles. Everyday metaphors, meanings, and experiences can also provide resources for understanding mathematical concepts. For example, elsewhere (Moschkovich, 1996) I have described how students used a metaphor drawing on everyday experiences (describing a steeper line as harder to climb than a line that is less steep) to compare the steepness of lines on a graph.

The two perspectives summarized above, *acquiring vocabulary* and *constructing multiple meanings*, have provided useful analytical tools. However, they can be employed in ways that have negative implications for equity in classrooms. If these perspectives are used to emphasize the *obstacles* that bilingual students face as they learn mathematics, they provide only deficiency models (Garcia & González, 1995; González, 1995b) of bilingual students as mathematics learners. Instead of emphasizing obstacles, we need to consider the resources bilingual learners use for learning mathematics. In the following section I explore how a sociocultural view can provide a more complex view of bilingual mathematics learners and shift the emphasis from deficiencies and obstacles to resources and competencies.

PARTICIPATING IN MATHEMATICAL DISCOURSE PRACTICES

The sociocultural perspective described here uses a situated perspective of learning mathematics (Brown, Collins, & Duguid, 1989; Greeno, 1994) and the notion of Discourses (Gee, 1996) to build on previous work on classroom mathematical and scientific discourse (Cobb, Wood, & Yackel, 1993; Rosebery, Warren, & Conant, 1992). This perspective implies, first, that learning mathematics is viewed as a discursive activity (Forman, 1996). From this perspective, learning mathematics involves participating in a community of practice (Forman, 1996; Lave & Wenger, 1991; Nasir, 2002); contributing to the development of classroom sociomathematical norms (Cobb et al., 1993); and using multiple material, linguistic, and social resources (Greeno, 1994). This perspective assumes that learning is inherently social and cultural "whether or not it occurs in an overtly social context" (Forman, 1996, p. 117); that participants bring multiple views to a situation; that words, representations, and inscriptions have multiple meanings; and that participants actively negotiate these multiple meanings.

Rather than defining a "bilingual learner" as an individual who is proficient in more than one language, a sociocultural perspective defines bilingual learners as students who participate in multiple language communities. As described by Valdés-Fallis (1978), "natural" bilinguals are "the product of a specific linguistic community that uses one of its languages for certain functions and the other for other functions or situations" (p. 4). Work in sociolinguistics has described code switching as one of the resources available to bilingual speakers. These studies have shown that code switching is a rule- and constraint-governed process and a dynamic verbal strategy in its own right, rather than a sign that students are deficient or "semilingual." This work also cautions that code switching should not be seen as a deficiency or a reflection of the ability to recall (Valdés-Fallis, 1978).

A sociocultural perspective views language as more than sequential speech or writing. Gee emphasizes how "Discourses always involve more than language" (1999, p. 25) and defines Discourses as much more than vocabulary or multiple meanings:

> A Discourse is a socially accepted association among ways of using language, other symbolic expressions, and "artifacts," of thinking, feeling, believing, valuing and acting that can be used to identify oneself as a member of a socially meaningful group or "social network," or to signal (that one is playing) a socially meaningful role. (Gee, 1996, p. 131)

Using Gee's definition, mathematical Discourses include not only ways of talking, acting, interacting, thinking, believing, reading, and writing but also communities, values, beliefs, points of view, objects, and gestures.

There is no one mathematical Discourse or practice (for a discussion of multiple mathematical Discourses see Moschkovich, 2002a). Mathematical Discourses involve different communities (mathematicians, teachers, or students) and different genres (explanations, proofs, or presentations). Practices vary across communities of research mathematicians, traditional classrooms, and reform classrooms. However, within these various communities, there are commonalities in the practices that count as participation in competent mathematical Discourse. Particular modes of argument, such as precision, brevity, and logical coherence, are valued (Forman, 1996). In general, abstracting, generalizing, searching for certainty, and being precise, explicit, brief, and logical are highly valued activities across different mathematical communities. Mathematical claims apply only to a precisely and explicitly defined set of situations, as in the statement "Multiplication makes a number bigger, except when multiplying by a number smaller than 1." Claims are frequently tied to mathematical representations such as graphs, tables, or diagrams. The value of generalizing is reflected in common mathematical statements, such as "The angles of any triangle add up to 180 degrees," "Parallel lines never meet," or "The equation a + b will always equal b + a." Imagining (for example, infinity or zero), visualizing, hypothesizing, and predicting are also valued mathematical practices.

MATHEMATICAL DISCUSSIONS

In this section I examine two mathematical discussions to illustrate the limitations of the vocabulary and multiple-meanings perspectives and to describe how a sociocultural perspective enriches our view of language, provides an alternative to deficiency models of learners, and generates different questions for both research and instruction. I selected the first example to illustrate the limitations of the vocabulary perspective and the second example to illustrate the limitations of the multiple-meanings perspective. The two examples, presented below, show the complexity that using a situated and sociocultural perspective as an analytical lens brings to the study of bilingual mathematics learners. The first example shows us how the vocabulary perspective fails to capture students' competencies in communicating mathematically. The second example shows that the multiple-meanings perspective can also fall short of a full description of the resources that students use.

In presenting these examples, I also show how to use a sociocultural perspective to identify student competencies and resources that instruction can build on to support mathematics learning. To uncover these competencies and resources, I use the following questions, selectively and loosely following Gee's (1999) questions for Discourse analysis: (1) What are the situated meanings of the words and phrases that seem important in the situation? (2) What are the resources students use to communicate mathematically? That is, What sign systems (speech, writing, images, and gestures) are relevant in the situation? In particular, how is "stuff" other than language relevant? And (3) What Discourses are involved? What Discourse practices are students participating in that are relevant in mathematical communities or that reflect mathematical competence?

Example 1: Describing a Pattern

A group of seventh- and eighth-grade students in a summer mathematics course constructed rectangles with the same area but different perimeters and looked for a pattern to relate the dimensions and the perimeter of their rectangles. Below is a problem similar to the one they were working on:

1. Look for all the rectangles with area 36 and write down the dimensions.
2. Calculate the perimeter for each rectangle.
3. Describe a pattern relating the perimeter and the dimensions.

In this classroom, there was one bilingual teacher and one monolingual teacher. A group of four students were videotaped as they talked in their small group and with the bilingual teacher (primarily in Spanish). They attempted to describe the pattern in their group and searched for the Spanish word for rectangle. The students produced several suggestions, including *ángulo* (angle), *triángulo* (triangle), and *rángulo* ("rangle").[5] Although these students attempted to find a term to refer to the rectangles, neither the teacher nor the other students provided the correct Spanish word, *rectángulo* (rectangle).

Later on, a second teacher (a monolingual English speaker) asked several questions from the front of the class. In response, Alicia, one of the students in this small group, described a relationship between the length of the sides of a rectangle and its perimeter. (Transcript annotations are between brackets. Translations are in italics).

Teacher B: [Speaking from the front of the class] Somebody describe what they saw as a comparison between what the picture looked like and what the perimeter was . . .

Alicia: The longer the ah, . . . the longer [traces the shape of a long rectangle with her hands several times] the ah, . . . the longer the, rángulo [*rangle*], you know the more the perimeter, the higher the perimeter is.

An analysis of this excerpt using the vocabulary perspective would focus on this student's failed attempt to use the right word, *rectangle*. Focusing on how vocabulary was an obstacle would not do justice to how this student successfully communicated a mathematical idea. If we were to focus only on Alicia's inaccurate use of the term *rángulo*, we might miss how she used resources from the situation and how her statement reflects valued mathematical Discourse practices. If we move from a focus on vocabulary, then we can begin to see this student's competence. Alicia's competence only becomes visible if we include gestures and objects as resources for communicating mathematically. This move is important for instruction because it shifts the focus from a perceived deficiency in the student that needs to be corrected (not using the word *rectangle*) to a competency that can be refined through instruction (using gestures and objects). This move also shifts our attention from words to mathematical ideas, as expressed not only through words but also through other modes. This shift is particularly important in uncovering the mathematical competencies of students who are learning English.

Alicia used gestures to illustrate what she meant, and she referred to the concrete objects in front of her, the drawings of rectangles, to clarify her description. She also used her first language as a resource. She interjected an invented Spanish word into her statement. In this way, a gesture, objects in the situation, and the student's first language served as resources for describing a pattern. Even though the word that she used for rectangle does not exist in either Spanish or English, it is very clear from the situation that Alicia was referring to a rectangle. It is also clear from her gestures that even though she did not use the words *length* or *width*, she was referring to the length of the side of a rectangle parallel to the floor.

Using a sociocultural perspective, we can also ask what mathematical Discourse practices are relevant to this situation. Describing patterns is a paradigmatic practice in mathematics, so much so that mathematics is often defined as "the science of patterns" (Devlin, 1998, p. 3). And Alicia certainly described a pattern correctly. The rectangle with area 36 that has the greatest perimeter (74) is the rectangle with the longest possible length, 36, and shortest possible width, 1. As the length gets longer, say, in comparing a rectangle of length 12, width 3, and perimeter 30 with a rectangle of perimeter 74, the perimeter does in fact become greater. Alicia appropriately (in the right place, at the right time, and in the right way) used a construction commonly used in mathematical communities to describe patterns, make comparisons, and describe covariation: "the longer the _____, the more (higher) the _____."

This example illustrates how a sociocultural perspective can open the way for seeing competence. This perspective does not emphasize the obstacles Alicia faced, but uncovers the ways that she used resources from the situation to communicate mathematically. Focusing on mathematical Discourse practices and including gestures and objects as resources make her mathematical competence visible.

Different implications for instruction follow from the vocabulary and sociocultural perspectives. Certainly, Alicia needs to learn the word for rectangle (ideally in both English and Spanish), but instruction should not stop there. Rather than only correcting her use of *rángulo* or recommending that she learn vocabulary, instruction should also build on Alicia's use of gestures, objects, and description of a pattern. If instruction only focuses on what mathematical terminology English learners know or don't know, they will always seem deficient because they are, in fact, learning a second language. If teachers perceive these students as deficient and only correct their vocabulary use, there is no room for addressing their mathematical ideas, building on these ideas, and connecting these ideas to the discipline. English learners thus run the risk of getting caught in a repeated cycle of remedial instruction that does not focus on mathematical content. Seeing mathematical communication as more than vocabulary implies that instruction should also focus on how students generalize, abstract, and describe patterns, rather than only on how students use individual words.

Example 2: Clarifying a Description

While the first example fits the expectation that bilingual students struggle with vocabulary, the vocabulary perspective was not sufficient to describe that student's competence. The second example highlights the limitations of the vocabulary perspective for describing mathematical communication and shows how code switching can be a resource for bilingual speakers. In the following discussion two students used both languages not for vocabulary, but to clarify the mathematical meaning of a description.

The example is taken from an interview conducted with two ninth-grade students after school. The students had been in mainstream English-only mathematics classrooms for several years. One student, Marcela, had some previous mathematics instruction in Spanish. These two students were working on the problem shown in Figure 6.1. They had graphed the line $y = -0.6x$ on paper and were discussing whether this line was steeper or less steep than the line $y = x$ (see Figure 6.2).

Giselda first proposed that the line was steeper, then less steep. Marcela repeatedly asked Giselda if she was sure. After Marcela proposed that the line was less steep, she proceeded to explain her reasoning to Giselda. (Transcript annotations are between brackets. Translations are in italics directly below the utterance in Spanish).

FIGURE 6.1. Problem for example 2

8a. If you change the equation y=x to y=-0.6x,
how would the line change?

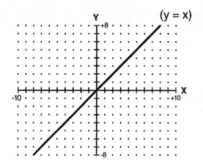

A. The steepness would change.
Why or why not?

		___ STEEPER
___NO	___YES	___ LESS STEEP

Marcela: No, it's less steeper . . .

Giselda: Why?

Marcela: See, it's closer to the *x*-axis . . . [looks at Giselda] . . . Isn't it?

Giselda: Oh, so if it's right here . . . it's steeper, right?

Marcela: Porque fíjate, digamos que este es el suelo. [*Because, look, let's say that this is the ground.*] Entonces, si se acerca más, pues es menos steep. [*Then, if it gets closer, then it's less steep.*] . . . 'cause see this one [referring to the line $y = x$] . . . is . . . está entre el medio de la "*x*" y de la "*y*." Right? [*is between the "x" and the "y"*]

FIGURE 6.2. Lines drawn by students

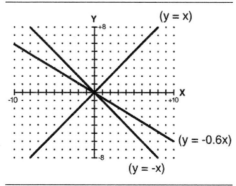

Giselda: [Nods in agreement.]
Marcela: This one [referring to the line $y = -0.6x$] is closer to the "x" than
to the "y," so this one [referring to the line $y = -0.6x$] is less steep.

The vocabulary perspective is not very useful for understanding what this student knows, describing how she communicates mathematically, or guiding instruction. Marcela, rather than struggling with vocabulary or using Spanish to fill in for a missing English word, used her first language to clarify a mathematical description. Her competence involved more than knowing the meaning of *steeper* and *less steep.* If we use a multiple-meanings perspective, we can begin to see that in this discussion the two students are negotiating and clarifying the meanings of *steeper* and *less steep.* We could say that Marcela used the mathematics register as a resource to communicate mathematically. She used two constructions common in the school mathematics register, "Let's say this is . . ." and "If _____, then _____."

The multiple-meanings perspective is also not sufficient for describing Marcela's competence. This becomes apparent when we focus on how this student used her first language, code switching, mathematical artifacts—the graph, the line $y = x$, and the axes—and everyday experiences as resources. The premise that meanings from everyday experiences are obstacles for communicating mathematically does not hold for this example. In fact, Marcela used her everyday experiences and the metaphor that the x-axis is the ground— "Porque fíjate, digamos que este es el suelo" (Because, look, let's say that this is the ground)—as resources for explaining her description. Rather than finding everyday meanings as obstacles for moving between two registers, she used an everyday situation to clarify her explanation.

Using a sociocultural perspective, we can also ask what mathematical Discourse practices are relevant to this situation. Marcela's explanations echo mathematical Discourse practices in several ways. First, Marcela explicitly stated an assumption, a discursive practice valued in mathematical Discourse, when she said, "Porque fíjate, digamos que este es el suelo" (Because, look, let's say that this is the ground). Second, she supported her claim by making a connection to mathematical representations, another valued discursive practice. She used the graph, in particular the line $y = x$ (line 5) and the axes (lines 5 and 7), as references to support her claim about the steepness of the line. A sociocultural perspective helps us to see that Marcela was participating in two discursive practices that reflect important values: stating assumptions explicitly and connecting claims to mathematical representations.

CONCLUSIONS

The three perspectives I have described make different assumptions regarding bilingual learners, define mathematical communication in different ways, and result in different recommendations for instruction (see Figure 6.3).

The first two perspectives have been important in understanding the relation-

FIGURE **6.3.** Comparing assumptions of the three views

Vocabulary	Multiple Meanings	Participation
Language		
Mathematical communication is principally about vocabulary.	Mathematical communication involves the mathematics register and multiple meanings for words, phrases, and constructions.	Mathematical communication involves more than words, registers, or multiple meanings; it also involves nonlanguage resources and discourse practices.
Bilingual Learners		
Are deficient in vocabulary proficiency when compared to monolinguals or native speakers.	Face additional difficulties and complications in learning to use the mathematics register and sorting out multiple meanings.	While bilingual learners are different from monolinguals, they are not deficient; they bring some competencies and use resources. These competencies and resources may be the same or different from those of monolinguals.
Instruction		
Should focus on developing students' vocabulary, perhaps as a prerequisite for studying particular mathematical topics.	Since the mathematics register and multiple meanings are the main obstacles, instruction should focus on developing students' mathematics register and awareness of multiple meanings.	Should focus on uncovering student competencies and resources and building on these.

ship between learning mathematics and language. They have also provided a basis for designing instruction for bilingual mathematics learners. A perspective that emphasizes acquiring vocabulary has been used to describe how students solve word problems and understand mathematical texts, and suggests that instruction should focus on vocabulary. A perspective that emphasizes constructing multiple meanings across registers has uncovered possible sources of misunderstandings in classroom conversations. This second perspective suggests that instruction can support bilingual learners in communicating mathematically by clarifying multiple meanings, addressing the conflicts between two languages explicitly, and discussing the different meanings students may associate with mathematical terms in each language.

As I have illustrated, the two perspectives have limitations. A focus on vocabulary does not capture the complexity of mathematical communication, ignores situational resources, and neglects important aspects of student mathematical competence. Assuming that students' everyday experience is an obstacle for learning mathematics obscures how everyday meanings can be resources for mathematical discussions. When these two perspectives are used to emphasize obstacles, they provide a limited model of bilingual students as mathematics learners that focuses on deficiencies. A more complete description of mathematical communication for bilingual students should include an analysis not only of the difficulties these students face but also of the competencies and resources they use to communicate mathematically.

The sociocultural perspective that I have presented expands the analytical lens to include nonlanguage resources and mathematical Discourse practices, thus expanding what counts as competent mathematical communication. The key assumptions on which this broader view of competence is based include the following:

- Mathematical communication involves more than language.
- Meanings are multiple, changing, situated, and sociocultural.
- Bilingual learners may be different than monolinguals but they should not be defined by deficiencies.

The two examples illustrate several aspects of learning mathematics in a bilingual classroom that only become visible when using a sociocultural perspective:

1. Learning to participate in mathematical Discourse is not merely or primarily a matter of learning vocabulary. During conversations in mathematics classrooms students are also learning to participate in valued mathematical Discourse practices such as describing patterns, making generalizations, and using representations to support claims.
2. Bilingual learners use many resources to communicate mathematically: gestures, objects, everyday experiences, their first language, code switching, and mathematical representations.
3. There are multiple uses of Spanish in mathematical conversations between bilingual students. While some students use Spanish to label objects, other students use Spanish to explain a concept, justify an answer, or elaborate on an explanation or description.
4. Bilingual students bring multiple competencies to the classroom. For example, even a student who is missing vocabulary may be proficient in describing patterns, using mathematical constructions, or presenting mathematically sound arguments.

A sociocultural perspective points to several aspects of classroom instruction that need to be considered. Classroom instruction should support bilingual students' engagement in conversations about mathematics, going beyond translating vocabulary and involving students in communicating about mathematical ideas. The examples presented here show that English learners can participate in discussions in which they grapple with significant mathematical ideas, even when they do not use the right words or switch languages.

Instruction for this population should not emphasize low-level language skills over opportunities to actively and repeatedly communicate about mathematical ideas. One of the goals of mathematics instruction for bilingual students should be to support all students, regardless of their proficiency in English, in participating in discussions that focus on important mathematical ideas, rather than on pronunciation, vocabulary, or low-level linguistic skills. By learning to recognize how bilingual students express their mathematical ideas as they are learning English, teachers can maintain a focus on the mathematical ideas as well as on language development.

It is not a question of whether students should learn vocabulary but rather how instruction can best support students learning both vocabulary and mathematics. Vocabulary drill and practice is not the most effective instructional practice for learning either vocabulary or mathematics. Instead, experts on vocabulary and second-language acquisition describe vocabulary acquisition in a first or second language as occurring most successfully in instructional contexts that are language rich, actively involve students in using language, require both receptive and expressive understanding, and require students to use words in multiple ways over extended periods of time (Blachowicz & Fisher, 2000; Pressley, 2000). To develop written- and oral-communication skills students need to participate in negotiating meaning (Savignon, 1991) and in tasks that require output from students (Swain, 2001). In sum, instruction should provide opportunities for students to actively use mathematical language to communicate about and negotiate meaning for mathematical situations.

Understanding the mathematical ideas in what students say and do can be difficult when teaching, perhaps especially so when working with students who are learning English. It may not be easy (or even possible) to sort out which aspects of a student's utterance are results of the student's conceptual understanding or of the student's English proficiency. However, if the goal of instruction is to support students as they learn mathematics, determining the origin of an error is not as important as listening for students' mathematical ideas and uncovering the mathematical competence in what they are saying and doing. Hearing mathematical ideas and uncovering mathematical competence is only possible if we move beyond limited views of language and deficiency models of bilingual learners.

NOTES

This work was supported in part by the National Science Foundation (Grant Number 96065) and by faculty research funds granted by the University of California, Santa Cruz.

1. Although there are differences between the labels *bilingual* and *English learners,* for the sake of simplicity I will use *bilingual* to refer to both populations.

2. I will use the term *sociocultural* to refer to a view of learning as inherently social, cultural, and situated. I use *situated* to mean "local, grounded in actual practices and experiences" (Gee, 1999, p. 40). Although in a previous article (Moschkovich, 2002b) I used the term *situated/sociocultural,* for the sake of brevity here I will use the term *sociocultural.*

3. I propose these three views as useful for understanding the relationship between learning mathematics and language. These perspectives are not meant to represent any one researcher, theorist, or school. Instead, I offer them as composite summaries of three theoretical stances reflected in work in this area. In critiquing the "acquiring vocabulary" and "constructing multiple meanings" perspectives, my purpose is not to point out how previous work was "right" or "wrong" but to examine the limitations we face when using these two perspectives.

4. The notion of *register* should not be interpreted as representing a list of technical words and phrases. This interpretation reduces the concept of mathematical register to vocabulary and disregards the role of meaning in learning to communicate mathematically (Moschkovich, 1998).

5. Although the word does not exist in Spanish, it might be best translated as "rangle," perhaps a shortening of the word *rectángulo.*

7

Building on Community Knowledge:
An Avenue to Equity in Mathematics Education

Marta Civil

This chapter presents my personal reflection on more than a decade of work in mathematics education in working-class, mostly Latino communities in Tucson. My research is driven by an equity agenda that capitalizes on building on the students' and their families' knowledge and experiences as resources for schooling. What are the implications for the mathematical education of these children, if we take their experiences and backgrounds as resources for learning in the classroom? In this chapter I address this question by paying special attention to the challenges in the pedagogical transformation of household knowledge into mathematical knowledge for the classroom. I focus on a critical reflection on the teaching innovations we carried out as we tried to link school mathematics with everyday experiences. In particular, I examine two aspects of our work:

- How do our values about what we consider to be mathematics influence the curriculum development? (Civil & Andrade, 2002).
- What resources and support mechanisms are needed for teachers to successfully carry out the implementation of such curriculum?

BACKGROUND: SETTING THE CONTEXT

Much of the work I describe in this chapter originated with my involvement in the Funds of Knowledge for Teaching (FKT) project (González, 1995a; Gonzáles, Moll, & Amanti, 2005), followed up by Project Bridge, which had a specific focus on mathematics (Civil & Andrade, 2002). These projects were collaborative research efforts between university researchers and elementary school teachers. The teachers worked in schools in working-class neighborhoods where the student body is largely composed of ethnic and language "minority" children. FKT is grounded on the theory that household and community knowledge can provide strategic resources for classroom practice. It is assumed that all households have historically accumulated and culturally developed bodies of knowledge and skills on which they draw

Improving Access to Mathematics, edited by Na'ilah Suad Nasir & Paul Cobb. Copyright © 2007 by Teachers College, Columbia University. All rights reserved. Prior to photocopying items for classroom use, please contact the Copyright Clearance Center, Customer Service, 222 Rosewood Dr., Danvers, MA 01923, USA, tel. (978) 750-8400, www.copyright.com.

for daily survival and well-being (Moll & Greenberg, 1990). As González (1996) writes, "This assumption is critical in terms of re-conceptualizing households, not as the source of barriers to educational attainment, but as repositories of resources that can be strategically tapped" (p. 3). Within the FKT project, instead of relying on a static, bounded definition of culture, teacher-researchers learned firsthand about the lived realities of students and their families (through ethnographic household visits), and then used this knowledge as the basis for curricular units (modules) within the classroom (González, 1995a).

In the following sections I address the two core questions of this chapter through examples from some of the modules that we developed. It is useful to consider the vision I had in mind for a teaching innovation that would be both mathematically rich and community based (for more on this vision, see Civil, 2002a). I was looking for situations in which students would engage in what one could consider "mathematics for the sake of mathematics"—for example, problem-solving situations that call for different approaches, tasks that require offering a mathematical justification, or activities that cut across different areas of mathematics (to highlight the connections). Yet, at the same time, I wanted the mathematics to be connected to community knowledge. This means two things: I was interested in activities that grew out of the community knowledge and experiences (such as the construction or the garden modules I will describe) and I wanted to capture the forms of knowledge and learning that we had seen in these communities, in particular the idea of apprenticeship learning. The FKT project had gathered evidence that at home and in their community, children were often active participants in the functioning of the household (e.g., acting as language interpreters for parents and other relatives; assisting in the child care of younger siblings; helping out in the economic development of the household, such as helping in the repair of appliances, cars; playing an active role in traditional ceremonies, such as Yoeme Easter). This active participation and the learning that accompanies it are quite different from what many of these students experienced in their traditional schooling (for the concept of transitions between home and school mathematics, see Civil & Andrade, 2002). So, I wondered, what might the learning environment look like if we were to develop a more participatory approach towards the learning of mathematics (similar to what these children experience in their out-of-school lives)?

WHERE IS THE MATHEMATICS?

One of the first modules on which I collaborated centered on the theme of construction in a second-grade classroom in a primary school (K–2) just outside a Native American (Yoeme) reservation. The teacher had conducted household visits the year before—when her students were in first grade; she stayed with them for second grade—and had realized the wealth of knowledge about construction that existed in most families. The teacher expressed an interest in emphasizing mathematics in this module. To this end, she and three university-based researchers (including myself) met several times during the month of July to plan the module. The meetings ranged over a variety of topics: how to integrate the different content areas while keeping in mind the required curriculum, how to assess the children's learning, how to bring in the knowledge from the home (e.g., whom to invite as guest speaker and when) (Civil, 1993, 2002a; Sandoval-Taylor, 2005).

The construction module provided quite a few opportunities for the children to engage in rich mathematics particularly in relation to patterns, measurement, estimation, and properties of different shapes (Civil, 2002a). Arithmetic was used in context and I witnessed children coming up with a variety of different ways to add and subtract numbers. The measuring activities led to some of the difficulties that children this age encounter when using a ruler (such as where to start reading the ruler and how to read a result that does not end in a whole number). Since these students were used to working with one another and to comparing ideas, they naturally engaged in dialogues about their different interpretations on how to use the ruler. These children were persistent and seemed eager to explore a question and engage in conversation about their work with me or any other adult who visited the classroom. On any given day, they were either constructing something, trying to guess someone else's pattern, working on a problem, talking to their partner about the task, or writing in their mathematics journal.

In this chapter, I focus on what I view as a possible tension that I describe as preserving the purity of the funds of knowledge, perhaps at the expense of mathematics. The teacher wanted her students to have ownership of their learning. A key issue was that the opportunities for mathematical exploration had to arise from the children's and their families' experiences. This was consistent with her view that "there is a lot that they know about mathematics, everything you do is mathematics." In Sandoval-Taylor (2005), she writes,

> I wanted the module to be inquiry-based, focused on my students' prior knowledge, and I also wanted the children to make the decisions and negotiate the curriculum. . . . For example, if a parent visited the class and brought up estimating how many nails are needed for a certain task, I wanted to be able to follow this with a mini-lesson on estimation. The parent would provide the focus and the set would already be there for this lesson. (pp. 154, 159)

This teacher was a firm believer in parents as resources. To me, this concept of resources, as reflected in the excerpt below, relates closely to the notion of parents as intellectual resources (Civil & Andrade, 2003), which I will come back to at the end of this chapter. In reflecting on how to assess children's learning in this module, she writes,

> I was satisfied with the assessment procedure but still felt that parents would contribute additional knowledge that would help students on the posttest, and I wanted

to reflect this in the assessment task. I knew students would grow when parents came in and particularly when students used them as resources to answer their own questions. (Sandoval-Taylor, 2005, p. 160)

During the planning meetings prior to the module implementation, we went back and forth on the issue of assessment. We soon reached agreement on one possible task to give the students. We asked them, "How do you build a house?" We chose six students to be individually interviewed (pre and post) and the rest of the children answered this question in writing (pre and post, too). A comparison of the pre- and postinterviews as well as of the pre- and post-write-ups showed clear growth in terms of literacy and general knowledge about how to build a house. Our dilemma during the planning meetings was how to assess the children's mathematical learning. What kind of task could we give them (as a pre and post) that would preserve the purity of the funds of knowledge? In order for us to respect the teacher's beliefs in building on the children's and the families' knowledge, we had to plan for different possibilities, while knowing that everything could change, depending on how the module evolved. I, however, wanted to make sure that we had in place what I would consider a mathematically rich task. At one of the planning meetings, I suggested that a possible activity could involve the children making something (e.g., a chair) for a doll or an action figure. This would allow us to discuss proportional reasoning. Then as a posttest, students could make something else for that doll/action figure. In reflecting over this suggestion, Sandoval-Taylor (2005), having just summarized my idea for assessment, writes,

> I was not sure that learning about proportion would emerge during the unit. From my experiences in my students' community, I thought that the unit focus would more likely be on constructing buildings. I thought this might be a better focus for an assessment prompt. Students could be asked, for instance, how to build an additional room on their homes. (pp. 159–160)

In reflecting back on this module and in particular on this assessment issue, I am not sure how mathematically appropriate the proportional reasoning task that I had in mind would be for second graders. I remember saying that it would probably have to be adapted, as I had only tried it with older children. But what caught my attention is that we never really discussed the appropriateness of the mathematical content; rather, our discussion revolved around whether making furniture (as in my example of the chair) and engaging in proportional-reasoning tasks would be something that would naturally emerge from the module. If it was not grounded directly on the funds of knowledge pertinent to this classroom, did we want to pursue it? In the excerpt above, the teacher suggests "how to build an additional room on their homes" as a more appropriate assessment prompt. But then my question would be, Where is the mathematics? I am not denying that in building an additional room, one uses mathematics, but would we be able to uncover it in asking children this question? Maybe my hesitations are the result of my content orientation. For example, I would have liked to see how these children tackled problem-solving situations in mathematics. The teacher and I talked about this, but my impression at the time was that she viewed these mathematics tasks as artificial and removed from the children's experiences. This potential tension between developing mathematics activities that reflected the funds of knowledge versus activities that would be more along the lines of mathematicians' mathematics was not unique to the construction module (for a discussion on different forms of mathematics, see Civil, 2002b). This example shows some of the challenges with trying to infuse the modules with what in my view would be rich mathematical tasks. I could not help but wonder, Where is the mathematics? and Did we do enough or did we just touch on superficial uses of mathematics? These dilemmas mostly relate to the teacher's and my views about what counts as mathematics and what it means to teach within a funds of knowledge perspective. But what about the students' views? In the following section I address this.

WHAT IS DOING MATHEMATICS IN SCHOOL?

For 3 years, another researcher and I collaborated with a fifth-grade teacher who was particularly interested in strengthening her students' mathematical knowledge to help them succeed in their transition to middle school. Our agenda was then to advance these students' learning of mathematics. We took a slightly different interpretation from the approach in the FKT project as we tried to ground the modules on the children's interests and experiences (rather than on their families, even though the teacher did conduct household visits). We put particular emphasis on other aspects of the FKT pedagogy, namely, inquiry-based learning and a participatory approach to instruction. As we tried to develop these approaches to mathematics instruction (in which we wanted to encourage students' sharing of ideas) we encountered several obstacles. At this school, many of the students had been together since kindergarten. Friendships and rivalries were well in place. Furthermore, the teacher was a newcomer to this school, one in which many of the teachers and staff had been there for years and had formed a close-knit community (for more details on the setting, see Civil, 2002b). These students were not used to engaging in discussions in mathematics. In an interview the teacher described the situation quite clearly:

> They didn't see the point of the discussion; they didn't like waiting on everybody to talk. You know, you have to have waiting time. A lot of the kids were very impatient about giving waiting time to their colleagues. They didn't feel like that was work. To them, work is filling out worksheets and turning the paper in and seeing if they got it right or wrong. So, hopefully this project little by little is helping them rethink what, you know, is work, when has work been done, what tasks are really important, and what tasks aren't.

Our biggest struggle was in relation to our efforts to change the social and sociomathematical norms (Yackel & Cobb, 1996) in these classrooms (Civil, 2002b; Civil & Planas, 2004). A related issue is students' beliefs about what they were willing to view as valid mathematics. As the teacher's excerpt above shows, these students were expecting a worksheet approach to mathematics teaching and learning. Our attempts to engage students in, for example, discussing the uses of mathematics in everyday life and in different occupations, or working in small groups on problem-solving-type tasks, were often met with resistance and even questions about what this had to do with doing mathematics. I know this is no surprise to anyone who has tried to develop a teaching innovation. My concern is with whether students viewed the mathematics embedded in the modules as "real" mathematics. By fifth grade, students have developed an idea of what to expect in school mathematics. After one year in a classroom where teacher and students try to base the learning of mathematics (and of other subject areas) on their everyday experiences and knowledge, these students usually move to a very different kind of classroom for the following grade. Students may have indeed been involved in rich mathematical opportunities, but if they did not see what they did as valid mathematics, is this problematic for their overall mathematics education?

Underlying these dilemmas are also my own beliefs about mathematics. As we tried to uncover the mathematical Funds of Knowledge through household visits and occupational interviews (Civil & Andrade, 2002), I realized how limiting my own training in academic mathematics seemed to be. Millroy's (1992) paradox rings particularly true for me: "How can anyone who is schooled in conventional Western mathematics 'see' any form of mathematics other than that which resembles the conventional mathematics with which she is familiar?" (p. 11) I knew what I did not want: superficial applications of "household" experiences. Although I believe in the pedagogical approach behind thematic instruction, I am concerned that often the mathematics in those themes is watered down. It is not challenging students' thinking in mathematics. After more than a decade of work in this area, I am still left wondering about the process of pedagogical transformation of mathematical funds of knowledge for classroom implementation (González, Andrade, Civil, & Moll, 2001). In the following section, I present one example of what in my view was a "successful" implementation.

WHAT DOES A "SUCCESSFUL" IMPLEMENTATION LOOK LIKE?

The household visits and interviews in both the FKT and the Bridge projects had consistently revealed a learning-by-participation approach to assisting children in their acquisition of the necessary skills for the tasks at hand. I have always been intrigued by the possibilities of bringing such an approach to learning to the school setting, particularly in mathematics. In a participation model of teaching and learning, the learner participates in a community of learners (Lave, 1996; Rogoff, 1994). Learning takes places through collaboration and engagement in activities that are important to the practices of the community. To a certain extent the construction module and the example I present next (the garden module) show attempts to re-create this participation model in the school. Furthermore, the garden module reflects our attempts to develop a mathematical apprenticeship in a school setting (van Oers, 1996), by embedding the mathematical learning in the "context of a sociocultural activity in which the pupils want to participate and in which they are able to participate given their actual abilities" (p. 104).

The example takes place in a fourth-/fifth-grade combination classroom. The teacher, Leslie, had been with the fifth graders since the year before. She was used to having parents come to her classroom and contribute their expertise. She viewed building on parents' and community knowledge as fundamental to the develop-ment of a sense of community in her classroom. What was new for Leslie was the development of a learning module that would focus on mathematics.

The Garden Module

This module grew out of a curriculum retreat during which we all brainstormed possible modules grounded on the findings from the household visits. Two of the teachers had uncovered funds of knowledge related to gardening within the fami-lies they had interviewed and decided that they wanted to develop a module around gardening. Hence, part of the retreat time was spent working as a group on what a garden module would look like and in particular what the mathematics opportu-nities might be in such a module. Leslie had made it very clear that her interest in the overall research project was to explore how "rigorous mathematics could be developed from household visits."

To me this was an intriguing prospect because, on one hand, Leslie had much in common with the second-grade teacher in the construction module in that she wanted the children to guide the curriculum. On the other hand, she wanted to make sure that we addressed key concepts in mathematics in her grade levels. Al-though the two objectives are not incompatible, my experience so far had been that the mathematics had not been as strong as I would have liked it, in part for the reasons discussed earlier in this chapter. The garden module became an opportu-nity to engage students in mathematically rich tasks (e.g., exploring how area var-ies given a fixed perimeter; discussing different ways to graph the growth of an Amaryllis, which included the concept of scale) by building on their gardening experiences throughout the module (for more on this module, see Civil & Kahn, 2001; Kahn & Civil, 2001). Here my focus will be on how the teacher involved the families and on some considerations related to building on everyday experiences.

Leslie was an experienced teacher (about 20 years in that school district) who had been at that school for 5 years. She was well liked and respected by the parents, and most likely this helped them give her a vote of confidence when she decided to try something different from what she had done in the previous years. She drew the parents in; they became co-constructors of the curriculum. The families were involved in many aspects of this module, contributing from actual resources (such as seeds and soil) to their expertise with gardening.

This offers a very different view from that of typical parental involvement. Leslie learned from the parents and families and had some of them come in as experts. She engaged with them in conversations and these conversations helped her shape the curriculum. This is one more aspect of seeing parents as intellectual resources.

A Look at Some of the Mathematics in the Garden Project

Leslie and I had a common goal: We wanted to combine everyday mathematics and academic mathematics (Civil, 2002b). For example, as the plants grew and the children refused to thin them or to get rid of some of them, we needed bigger gardens. Each group of 4 or 5 children had a garden enclosed with chicken wire. How could we make those gardens bigger without adding any more chicken wire? From the point of view of an out-of-school problem, one could argue that the mathematics is limited: By just pulling here and there on the chicken wire, the different groups were able to make their enclosures bigger. By doing this, most gardens ended up in a somewhat square/circle shape. But we did not think that this would be enough to make the mathematical connection. So we developed an artificial activity: The students made a garden enclosure using a 3-foot-long string that each student glued to paper in any shape that he or she wanted to make. The challenge then became to find the area of that shape (students had different tools around, including cubes and tiles to cover the area and then count, as well as rulers). The different shapes with their area were displayed and a discussion of what shape would give the largest area followed. Because the activity was grounded on the students' experiences with the garden, we believe that despite its artificiality, the students were intrigued and curious about the problems of how to find the area of an irregular shape and how to maximize the area while keeping the perimeter fixed (see Civil & Kahn, 2001). The students' experience with the in-class activity made its way into their gardens. As the need for bigger gardens continued, many of the groups started working toward making their garden circular (although some children realized that a circular design could be problematic in terms of access to their plants).

The idea of grounding in-school mathematics activities on everyday experiences is not unproblematic. For example, once the out-of-school activity is brought into the school, it may loose its appeal. Further, as Schliemann (1995) notes,

> to bring to the classroom problems that can be related to their everyday practice does not seem to be the answer since these will also be limited and will not help exploring new facets of mathematical knowledge which are not part of everyday situations. Moreover, once transposed to the classroom cultural setting the problem is no more the same. (p. 57)

The garden project gave us an indication of a potential interference situated between everyday experiences and school mathematics. At the end of the year I conducted task-based interviews with four students (two fourth graders and two fifth graders) to gain some perspective on these four children's views on the garden project, as well as to assess some aspects of their mathematics learning. One of the tasks involved revisiting finding the area of an irregular shape (a "garden" made with 1-foot string) and discussing what shape would have the largest area (given this perimeter). One of the students kept going back and forth between whether the garden with largest area would be a circle or a square. His reasoning was based on the shape of the pots. Since the pots for the real garden were circular, he argued that a circle would be the best shape; but for the one in class (as well as during the interview), which used square tiles as the "pots," he argued that a square would be a better shape because "I think that it would have to be like a square this way, to hold more because they are square units. Because, I mean you can't cut a plant holder in half. . . I mean you can fit circles into squares, but it is hard to fit a square into a circle."

Another student, who was also undecided between a circle and a square for larger area, leaned toward a circle as the one having the largest area, but in practice (i.e., in real life) she seemed to prefer a square. Below is an excerpt from that interview (K is the student):

> *Marta Civil:* OK, so do you think if you have to choose between a circle and a square do you think it will make a difference or would you choose actually, one of them?
>
> *K:* I would choose square.
>
> *Marta Civil:* You would choose a square. And why would you choose a square?
>
> *K:* Um, it looks . . . then you can put it in rows.
>
> *Marta Civil:* OK so I see. So . . .
>
> *K:* In the garden we had to put rows. With a circle you have to maybe put them around it like that in a spiral sort of. . . . It [the square] is easier to work with.

In my view, these two students were using practical reasoning to justify their answers. They seemed to understand that in real life other factors may have to be taken into account. Whether it was the shape of the pots or issues of access to the center of the garden, these students were making connections to the reality they had experienced through the garden project in their assessment of what the most efficient shape was. These two students, however, were also able to play the school game and explain why a circle would have the largest area. But I wonder about the possibility of other students bringing in the real-life experiences to bearing in school settings and not knowing how to play the school game, hence saying that a square would be the best shape (even though the "expected" answer is a circle). The research by Cooper and Dunne (2000) illustrates some of the problems that may occur when children (particularly working-class children) try to "import their everyday knowledge when it is 'inappropriate' to do so" (p. 43).

The garden project was a learning ground not only for the students but also for the teacher and for me. For example, Leslie had prior knowledge about a circle's having the largest area (among shapes with the same perimeter). She intuitively used this knowledge to guide some of the groups in making their gardens more or less circular. But in her journal she wrote:

> After each group planted as many pots as we had seeds for, they made a little enclosure with chicken wire. B [one of the fathers helping out that day, and an expert gardener] helped many of the groups with that. His group also made a rectangle instead of a circular enclosure. He was right about that, because it is easier to water the plants in the middle and the circles are harder to water. M [one of the research assistants] is going to do a lesson on planning a garden as if it were in rows. This is the perfect reason to do this. As the plants get bigger and we're transplanting, the kids need to be able to reach their plants. So it's amount of chicken wire versus convenience of watering. (October 19)

Leslie's experience is particularly significant for me because I would have done the same thing. That is, I would have let my academic knowledge of mathematics guide my thinking in the design of the gardens. Yet that may not have been the most efficient path to take from a gardening point of view. In González et al. (2001), we discuss in more depth the issue of how our background in only academic mathematics may in fact limit our understanding of the mathematics in the household, which is often embedded in the practice itself (e.g., gardening).

The journal excerpt shows another example of how work in this project proceeded. Leslie turned this design issue into a learning opportunity by asking one of the research assistants, who was a graduate student in mathematics, to help her develop a lesson around the geometry in garden design. I think that one reason for the success of the garden module—and by *success* I mean our ability to capture the mathematical moments and turn them into learning opportunities—was the amount of resources available (e.g., people with different kinds of knowledge). Not only did we have parents who contributed their expertise and resources, but also there were several other adults around with different ranges of expertise (including mathematics and mathematics education). Leslie welcomed the different contributions, as she viewed them as a way to break the isolation that often characterizes a teacher's life.

In an end-of-the-year reflective piece Leslie wrote,

> Marta helped me figure out scaling the information down [on the amaryllis] so that it would fit into their notebooks, because it was becoming

unwieldy. Marta also helped me take the risk of doing a perimeter/area experience with my students that helped me to assess just how much these kids knew in terms of how shape affected area. . . . Are there things that my students haven't gotten to mathematically? Yes, and that bothers me, too, but I have proven a point to myself. Much of the math that the kids did this year, was both authentic and valid for what we were doing. And that was the whole reason that I wanted to participate in this project. (April 10)

A Mathematical Apprenticeship

In my view, the garden module succeeded in engaging the students in doing challenging mathematics. This happened in part because "doing mathematics in school" took on a different meaning. As Nunes (1999) writes:

> The nature of the social interactions in school in such that a problem is not solved for the student's sake, because of his personal interest in it, but for the teacher's sake, so that teachers can verify whether learning is taking or has taken place. (p. 48)

Students had a personal interest in the tasks and the outcomes. They became attached to their gardens; some students would get upset when they could not go out to work on them. As the teacher wrote in her journal, in relating the case of a student who became really upset when one of his plants died and blamed one of his peers for not covering it properly, "To me they are truly just plants, but to the kids they mean something else entirely."

I think that because of the overall inquiry approach that the teacher developed around the garden theme, the children took a personal interest in the mathematics problems that we posed in the classroom (e.g., graphing the growth of the amaryllis or finding the area of irregular shapes). The garden module reflects the key characteristics of out-of-school learning, which are (a) learning gained through apprenticeship; (b) work done on contextualized problems; (c) control remaining largely in the hands of the person working on the task (i.e., he or she has a certain degree of control over tasks and strategies); and (d) mathematics being often hidden, not being the center of attention, and perhaps even being abandoned in the solution process (Brown et al., 1989; Lave, 1988, 1992). As Lave (1992) writes, "Math learning in everyday practice is situated, dilemma-driven and the process for 'mucking about' with quantitative dilemmas are improvised in the process" (p. 80). Although the mathematics could have remained hidden, we had specific ideas about the content of the mathematics we wanted the students to explore, and thus we made sure that we somehow forced those "improvisations" and ensured "that these actions [were] systematically included in this shared mathematical learning activity" (van Oers, 1996, p. 105). In so doing, we developed examples of what a mathematical apprenticeship in a school setting might look like.

González (1995a) writes:

> The basic premise of [FKT] is that classroom learning can be greatly enhanced when teachers learn more not just about their students' culture in an abstract sense but about *their particular* students and their students' households.... The teachers then draw upon that knowledge to develop curricula and teaching innovations that have roots in the experience and forms of knowledge of the students and of the community. (p. 3)

The idea of developing teaching innovations that build not only on the knowledge and experiences in the community but also on its *forms* of knowledge (e.g., apprenticeship) is key to the equity agenda that drives my work in mathematics education. The construction and garden modules discussed in this chapter are examples of apprenticeship-like approaches to classroom instruction. I argue that this apprenticeship approach is critical to support the pedagogical shift that took place in both classroom practices. Through this shift we were able to engage students in what I described earlier as mathematically rich situations (e.g., in the garden module, exploring maximizing area of shapes with a fixed perimeter).

CONCLUSION: BUILDING ON COMMUNITY KNOWLEDGE

The focus of this chapter has been on the development of approaches to the teaching and learning of mathematics that build on students' and their families' backgrounds and knowledge. The work presented here took place in schools in working-class, ethnic and language "minority" communities. One of the key characteristics of our work is the approach we take to involve the community. To me, the fundamental contribution of FKT and Bridge is the involvement of teachers as researchers with the goal of learning about the community and about the resources and knowledge in their students' households. This is not about teachers applying generalities about different cultural groups. It is about teachers learning firsthand about the lived experiences of the community and about their developing rapport and trust (*confianza*) with their students' families. As Leslie wrote in reflecting on the impact of household visits,

> Bridge has given teachers a chance to change the way they teach as they become more informed about the homes of their students. While we have much to do and little time to do everything, the household visit serves us well. It gives us a chance to connect with one family and through them a much larger community. It lets the family know who we are and by doing so we learn a lot about ourselves, ... the way we respect other cultures and how we think about the classroom and its place in the community. Further, it provides a real look at the whole child. (From teacher's journal, January 2000)

These teachers viewed parents (and other adults who were important in the lives of their students) as resources in the development of the modules. For example, in the construction module, the teacher talked about how her students would "grow" when parents came in and how they would use them as resources to answer their questions.

Parental involvement in working-class, ethnic, and language "minority" communities tends to be in tasks such as monitoring the cafeteria, helping out with bulletin boards, and raising funds. Parents may be present in the classroom but it is usually to assist with logistic and bureaucratic activities, not to contribute to the academic content (Civil & Andrade, 2003). Instead, the examples presented in this chapter show parents contributing as academic resources. This idea of involving parents (and other community members) as direct contributors to the curriculum is what we describe as *parents as intellectual resources*. We seek to learn from the community and to build our mathematics instruction on these adults' knowledge and experiences as well as on their forms of knowledge.

NOTE

The research reported here was funded in part by the National Center for Research on Cultural Diversity and Second Language Learning and by the Center for Research on Education, Diversity and Excellence (CREDE), through the Office of Educational Research and Improvement (OERI) of the U.S. Department of Education, under Cooperative Agreement No. R117G10022 and PR/Award No. R306A6000. The contents, findings, and opinions expressed here are those of the author and do not necessarily represent the positions or policies of OERI, NIEARS, or the USDoE.

8

Social Valorization of Mathematical Practices: The Implications for Learners in Multicultural Schools

GUIDA DE ABREU & TONY CLINE

INTRODUCTION

In this chapter we synthesize our work illustrating how the notion of social valorization was incorporated into our research on mathematics learning and discuss its relevance to the analysis of equity in mathematics education. We are specifically concerned with issues of equity relating to cultural diversity. In England there have been concerns about ethnic-group differences in educational achievement over a very long period (Rampton Committee, 1981; Select Committee, 1977; Swann Committee, 1985). National statistics continue to suggest that some groups under-achieve, though some recent researchers have emphasized that there are local variations in group profiles (Gillborn & Mirza, 2000, pp. 8–11). Monitoring of achievement is a useful tool for pointing out problems of equity, but it does not clarify the underlying processes through which these differences are perpetuated. We argue here that new insights into these processes can be obtained by exploring the impact of society's valorization of distinct school and home and other out-of-school mathematical practices on learners. Our thinking is situated within the field of sociocultural-developmental psychology (Cole, 1995; Goodnow, 1990, 2000; Nunes, Schliemann, & Carraher, 1993; Saxe, 1982; Valsiner, 2000; Wertsch, 1991).

Theories that explain the effects of cultural factors on human learning in terms of a cultural deficit that afflicts some groups and not others are not now influential in developmental psychology. They have been replaced by a "cultural difference" explanation, which is less ethnocentric (Cole & Bruner, 1971). The cultural-differences explanation promoted new ways of understanding diversity between cultures. It stimulated research investigating the impact of the tools available in a particular culture, such as measuring and counting systems, and on the way individual members of that culture learn, think about, and use mathematics (Cole, 1977, 1995). Researchers also realized that these differences existed between communities of practices within the same culture. However, when this theory was used to revisit the learning of school mathematics, issues related to the relationship between practices emerged.

In this chapter we set out, first, to show how our work on the social valorization of mathematical practices has addressed these issues, explaining why we introduced the notion of social valorization as a key conceptual tool. Second, we focus on the development of our thinking on conceptualizing valorization, highlighting the relational nature of valorization, which in our perspective contributes to the understanding of groups and psychological diversity and has value in informing the analysis of learning practices aimed at promoting equity. Third, we refocus on empirical work conducted in multiethnic schools in England. We explore the extent to which the proposed social-valorization perspective can offer insights into the learning of students and the analysis of teaching-staff views. In the presentation of our findings and conclusion, we consider the implications of this argument for strategies to underpin the development of teaching environments that promote equity.

THE INITIAL APPLICATION OF THE CONCEPT OF "SOCIAL VALORIZATION" TO MATHEMATICAL PRACTICES

Abreu (1993, 1995, 1999) initially introduced the notion of social valorization of mathematical practices to explain the results of empirical studies with farmers and schoolchildren in a sugarcane farming community in the northeast of Brazil. In this community the farming of sugarcane involved the use of a specific body of mathematical knowledge and practices distinct from school mathematics. Furthermore, historically farming mathematics preceded the introduction of universal schooling in the community. Interestingly, the introduction of schooling did not replace the traditional mathematical practices of the community. Schooled farmers continued to use their traditional mathematics in their everyday practices. However, this coexistence was not a simple matter of appropriating distinct mathematical tools and applying them in each context. There was a complex relationship between the farmers' traditional practices and modern schooling, which resulted in Abreu's introduction of the concept of social valorization. Observations that emphasized that complexity included noting that farmers often passed on traditional knowledge to new generations in a selective way so that it was more likely to be passed to a child who failed at school than to a successful one.

It was thus apparent that the distinct forms of mathematics associated with different communities of practice in this rural society were accorded varying status by adults and children. In fact social valorization of the forms of mathematics of specific communities was a key dimension in the way members of these communities constructed their understanding of their practices. These valorizations were understood in terms of the position of the community of practice in the wider social structure—farming mathematics was lower status, not legitimated at school, and less powerful in the context of technological innovation. School mathematics had a higher status than what might be called in Anglo-Saxon terms "peasant mathematics." In addition, social valorization was expressed in terms of the social identities ascribed to the participants in the practices. The low status of the practices was extended to the people participating in the practices in terms of negative social identities (Tajfel, 1981). These observations were further elaborated in a subsequent study in which Abreu investigated how schoolchildren in this farming community experienced the relationship between home and school mathematics (Abreu, 1993).

As with the farmers, field observations from the study with the schoolchildren brought to attention the fact that whenever there was a reference to farming mathematics in relation to other school-based mathematics practices, a salient aspect of the relationship was the status of the practice and the associated "social identities." For instance, when Abreu (1993) asked a primary teacher if she helped the children to bridge the gap between their home and school mathematics in her teaching, she replied:

> No. I had never worked with them on weighing, measuring. . . . It will be good if they happen to become rural workers. But, it is too unlikely that any of them [her students] wants to be a rural worker. . . . In the lesson about professions, I explained the value and objectives of the work. Afterwards I asked: "What profession would you like to enter?" The majority of the girls wanted to be teachers, the boys motorists, airforce, but no one mentioned rural worker. . . . I believe that what they most repudiate is knowing that their fathers work the whole week, and at the weekend have no money to buy food. (Abreu, 1993, p. 148)

One of the youngest students of this teacher was an 8-year-old boy called Manoel. When asked if children having a mathematics lesson at school could learn anything that was important in helping their parents in agriculture, he replied:

> No. Well it could be important to teach their parents to do some mathematics. [Researcher: To help in farming?] It is important because they can get away from working in farming. (Abreu, 1993, p. 194)

It is apparent from these extracts that neither the teacher nor the student viewed "school mathematics" as merely cognitive tools. Both stressed the link between mastering specific mathematical tools and the identities these tools afforded. Social valorization of the practices was a key aspect of the way the link was expressed. For the teacher, farming mathematics was associated with a type of "person" the children did not want to become. The difficult life conditions of the farmers in the present led their children to exclude "being a farmer" as one of their projected professions. Manoel, by contrast, perceived the appropriation of high-status school mathematics as a tool that would enable members of the farming community to exit these low-status jobs.

Up to this stage of Abreu's research, Vygotsky's ideas had provided an effective framework for understanding the sociocultural foundations of the uses and learning of mathematics in local practices. However, issues of valuing (and devaluing) mathematical knowledge associated with particular cultural practices and development of identities, as illustrated above, have not been addressed in mathematical research following such a framework. To address these issues, Abreu (1993, 1995, 1999) tentatively introduced the notion of social valorization, which we then further developed in our joint work on mathematics learning in multiethnic schools in England (Abreu, Cline, & Shamsi, 1999; Abreu & Cline, 2003b).

The concept of social valorization helped to explain how social groups and individuals understand value differences in the status of mathematical practices. It is also, in our view, a dynamic concept because it captures not only dominant views on the social value of a practice in the context of a whole society, but also the local views of specific communities within the society. We needed a dynamic concept to explain how knowledge can be transmitted in different ways within a single community of practice: Why do some families willingly engage in practices aimed at transmitting their knowledge to their children while others do not? We also found this concept useful in attempting to account for the diversity among the children, both in their participation in the practices and in their social identities. Why do some children align themselves with these practices, while others seem to resist? Over time we have been able to make explicit some aspects of the notion of valorization, which clarify its nature and seem to throw some light on the questions we just raised.

CONCEPTUALIZING SOCIAL VALORIZATION

Our understanding and use of the concept of social valorization to inform our empirical research involves two main dimensions. First, we see social valorization as relational. It is one of many factors that position individuals and groups in relation to one another in the wider society. Second, we see social valorization as having a social-identification dimension in that it influences the way groups and individuals define who they are. The examples discussed in the previous section may have given the impression that the social valorization of a practice is fixed and static, but this is not the way we view it. Rather, we see social valorization as fluid and dynamic. Valorization is a relational construct. The same practice can be valorized or devalorized, depending on its positioning in a web of social and historical relations, which is relevant for the group or participant in a practice. Like currency, valorizations are not fixed. At a particular point in time they can change, depending on the positioning one takes on. In Abreu's study the same farmers could both valorize their farming mathematics knowledge, when talking from the perspective of its usefulness in their daily practices, and devalorize this knowledge, when talking as parents of schoolchildren. Moreover, within the same communities, practices are differently valued over time. New technologies and knowledge may bring in more efficient ways of dealing with certain practices and be valorized. One has, nevertheless, to be careful in taking account of power relations. Who decides that one technology or way of knowing is superior to existing practices? For whom are the novel approaches more efficient than the traditional practices?

Understanding the relational character of social valorization is of crucial importance for its application as a tool that both enables understanding of groups and psychological diversity and at the same time has a value in informing the development of learning practices that promote equity. Its relational character makes it possible to ask questions about schooling practices that ignore valorization, such as, Does the differential valorization of children's home experiences have a negative impact on the development of their identities as learners? Most important, it also points toward questions about the positive effects of taking valorization into account, such as, If the dominance of certain social representations of mathematical practices were challenged, would this empower the development of an integrated sense of identity by children in marginalized communities and help to promote equity?

Having discussed the broad relational nature of social valorization, we will now attempt to explore what we called the social-identification dimension of valorization. In doing so we will show how it is related to ideas in Tajfel's social-identity theory. A main reason for drawing these links was that we observed that social valorizations were often expressed when research participants were talking about their membership in communities of practice and the social identities associated with that. We took the view that mathematical practices as products of a cultural heritage do not exist in a social vacuum, but are owned by social groups, which have a position in a social order. This enabled us to theorize the process of mathematical learning in social-psychological terms. In particular it enabled us to draw on Tajfel's notion of social comparison (Tajfel, 1978) to explain the relationship between the valorization of mathematical practices at the social level and its reconstruction at the psychological level. For Tajfel it is almost inevitable that when a person learns about social categories, he or she also learns about associated values and therefore engages in comparisons. He saw the processes of social categorization, social comparison, and social identity as complementary. The first two of these processes reveal understanding of one's social world, while social identity corresponds to the subjective plan of how the individual views and positions him- or herself in the social world. He defined *social identity* as "that part of an individual's self-concept which derives from his knowledge of his membership of a social group (or groups) together with the value and emotional significance attached to that membership" (Tajfel, 1978, p. 63). Furthermore, he argued that in circumstances in which their group membership is devalorized or given a negative social identity, groups and individuals will seek strategies to establish a positive social identity.

To sum up, Tajfel's theory provided insights and concepts that enabled us to explore social valorization in a framework that was compatible with the Vygotskian perspective we had adopted in our studies (Abreu, 2002; Vygotsky, 1978). In

Vygotskian theory, knowledge first exists in the social sphere before being appropriated by the individual and becoming a cognitive tool. In Tajfel's theory, social groups occupy positions in the social structure, which will influence their social development and the way in which individuals construct their social identities. In both theories the sociocultural origins of psychological development are of fundamental importance. These two theories come together when one adopts the view that mathematical learning and thinking develop through forms of participation in the practices of specific communities, each of which has a position in the structure of the society that is often well understood by all.

STUDIES IN ENGLAND: SOCIAL VALORIZATION OF MATHEMATICAL PRACTICES AND IMPLICATIONS FOR LEARNERS' IDENTITIES

When we were searching for new settings in which to explore further the impact of social valorization on schoolchildren's mathematics learning, multiethnic primary schools in England seemed to offer an interesting choice. These schools have some similar characteristics to the Brazilian schools in the original studies that generated the development of the theory (Abreu, 1993, 1995, 1999). First, previous studies of ethnic-minority students in England have highlighted wide gaps between their lives at home and at school (McIntyre, Bhatti, & Fuller, 1997). Second, though most parents with children in multiethnic schools in England have themselves attended school, unlike the Brazilian farmers, these parents had often learned about learning in a different culture and a different school system. Finally, though some of the schools had enrolled children from ethnic groups who, on average, underachieve at school, there was heterogeneity within each group (Gillborn & Mirza, 2000). So the conditions for our investigations were potentially present. There was potential for the child to live in a family, or come from a home background, with home mathematical practices different from those of the school. In these conditions it was also likely that there would be a value placed on the practices and related competencies in each of these practices. Our hope was that this would provide us with an environment where we could explore how valorizations develop and how they affect the learner.

Our empirical studies have been predominantly qualitative and conducted with relatively small numbers of participants. To caution against stereotyping minority ethnic groups on the basis of a taken-for-granted cultural heritage we adopted several strategies. First, in some of our studies we also included White British participants. This measure was built in to help to distinguish between differences associated with a minority ethnic heritage, and differences that may apply to all participants and be a result of other factors, such as curricular changes, home-school policies, and so on. Second, when selecting children for case studies we included both girls and boys, and high and low achievers from each ethnic group.

This allowed us to recognize existing heterogeneity within each group. Third, we selected the participants from the same schools and home areas, as a rough measure of socioeconomic conditions of the families. Fourth, we combined this careful selection of participants with an ethnographic approach to data collection, which included gathering data from the pupils, their teachers, and their parents, using interviews, observations, and structured tasks. Applied across several studies these strategies have provided in-depth descriptions of how children from a variety of minority ethnic groups represent and experience their home and school mathematical practices.

To examine the extent to which the notion of valorization is relevant to the way children construct their participation in their society's mathematical practices, the following questions have been included in our studies: (1) Do children exposed to different mathematical practices gain understanding about the valorization of these practices? What are the processes involved? (2) Does valorization play a part in the way children experience their participation in school and home mathematical practices? and (3) How do teaching-staff views and valorizations of students' home background and home practices influence school practices and affect equity?

CHILDREN'S UNDERSTANDING OF THE VALORIZATION OF MATHEMATICAL PRACTICES

When children are exposed to different mathematical practices, they appear to develop an understanding of how these practices are valorized. In this section we aim to illustrate the underlying psychological processes through which social valorizations, which exist in the social plane, are reconstructed by individuals. Following Tajfel (1978) we assumed that this understanding could be empirically examined through processes of social categorization and social comparison of mathematical practices. Categorization would reflect a position that a community of practice occupies in a wider social structure (institutional or societal). At the same time, social comparison would lay the basis for an understanding of the social identities associated with mathematical practices ("given identities").

In our studies children's *categorizations* of mathematical practices were explored through tasks that required them to sort pictures of local practices into situations in which people need to use or do not need to use mathematics. The *comparisons* were explored by asking them to choose who in the pictures was the best and who was the worst student in mathematics when at school. The pictures included practices believed to have different social status, including blue-collar and white-collar jobs. The findings from two studies (Abreu, Cline, & Shamsi, 1999; Abreu, Cline, & Cowan, 2000) first confirmed that children do understand the categorization of practices as requiring greater or less use of mathematics. Thus, for instance, while the practice of working as a shop assistant is constructed by a large number of children as involving the use of mathematics, driving a taxi is not. Second, when required to make *comparisons,* most of our participants chose as likely to have been the best student in mathematics a person in a high-social-status job (the office administrator) and as likely to have been the worst student a person in a low-social-status job (the taxi driver). Identity as a mathematical learner in school is not constructed as restricted to school practice, but instead is constructed as a passport to gain entry into practices that enjoy different status in the wider society.

Children's justifications for their choices were also revealing. When talking about a social actor who was an adult, they tended to emphasize the status of the person's job (social valorization of the practices) as the key factor in their comparisons. The following extract from an interview with a Year 6 boy of Pakistani origin illustrates a common justification relating to the importance of a job.

> *Interviewer:* Why do you think then that he was the best at maths?
> *Child:* Because look at him [office administrator], all wearing flashy clothes and like he looks like a rich . . . and he's got such a good job, and him, he's . . . nothing he has to do taxi. . . . Like if he's ain't good at something he'd have been like him [taxi driver], like he's probably not good at anything. He's [taxi driver] probably came from Pakistan.
>
> (Abreu & Cline, 2003b, p. 23)

The valorization of the practices was a key component in the way this student came to identify the other, or developed representations of social identities associated with competencies in school mathematics. In addition, the reference to the cultural group ("came from Pakistan") may have personal implications for this student's social identification as a member of this community. Being a taxi driver for the students in this study had a status that was not different from that of being a sugarcane farmer/worker in the Northeast of Brazil (Abreu, 1999). Similar arguments were put forward in Brazil, for example:

> "I see that he is in a good job [office administrator]. I think he was good at mathematics, because he needs a lot of mathematics to do that."

> "Because if he was good in mathematics he would not be working in the field. He would be in another job."

> "If they [sugarcane workers] had been to school they would not be there working in that place. That is an example of someone who has never been to school, *like my father.*"
>
> (Abreu, 1999, p. 30)

In both studies the impact of the valorization of the practices was expressed in processes of identification of the other—how students in the communities studied came to represent the social identities afforded to those who participate in particular social practices. It was also the case that for some students the identification of the other posed questions for their own self-identification. For these students the devalorization of practices linked to their home community may have prevented them from constructing their participation in home and school as inclusive, as affording social identities that can coexist and enrich their social experiences.

Reflecting on the preceding findings from a methodological perspective, we argue that the reason for similarities between the findings in England and Brazil lay in the background conditions (Valsiner, 2001). When students live or belong to communities where their home practices enjoy a status lower than that of their school, they will develop an awareness of the differential valorization, and this will become a mediator in their own construction of identities and participation in learning practices. This means that the findings cannot simply be generalized across populations, such as children from a particular ethnic or social background, but need to be viewed as manifestations of the positioning of social practices in the wider social structure. Social categories and associated valorizations need to be seen as social-historical constructions and therefore as bound to change.

SOCIAL VALORIZATION AND CHILDREN'S EXPERIENCE OF MATHEMATICAL PRACTICES

In addition to the point we just made that our findings in the studies described above reflect the dominant representations within a community or society, there is another point that needs to be considered. Our second point refers to the impact of valorization on the way children participate in their mathematical practices. Abreu's previous study in Brazil suggested that this influence is not a one-way process. In her observations of mathematical practices at school it was apparent that the children's home mathematics was excluded (teachers tended to ignore that it existed at all). So, in these schools, the hidden message pointed to one unique route for positive self-identification, which required the suppression of the low-status home ways of dealing with mathematics. In spite of this, not all the children "abandoned" their home mathematics. The circumstances of life of these children's families required them to continue participating in their family practices. On the surface, the main reason for this participation was economic, but one cannot disregard other reasons, such as family attachments to their land and traditions, which were not explored in the study. With these considerations in mind we turn again to the situation in England.

In our studies in England we found that both children and parents often identify the significance of differences between their home and school mathematical practices, while teachers give importance to these differences less often and may even show no awareness that they exist (Abreu, Cline, & Radia-Bond, 2001; Abreu, Cline, & Shamsi, 2002; Cline et al., 2002). A major reason for the salience of the differences for the children and the parents emerges from their "direct experience." They have to confront the fact that sometimes the way they have learned to address a mathematical task is different from the way it is taught at school. Still, one has to ask the question, Why don't teachers report experiences of children using their home ways of doing mathematics at school? Is it because the children do not bring their home maths into school? If that is the case, why do they not do so?

Another finding in our studies is that among the children (and parents) who experience home and school mathematical practices as different we have found many children who devalue their home mathematics but also some who see it as a legitimate alternative to school mathematics. Overall, however, children tend to share the view that their home mathematics should not be openly displayed at school. Eileen, a 10-year-old, Year 4 child is an example of a student who devalues her mother's mathematics, describing it as old-fashioned:

> *Interviewer:* Okay, and which do you think is the proper way of doing it, the way that you do it with the teacher at school or with your mum at home?
> *Child:* At school.
> *Interviewer:* Why is that?
> *Child:* Because they're telling us how we're meant to do it, and my mum's telling me the old way of doing it.
>
> (Abreu & Cline, 2003a)

Eileen's mother confirmed that her daughter resisted her teaching when she perceived it to be different from the school's way. The case study of Eileen stressed the resistance of students to home practices as an expression of their subordination to school practices. However, we also found examples of this subordination being orchestrated by parents, who did not necessarily devalue their own knowledge, but had concerns that it might not be valued by their children's teachers. Aware that their ways of doing school mathematics could be different from the ways their children were learning at school, these parents used strategies to hide their procedures (ways of thinking) from their children. One may say that these parents tried to promote home practices that were an extension of what the child was doing in school mathematics, and that in doing so they were also trying to support the child's participation in their school mathematics in a way that was as close as possible to the expectations and methods used by the teacher.

While some parents show concern about exposing their children to home practices that are perceived as different from those of the school, others intentionally promote their practices and expect their children to value them. These parents do not accept the superiority of their children's school mathematics. In fact, some perceive some aspects of it as less efficient and less conducive to what they view as the basis of mathematical competence. It is in these families that we found examples of students who equally valued their home and school practices, constructing them as alternative practices (Abreu & Cline, 2003a). Nevertheless, students in these circumstances still subscribe to the view that it is better to stick with the school's ways of doing mathematics when at school. These students will often avoid showing their teacher how they learned at home. As illustrated in the following extract from an interview with Saeeda, a girl from a Pakistani background and a Year 6 student (age 11), they may develop identities of participation that separate the two practices.

> *Interviewer:* Okay, and when you did it with your dad at home, . . . when you had learned how to do it, did you do it at school in the same way in the class with your teacher? Did you show the teacher how you . . .
>
> *Child:* No because it was like kind of the same, all that was different was how they setted it, specially like normal division. That was quite different because there's two numbers, like there's one number and then if you can't take away, you go for that number. But I don't do it like that, I like put it on and on and on till I get, until there's nothing left and I've got the answer.
>
> *Interviewer:* Okay, and that's how you'd learned from your parents at home.
>
> *Child:* Yes.
>
> *Interviewer:* And do you still do it like that your division, the long division?
>
> *Child: I can do it both ways so when I'm at school I do it that, the school way, and when I'm at home I do it the home way.*
>
> (Abreu & Cline, 2003a, emphasis in the original)

While the trajectory adopted by Saeeda, keeping each practice in each setting, works for her, it disadvantages students whose mathematical competence is more developed in practices distinct from those of their current school. This is particularly acute for immigrant students who have attended school in other countries before coming to England.

In another study, Liliana, an 18-year-old student born in Portugal who came to England at the age of 15, talked about how the differences affected her identity in school mathematics:

> "Maths was one of my biggest problems because I was a really good student in Maths in Portugal. I was an 'A' [standard] student and when I came over here because they did everything so different, I couldn't understand. I felt completely lost and that was the worst thing because I thought, oh at least I can do good in Maths because it's just numbers, but no." (Abreu & Lambert, 2003, p. 195)

One common feature across the examples presented here is that home mathematical practices (in the broad sense, to include family maths and maths a student learned in another country) were experienced as subordinated to school maths. This clearly indicated that schooling in England was not perceived by the students in our studies as valuing diverse mathematical practices. This influenced the way the students constructed forms of participation in these practices. Those who aligned with school practices as superior and devalued home practices then engaged in forms of participation that attempted to suppress the latter. Those who valued both practices, but still showed an awareness that valorizations were relative, engaged in forms of participation that minimized potential conflict, such as keeping each practice separate and restricting its use to the context to which it "belonged." Although we can report examples of students who succeeded in their school mathematics with both approaches, we argue that for some these constraints may limit their opportunities for learning and thus pose equity issues. To discuss these further we turn to the teachers and in particular try to explore possible reasons for the asymmetrical valorization of home and school mathematical practices.

TEACHING STAFF VIEWS ON EQUITY AND VALORIZATION OF CHILDREN'S HOME PRACTICES

In the past the neglect of home mathematical practices by schools has been attributed to the dominant "view on the nature of mathematics" as a culture-free and universal field of subject knowledge (see, e.g., Bishop, 1988). When we interviewed mathematics coordinators in secondary and primary schools in England with relatively small numbers of minority ethnic pupils (Cline et al., 2002), we found that views on "equity" were sometimes an important factor in this neglect, as illustrated in the following examples. In the first example, the head of maths in a secondary school refers to treating "everyone as equals" based on their "merits," and in the second example the primary school teacher explicitly referred to "the child's ability."

> "I certainly think that within our department that we do extremely well and treat everyone as equals, everyone on their merits. There is no prejudice whatsoever that I have ever picked up here with regards to the different ethnic minorities. I think that is part of the reason that we haven't really considered that. We do a lot of results analysis. That is a big thing at the moment. We have never really looked at the ethnic minority. I know you are compiling data about how the ethnic minorities do at the GCSE's. We have never done that. Really it has never come to our minds because we do see everybody as equals." (Cline et al., 2002, p. 101)

In the same study a primary school numeracy coordinator said:

> "As far as I'm concerned, you teach Maths according to the child's ability—not their ethnic minority [laughs] . . . I don't treat them any differently to any other . . . and I wouldn't expect them to behave any differently to any other child." (Cline et al., 2002, p. 101)

Neither the secondary nor the primary maths coordinators realized that their views of equality could in fact be fostering inequities. By not recognizing that children reflect a diversity of home backgrounds that sometimes involve dealing with mathematical practices in ways that differ from those adopted by the school, teachers were not providing opportunities for the children to openly negotiate the differences. In doing so they may also have communicated implicit messages (whether intentional or not) about which mathematical practices were valued in the school and which were not. According to Sasha, a minority ethnic classroom assistant, interviewed in another study (Abreu, Cline, & Shamsi, 1999), school practices that do not support the child's bridging between home and school can contribute to their feeling isolated. Sasha's awareness of home background as an identity mediator seemed to be rooted in her own experiences of when she was a child in an English school. To survive school she had to exclude and silence her Pakistani home culture.

In a follow-up study (Abreu, Cline, & Radia-Bond, 2001), another teacher from a minority ethnic background talked, like Sasha, about her childhood experiences as influencing her current positioning. Mina, as the only Pakistani child in an English primary school, had felt isolated and embarrassed to share her home cultural practices. As an adult professional with a bicultural background she saw no reason why this should be the case and was able to use her experiences as a source of inspiration for a more culturally sensitive strategy. Strategies such as allowing a child to count in the language he or she is more familiar with, are then conceptualized not only as cognitive, but as contributing to the child's identity development.

Sasha and Mina had personal experiences that were close to those of the parents and the minority children they currently taught. They were both exposed to school practices that silenced their home identities. Many of the students we interviewed in these studies were still having experiences and feelings similar to those of Sasha. They hid their home practices from school. In doing so they developed identities of participation that can be seen on a continuum, where one of the extremes is the devalorization of home practices and their subordination to those of the school, and where the other involves the valorization of home practices and resistance to the hegemony of the school's influence. In the middle there is an understanding of the relative valorization of the practices and an appreciation that each may have its place in one's life. This middle position is represented by schoolchildren, such as Saeeda, and parents who understood the importance of a home practice in fostering understanding of a particular mathematical subject, but at the same time were aware that their home practices were not legitimated in school. Teachers such as Sasha and Mina, who come from a minority background, represent a small number of teachers. Even in schools with a high proportion of minority ethnic students the staff we interviewed often expressed views on equity along the lines of those described above as prevalent in mainly White schools. Clearly the prevalence of these views is maintained in part because of a lack of professional training on issues around teaching for cultural diversity (Cline et al., 2002).

CONCLUSIONS

Although we have argued that valorization is relational, our data have consistently depicted school practices as being categorized and experienced as superior. The predominance of the pattern in which home learning is devalued by professionals and other stakeholders places the situations that we have studied in England closer to the situation studied by Abreu (1995, 1999) in Brazil. The comparatively high valorization of school practices reflects, in fact, a dominant position in how cultural (and psychological) diversity is understood by many majority professionals and parents as well as by many minority parents. The main voices outside this consensus in our studies proved to be a small number of bilingual school staff from minority ethnic backgrounds. For others the valorization of school practices was not questioned because it was taken for granted that the cultural tools and ways of using mathematical tools as taught in school were socially superior. The often unquestioned, implicit, taken-for-granted character of valorizations of mathematical practices does not, however, prevent it from exerting a strong influence on the way these practices are organized and experienced. Valorizations influence how social identities associated with mathematical practices are constructed, both for relevant others (members of communities) and for the learners themselves. We argue that it is not possible to account for and reduce group differences in school mathematics performance and for the uncertain results of initiatives in home-school collaboration without taking into account the devalorization of home learning practices and taking active steps to combat that process.

9

Identity, Goals, and Learning:
The Case of Basketball Mathematics

Na'ilah Suad Nasir

The relation between culture, race, and mathematics learning has increasingly been of interest to the math education community. One approach to this topic has been to compare the mathematics achievement of different racial groups. Studies from this perspective have repeatedly indicated that African American and Latino students score lower on tests of mathematical knowledge (Johnson, 1984; Lockheed et al., 1985; Reyes & Stanic, 1988) and take fewer and less advanced mathematics courses (Campbell, 1986; Secada, 1992) than do White and Asian students. However, these achievement statistics only tell a partial story—they do little to help us understand the causes of the inequities or the processes that underlie them.

Recent research in both mathematics education and on culture and schooling more generally have made important contributions toward the development of a more complex and textured understanding of the relation between culture, race, and mathematics learning. In mathematics education, scholars have argued that learning mathematics is more complex than can be represented by grades and standardized-test scores (Heibert & Carpenter, 1990; Martin, 2000). Studies have shown that many students can "do" mathematics (that is, they can apply formulas to get numerical answers), but may not understand the concepts behind the procedures they learn to apply. Deep understanding also includes the concepts and mathematical relations that underlie those procedures (Ball, 1993; Lampert, 1990). Further, research in math education has viewed teaching as involving socializing students into the norms and discourse practices of the mathematics class (Cobb, Wood, & Yackel, 1993; Greeno, 1998) as well as fostering students' ability to see themselves as "doers of mathematics" (Boaler, 1999, 2000a). As such, work in math education differentiates learning (as a process) from achievement (as a static outcome) and emphasizes the importance of viewing math classrooms as *communities of practices* (Lave & Wenger, 1991; Wenger, 1998), thereby highlighting new concerns around how students become (or don't become) part of these communities.

Research on mathematics learning outside school has also focused on the relation between culture and learning. In studies of a number of activities including carpet-laying (Masingila, 1994), farming (De Abreu, 1995), construction work (Carraher, 1986), dairy-case loading (Scribner, 1984), and candy selling (Saxe, 1991), scholars have used a sociocultural perspective to focus on how mathematics learning is linked in fundamental ways to the cultural practices in which it occurs. One important and consistent finding in this research has been that mathematics occurs as individuals carry out goals in the course of everyday activity (e.g., to buy a week's worth of groceries)—activities that may not themselves be inherently mathematical in nature.

These explanations of how and when cultural activities give rise to mathematics learning have helped researchers to view math learning through a cultural lens and to better understand how mathematical activity is embedded in culturally defined local practices. However, without an analysis of how individuals develop identities as members of communities of practice of which mathematics is a part, it may be difficult to readily apply these frameworks to explain how mathematics achievement is unevenly distributed across racial groups.

In this chapter, I extend prior findings by drawing on the concepts of the *goals* individuals construct as they participate in cultural activities and the *identities* that students develop concurrently. I argue that the formation of goals and identities in practice are related processes that are central to learning. Specifically, I draw on findings from a recent study of the cultural practice of basketball in which some African American students construct mathematical knowledge. It is my contention that better understanding the link between goals, identities, and learning in practices can offer important analytical tools for both understanding the learning of minority students within the cultural practice of math classrooms, and thinking about how to improve such practices.

With this in mind, my goal in this chapter is to address the issue of race, culture, and learning in two ways. I will offer an example of the nature of mathematics learning in an out-of-school practice (basketball), common among some urban African American children and adolescents. On one level, this analysis offers a viewpoint on how successful mathematics learning is organized in this cultural practice (and how it develops), an issue of particular interest given the poor school math achievement of the participating students. On another level, the analysis shows how relations between identity, goals, and learning play out and how analysis of these elements of practice can help us understand the dynamics of race, culture, and math learning (or the failure to learn) in any setting, including school mathematics.

In the sections that follow, I first discuss the theoretical frame and elaborate on the role of goals and identities, describing the relevance of these concepts for the study of learning. Then I turn to an analysis of the practice of basketball, describing developmental shifts and the emergence of mathematical goals and practice-related identities over time. Finally, I turn the discussion to how the issues raised by this analysis are relevant to mathematics education in general and to African American and other minority children in particular.

STRUCTURING GOALS IN PRACTICE

The first critical component in understanding learning is goals. The perspective that human behavior is fundamentally goal directed is linked both to traditions in

Soviet psychology concerned with understanding the influence of society and cultural activity on thought processes, that is, to the work of Leontiev (1978), Vygotsky (1934/1962, 1978), and Luria (1976) and to that of other early psychologists seeking to understand the developing mind in relation to social and cultural context (i.e., the work of Stern, Lewin, and Werner). More recent accounts from the sociocultural perspective reiterate the importance of goals as a mediating link between society, culture, and thinking (Cole, 1996; Engestrom, 1999; Saxe, 1999; Werstch, 1991). For instance, Saxe has used the Emergent Goals Framework (Saxe, 1999) that takes goals as a central focus and has outlined various ways in which cultural practices mediate the practice-linked goals constructed by children. A number of scholars have also argued that goals are important in understanding the school failure of some minority students. For instance, the work of Ogbu (1987) on African American students describes the development of an "oppositional" frame of reference—a purposeful rejection of mainstream goals and values for the preservation of a cultural identity. In this model, school failure becomes the overarching goal, giving rise to other smaller goals (e.g., to be disruptive in class, to refuse to complete assignments). Because human action serves the function of accomplishing goals in the context of culturally organized activity, and because these goals help structure the nature of thought and problem solving of individuals, I argue that an account of the goals—both cultural and cognitive—that students construct in practice is critical to understanding how students construct and negotiate mathematical knowledge in cultural settings both in and out of school.

STRUCTURING IDENTITIES IN PRACTICE

The identities that students construct in relation to their participation in practices is a second critical component of understanding learning. In research on the learning of minority students, the relation between identity and schooling has long been viewed as critical. Beginning with the early doll studies of Kenneth and Mamie Clark (1950), which demonstrated that when given a choice, Black children overwhelmingly chose White dolls over Black dolls. The Clarks interpreted these findings to mean that these students (all of whom attended segregated schools) suffered from a damaged sense of themselves as a result of segregation. Ogbu's work also supports the critical role of identity in students' learning. Fordham and Ogbu (and others) argue that under certain conditions, minority students disidentify with school, resulting in school failure (Fordham & Ogbu, 1986; Graham, Taylor, & Hudley, 1998; Osbourne, 1997). Other research has shown that when students are encouraged through consistent instructional practices to build strong identities with school, learning and achievement are enhanced (Mehan, Hubbard, & Villanueva, 1994).

In addressing issues of identity in this chapter, I take a sociocultural perspective and view identity as being constructed by individuals as they actively participate in cultural activities. Drawing heavily on the work of Wenger (1998) and

Holland, Lachiotte, Skinner, and Cain (1998), in which identity is elaborated from a perspective that focuses on individuals in the course of everyday cultural activity, I view identity as a fluid construct, one that both shapes and is shaped by the social context. Indeed, identity is not purely an individual's property, nor can it be completely attributed to social settings. From Wenger's (1998) perspective, identity develops both through individual agency and through social practice. Further, the development of identity, or the process of identification, is linked to learning, in that learning is about becoming as well as knowing. It is my view that this issue of how learning settings afford ways of becoming or not becoming something or someone is central to understanding culture, race, and learning, particularly given the multiple ways that race (as well as social class) can influence both the kinds of practices within which one can "become," as well as the trajectories available in those practices.

Wenger argues that three modes of belonging characterize how identities are constructed within communities of practice. He terms these modes *engagement, imagination,* and *alignment. Engagement* refers to how one participates in a community of practice. *Imagination* refers to how one sees oneself as being connected to a broader community of "doers," and *alignment* refers to how actions within that community come to be aligned toward a broader common purpose.

In the following sections, I will describe the practice of league basketball among African American students, exploring how mathematical thinking develops in the context of this practice and attempting to understand the relation between the nature of students' mathematical thinking and their shifting goals and identities within this cultural practices.

IDENTITIES AND GOALS IN BASKETBALL

The data presented in this section draws on a study (Nasir, 1996, 2000) of middle and high school African American male basketball players. The focus of this research was on documenting how basketball (specifically, the use of statistics in evaluating the quality of play) led players to construct mathematical goals as a part of their practice. The study used ethnographic techniques, focused interviews, and mathematics tasks (in two formats: basketball problems and school problems) to understand the mathematical knowledge players constructed, how that knowledge shifted with age, and the relation between practice participation and knowledge construction.

In this chapter, I highlight the importance of goals, identities, and their interaction in understanding learning. I will first situate the analysis in the experience of basketball play. I will then discuss the importance of goals in understanding the shifting nature of mathematical understandings in play (as players move from middle school to high school play). Finally, I will explore the critical role of identity (as gauged by engagement, alignment, and imagination) as an aspect of learning.

The Practice of Basketball

Like any practice, that of basketball has many components. There is the actual game play—the crowded gymnasium, friends and family cheering, band playing—an immersion in sound and movement. Then there are the more mundane aspects of play—the daily practices, when drills are repeated until plays and moves are carried out with perfection; when players are corrected, cajoled, and screamed at; when tempers occasionally flare and laughter is interspersed with intense concentration. There is also the informal time—when players congregate before and after games or practices, to talk, to check their "numbers," to shoot around, to compare their own play and that of professional and college players. It is in this space that statistics become integral to the practice.

In basketball, statistics, or "stats," are one means by which players evaluate performance. Numbers—such as percentages of shots made from the free-throw line or average number of points scored per game—offer an objective means by which players can be compared. However, these quantitative measures, while informative, are weighed with qualitative judgments as well. One player sums up the balance nicely: "Oh, they're [statistics] important, but they're not, see, you can't ever really see how good the player is unless you come and see him yourself. You can see somebody's statistics and maybe they average 20 points, and they have five rebounds and five assists and you go see them, and they might do that, yeah, but they might be playing some little wack team that don't really matter anyway" (cited in Nasir, 2000).

Goals in Basketball

In basketball, the goals with which players approach the game, and the goals that they structure and restructure in play, are critical in understanding the nature of the mathematical learning that occurs. This analysis explores goals at two levels—goals linked to the practice of basketball and the use of statistics generally, and goals linked to mathematical problem solving more specifically. As players move from middle school to high school play, both of these types of goals shift in nature, resulting in a concomitant shift in the kinds of mathematical knowledge that students develop. In this discussion, I conceptualize goals as being a unit of analysis that incorporates both the way in which goals are afforded by the setting as well as how individual players take up or appropriate these goals.

Practice-Linked Goals

One indication of how goals shift from middle school to high school play was revealed in observations of the purposes for which players engaged in the practice. For many middle school players, play in basketball could serve varying purposes. For some, the basketball program kept them occupied for 2 extra hours after school.

Others played because basketball was just one of many sports they participated in, though some did have a special commitment to basketball.

In contrast, high school players were uniformly highly committed to the sport of basketball. For them, play was more than simply a fun pastime—for them, basketball was a central part of a long-term life trajectory. In fact, the majority of high school students said that they saw themselves going on to at least college basketball and possibly professional basketball (Nasir, 1996).

These goals are not simply individual constructions, created by players out of thin air. The goals that players purport at both middle and high school levels are afforded by the structure of the practice of basketball at these two levels (Nasir, 2000). For example, high school basketball practice was structured in such a way that the stakes for winning and losing games were high, and a player's individual stats profile was of great importance. At the middle school level, there were few, if any, consequences for a losing record or poor individual play. Differences also existed in the artifacts that became a part of play at the two levels (e.g., a sophisticated scoreboard at the high school level, and no public scoring record in middle school games) (Nasir, 2000).

These differences in the purposes of play were related to differences in the extent to which and the way in which players used statistics as a means of evaluation (Nasir, 1996, 2000). For players at both levels, both quantitative (e.g., statistics) and qualitative evaluations were important to get a feel for the strengths and weaknesses of a player. Where middle school and high school players differed was in the way they used quantitative evaluation—and the goal toward which they employed it. Middle school players used quantitative evaluation to compare their own play to that of their peers or to compare the play of one professional (or college) player with that of another. These comparisons tended to take place in relation to statistics that involved counts (i.e., number of points scored).

At times, high school players used statistical information for similar purposes, but in addition they used statistics to compare themselves to a norm or standard (a statistical profile) for the position that they played. They also discussed statistics in the context of talk about how recruiters and coaches might evaluate a player's "numbers"—both to compare across players and situations and to compare players to a standard for a particular playing level or position. In doing so, they relied on statistical measures that involved proportional relationships as well as counts, including averages and percentages. For example, one often-cited statistic was points scored per shots taken, both from the free-throw line and from the field.

Mathematical Goals

These differences in practice-linked goals were related to differences in mathematical problem-solving goals for players. In order to illustrate these differences, I will draw on players' answers to the basketball-format mathematics questions. Consider the following players both solving this problem: You are at the free-throw line. You take five shots and make two of them. What is your percentage from the line?

A middle school player, Anthony, answers that the free-throw percentage is 10%. He explains, "I multiplied 2 times 5 and got 10. That's an easy number." This answer was very typical of middle school players who, by and large, performed operations on the numbers without much regard to the nature of the problem. In contrast, many high school players solved this problem as did David, who explained, "It would be about 40%. It didn't make half, so it wouldn't be over 50%" (interview, 1996). David used his knowledge of a common percentage, half, to reason about the probable percentage of two shots out of five.

These solutions reveal different mathematical goals, with middle school players seemingly having the goal of producing a mathematical answer using the numbers in the problem. High school players' goals were more grounded in their practice— they seemed to want to find a solution that made sense in the context of the basketball scenario. High school players engaged mathematical problems as a normal part of their practice—hence their solution to basketball math problems is accomplished by using statistical information practically (Nasir, 2000).

Middle school players do not have the same kind of practical experience with complex statistics, so while they are exposed to these statistics, they do not use them in their everyday practice to the same extent—and they rarely, if ever, have occasion to calculate their own statistics (Nasir, 1996, 2000). Further, they don't have a "basketball" framework with which they make sense of the problems—so they linked the questions to their knowledge of school-type problems, in which answers are sought by carrying out a calculation with the numbers in the problem statement.

Identity in Basketball

Just as goals are constructed by players in the course of their play, so too do players' identities emerge as a product of their participation in basketball. Coming to identify themselves as "ballers" in line with basketball players all across the country is one way that young basketball players' lives change through their participation in the sport. In this section, I will discuss the shifts from middle school to high school play, organizing my discussion in terms of Wenger's (1998) three modes of belonging.

Engagement

In basketball, players' level of engagement is a defining aspect of their practice. High school players were deeply engaged in the practice of basketball. As illustrated in the section on emergent goals, high school players took their participation in basketball seriously. This engagement is manifested in players' dedication to winning, the relentless practice of their skills, and the professional manner with which they approached games and practices. In contrast, middle school players were not as intensely engaged in the sport, seeing it, rather, as an interesting and fun pastime (Nasir, 1996, 2000).

The nature of players' engagement is also evident in the way that players interacted with one another and the nature of the relationships they built. Both groups of players learned to play with one another as teammates and made special friendships among other team members. However, the deeper engagement at the high school level was reflected in the fact that team members seemed to develop a particular bond with other players in the course of their practice. They came to know and trust one another on the court—anticipating certain plays and particular styles of play, knowing when to expect a pass or a long shot from the field. These on-the-court relationships both helped structure and reflected high school players' engagement in their practice. In contrast, middle school players' relationships with one another were substantive, but not specific to knowledge of one another in the practice of basketball (Nasir, 1996, 2000).

Imagination

Wenger describes the role of imagination in the construction of identity as "the ability to dislocate participation . . . in order to reinvent ourselves, our enterprises, our practices, and our communities. Imagination requires an opening, the energy to explore new identities, and new relations." Hence imagination involves developing understandings and possibilities beyond the present state. It includes defining a trajectory that connects what we are doing to an extended identity and seeing ourselves in new ways. Imagination requires the ability to explore other ways of doing things, generating scenarios, and conceiving of other possible worlds. In the case of basketball, high school players' evolving engagement was related to the way the differing nature of their practice afforded their perception of their community and their place in it. In contrast, the practice of middle school players and their engagement in that practice neither emphasized nor fostered players' connections with communities of basketball practice beyond their own.

High school players, in accord with their ideas about their basketball trajectories, imagined themselves (with the support of their coaches) as a part of a larger community of basketball players, both within the school and in other settings; their doing so gave them a sense of connection with players on other teams. For instance, while both middle and high school players knew the rankings of college and professional players well, and kept abreast of game outcomes, high school players were more likely than middle school players in interviews to mention players from their neighborhood who went on to play professional or college ball as their favorite players. This recognition of those who have gone before them demonstrates an imagined connection to the sport via these other players. This sense of place (and life trajectory) within a broader system fostered high school players' identities as basketball players. All but one high school player saw themselves as going on to play basketball in college and many articulated that basketball was one way to get to college in spite of limited funds.

Alignment

Another important component of developing identities in communities of practice is alignment. Alignment is a process of translating imagination into action and involves the ability to coordinate perspectives and actions in order to direct energies to a common purpose. In practice, alignment is the coordination of action across communities of practice. This coordination of action both reflects and constitutes identity—as participants in one community align their actions with participants in other communities, the nature of their participation changes.

In basketball, alignment becomes a part of identity when players draw on their imagination about their future in other communities of basketball practice to structure their actions in the present. In other words, it is in part because of their intended future in higher levels of basketball play that players align their daily actions with those of college and professional players. This alignment occurs to some degree in both middle and high school play—both sets of players read basketball magazines and keep track of the outcomes of professional and college games (Nasir, 2000). At times, this process of alignment involves statistics (and comes to shape mathematical goals) when players compare their own stats to that of college or professional players.

However, as the level of engagement and imagination varies from middle to high school, so does the level of alignment. While both sets of players align their actions with the broader basketball community through practices such as keeping abreast of basketball news, they differ with respect to how they align their actions in the play of the sport itself. High school players (but rarely middle school players) discuss their attempts to emulate the play of the professionals whom they respect—thereby aligning their play style and choices during play with the professional players whom they hope to emulate (Nasir, 1996).

Alignment also takes place in more mundane ways as players wear basketball clothes and shoes that identified them as "ballers" to the rest of the school community. One extreme example of this is the call by certain shoe companies not only that players align their athletic shoes with the practice standard, but also that the players themselves help to create this standard. In this role, high school players choose shoe styles and storyboards and make recommendations about potential celebrity endorsers for an athletic-gear company.

GOALS AND IDENTITY IN PRACTICE

The previous analysis shows how goals are structured in alignment with the identities that players' structure in practice and, conversely, how the structuring and accomplishment of new goals in practice constitutes a shift in identity. As basketball players move from middle school to high school play, they become engaged in the practice in increasingly intense ways—they take the sport more seriously, they easily imagine their own connection to a broader basketball community, and they align their actions in play with players at higher levels. This process of increasing identity as "ballers" co-occurred with shifts in players' practice-linked and mathematical goals.

These shifts in goals and identities were also associated with changes in mathematical learning. Players' mathematical goals shifted from understanding basic statistics involving counts in middle school to calculating relatively complex statistics with percentages and averages in high school.

In many ways, the treatment of goals, identity, and learning presenting in this chapter both synthesizes and reaffirms what we have learned in the field from sociocultural accounts of learning. The data presented highlight the idea that mathematics in everyday practices is embedded in the context of meaningful activity. In part, this meaning is derived as individuals become members of a community of practice. Further, cultural practices structure the nature of the mathematics (via the goals players construct and the activity afforded) in fundamental ways.

However, the data presented in this chapter also suggest new insights. To date, sociocultural accounts of learning have offered good descriptions of how individuals move through cultural practices that are fairly stable in nature—that is, how newcomers come into using the established practices of "old-timers" and come to be increasingly substantial participants (and learners) in these activities (Cain, n.d.; Lave & Wenger, 1991; Rogoff, 1990). However, the data on basketball show us that, indeed, the nature of the practices themselves may shift in relation to the expertise of the participants. In fact, one important contribution of this work is the potential for gaining a better understanding of learning in cultural practices from a developmental perspective. The research presented in this chapter makes clear that development occurs both at an individual level and at the level of the practice itself. In fact, in basketball, as in many other practices, the skills and developmental levels of the players were inextricably linked to the way the activity was carried out among those players.

Despite the differing skill and understanding levels at the different ages, play was maintained as an intact, complete activity, with players carrying out all aspects of the practice. What differed, then, was a matter of degree, whereby older and more expert players carried out the practice with a more complete understanding of it and in more deliberate ways. These changes occurred along several dimensions.

CHANGES IN ENGAGEMENT, IMAGINATION, ALIGNMENT, AND GOALS

Engagement changed with development in several significant ways. First, engagement took on a new character in the practices with older players. This was evident in the smoother flow of play, greater attention to the task at hand and the game overall, and greater enthusiasm. Also, the nature of the relationships between players changed, with increased social ties and refined expectations for performance within practices. Players came to interact in increasingly practice-specific ways, distributing game tasks differently. This newly emerging set of social relationships also seemed to be related to an expanding set of shared historical experiences between players, resulting in better-defined game roles and expectations.

Imagination also shifted in key ways. Older and more experienced players tended to have a stronger sense of the trajectory involved in becoming expert at their practice and were more committed to playing out this trajectory. This increasing awareness was linked to shifts in the practice that supported these imagined trajectories. In fact, high school players' practice supported their conceptualizations of their play.

These shifts in imagination were closely related to changes in alignment. More experienced and older players became better able and more motivated to take on the practices associated with those broader communities of practice and to conceptualize their place in this broader community in increasingly complex ways. Similarly, their practice shifted in ways that increasingly aligned their activities with those of players in basketball practice at the next level.

Changes in players' goals with increasing levels of practice reflect changes in engagement, alignment, and imagination. Players' goals shifted from lower-level, less complex goals to higher-level, more sophisticated goals. These goals reflected their understanding of and the nature of the practices in which they took part. In this analysis, I have noted two kinds of goal changes—changes in overarching goals of play and concurrent changes in related mathematical subgoals. Overall, shifts of both types were characterized by increasing sophistication and differentiation. These shifts consisted of a process of refining, of committing to, of becoming one of—encompassing both cognitive processes (what you need to know to become) and social processes (how becoming one of implies a set of values, norms, and practices that guide behavior).

The results of this research portrays a complex developmental landscape, with much intertwining, that contrasts sharply with approaches to development that tend to isolate and highlight only individual developmental changes. It is critical to note that the developmental shifts of players in basketball were fostered by concomitant changes in the nature of the practices at the level of activity. It is also important to understand that this was not a unidirectional influence; indeed, the new ways that practices were organized afforded development at the individual level just as players' increasing capabilities made new ways of organizing practices possible.

THE INTERTWINING OF LEARNING, IDENTITY, AND GOALS

The data presented in this chapter also push our understanding of the intertwining of goals, identities, and learning in practices. In this work we saw how changing identities were related to shifts in both practice-linked goals and learning. I argue that these relations can be represented by Figure 9.1.

Figure 9.1 illustrates the multifaceted, bidirectional relations between identity, goals, and learning. I will discuss each of the three sets of relations in turn.

Learning Creates Identity and Identity Creates Learning

As members of communities of practice experience changing (more engaged) identities, they come to learn new skills and bodies of knowledge, facilitating new ways of participating, which, in turn, helps to create new identities relative to their community. We saw this in the data, where, as basketball players became more engaged with the sport, they became more skilled with statistical calculations and, in turn, became even more engaged in the basketball community and established stronger identities as "ballers." In one part of this dynamic, new skills support the construction of more engaged identity. In the other, increasing identification with an activity or with a community of practice motivates new learning. However, these shifts in learning and identities do not occur purely as an internal, intrapersonal process. Rather, they occur as a part of a socially distributed, interpersonal process, whereby practices shift in ways that afford (and indeed require) new sets of skills, knowledge, and participation.

Learning Creates Goals snd Goals Create Learning

Learning in practice also involves considering new kinds of problems and reconceptualizing old problems in new ways. As individuals learn, they come to construct new problem-solving goals—goals that are in line with an increasingly sophisticated knowledge base and that are afforded by shifts in broader practice-linked goals. For instance, increasing knowledge about the game of basketball and statistics caused players to set new and different kinds of goals in high school play.

It is also true that goals create learning. Through increasing participation in practices (and the identities associated with those practices), people come to construct (and practices come to afford) new goals in their activity. Often, to carry

FIGURE **9.1.** Bidirectional relations between identity, learning, and goals

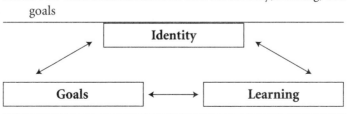

out these new goals requires learning: ways of interacting, bodies of knowledge, and ways of doing.

Identity Creates Goals and Goals Create Identity

New goals are often structured in line with emerging identities in practice. As participants take on new identities vis-à-vis others in the practice and in relation to the activity at hand, they begin to construct more sophisticated practice-linked goals (increasingly aligned with those of "experts"). This was the case when as older players identified more strongly with the sport, they began to take on (as the play context afforded) more sophisticated goals in the context of their activity—one of which was to learn to understand and calculate players' statistics. Conversely, new goals lead to new identities. Here, participants (through the alignment of their goals with experts) begin to see themselves as more expert, hence changing their identity in relation to the practice.

IMPLICATIONS FOR SCHOOLING
AND MATHEMATICS LEARNING

The idea that both cultural practices and the children who take part in them develop in important and complementary ways may be a valuable one for educators. School is a practice in which groups of novices come together to perform academic activities—quite different in nature from other practices in which one newcomer enters an already established group of old-timers and others in varying stages of becoming old-timers. From this perspective, we can understand learning as novices moving through a set of increasingly complex activities within which they develop corresponding competencies. This reconceptualization may be particularly appropriate in the case of schooling as a key question then becomes how to structure this successive set of activities in a way that maximizes learning and cognitive developmental outcomes.

In school practices, the developmental trajectory often proceeds in a piecemeal fashion, with one set of skills building on prior ones. In basketball, the practice was not broken up into its constituent parts—for instance, basketball players did not learn how to dribble, then how to pass, then how to interpret stats. In these practices, authentic practice is not an end point of the learning process; rather it is a part of the learning practice all along the way.

This raises questions about what teaching and learning practices might look like in school, and in mathematics in particular, were they to reflect this model. Children would solve authentic problems, messy ones without clear right or wrong answers, perhaps in the service of a nonmathematical goal. In many ways, this maps nicely onto recent reform curriculum packages and practices in mathematics.

This research also points to the importance of attending to some key "meta" mathematical issues, such as how schooling environments support children's developing identities as students, through the nature of their engagement. In this process, the extent to which students' activities are aligned with a broader community of practice (of students or of math students) and the extent to which students imagine themselves as being committed to that community may be important factors in learning.

IMPLICATIONS FOR AFRICAN AMERICAN CHILDREN

In this chapter, I have discussed an example of a practice trajectory in which some African American students developed stronger affiliations with age and experienced concomitant shifts in their mathematical goals and associated mathematical knowledge. This trajectory of increasing participation and learning is quite different from the trajectory that many African American students exhibit in school. In fact, researchers have documented the opposite pattern in the schooling trajectories of African American and other minority children, in which students increasingly disidentify with schooling (Graham et al., 1998; Ogbu, 1992a) and with mathematics classes in particular (Ginsburg & Russell, 1981; Martin, 2000).

This research offers important evidence for how these patterns of decreasing identity may be composed of engagement, alignment, and imagination processes on a local level, and related to the mathematical goals students do and do not construct in the classroom—goals that are fundamentally linked to students' learning of mathematics. Hence, the model elaborated in this chapter offers a concrete explanatory link between identity and learning, which could be used to better understand students' mathematics success and failure. Ultimately, the theoretical approach put forth here offers a viable alternative to deterministic environmental explanations, while still allowing for the critical role of sociohistorical factors (such as cultural ideas and stereotyping) in shaping African American and other minority students' mathematical achievement and learning.

10

Mathematics Learning and Participation in the African American Context: The Co-construction of Identity in Two Intersecting Realms of Experience

Danny Bernard Martin

> *I have further argued that the task of achievement is fundamentally shaped by the very identity of African Americans as African Americans. . . . The most important thing schools, families, and communities can do is to figure out how to develop among African-American children identities of achievement.*
> —Theresa Perry (2003, pp. 87–100)

> *My children are exposed to things. . . . So, my son could see how math relates to what he is doing right now. . . . The point I'm making is that when you're exposed to things early on and have role models and this is just banged in your head early on, you turn out to be a completely different person. . . . I honestly feel that through my struggles and working and living as long as I have so far that math is an essential foundation for everything.*
> —Keith, African American parent

The second quote presented above is from an interview that I conducted with a 37-year-old African American father named Keith and reflects his belief that one's mathematical experiences are a fundamental contributor to one's identity and sense of self. Readers will learn of the struggles that Keith and African Americans like him endure in order to maintain and merge positive identities in the contexts of being African American and being a learner of mathematics. This struggle is brought on by a number of forces that racialize the life and mathematical experiences of African Americans.

At the time of the interview, Keith was employed full time but was also taking courses at a local community college after many years away from school. He was taking one of those courses, beginning algebra, both for career advancement and to continue to help his two school-age children. Because he was a student in my class, I was able talk with Keith informally about his life and mathematical experiences. Based on those observations and conversations, I invited him to participate in an ongoing research study that focused on African Americans and mathematics (Martin, 1998). I subsequently interviewed Keith on two occasions for a total of about 4 hours. While constructing what amounted to a condensed life history, Keith was able to narrow the discussion and focus on his struggle for mathematics literacy. Like many other African American adults whom I have interviewed, he highlighted his strong beliefs about the role of his African American status and identity in his struggle for mathematics literacy. In Keith's view, this status and identity, and the meanings assigned to them by Whites, created boundaries (both real and perceived) that limited his opportunities in the larger social structure, and in mathematics in particular. Yet Keith did not accept these boundaries passively but instead exhibited a range of positive, agency-related behaviors. What I also found remarkable was that despite the negative connotations assigned to his being African American both in and outside mathematical contexts, Keith had maintained a strong African American identity and a firm belief in the importance of mathematics literacy for both himself and his children. Keith's struggle to transcend these boundaries also revealed how closely his identity as an African American[1] and his identity as a learner of mathematics were *linked*. His struggle for mathematical literacy continued to shape his sense of self as an African American. His strong African American identity made him more committed in his struggle for mathematics literacy.

My interactions with African American adults such as Keith reveal that the experiences and motivations characterizing African American struggle for mathematics literacy often extend well beyond the school context. On the one hand, this struggle is often linked to a desire for meaningful participation in the larger opportunity structure. On the other hand, it is emblematic of a philosophy of education that has been passed down in the African American narrative tradition: *literacy for freedom and freedom for literacy* (Perry, 2003). This narrative tradition includes "stories about struggles for literacy, stories about the purpose of literacy, stories about what people were willing to do to become literate, and stories about how people became literate so that they could 'be somebody'" (p. 92). According to Perry, these stories are also important because they "link literacy and education to the social identity of African Americans, to the very notion of what it meant to be African American" (p. 105).

Against the backdrop of Perry's claim and the experiences of African American adults such as Keith, the goal of this chapter is to address participation in mathematics among African Americans employing the analytic lens of *identity*. I focus specifically on the construction of identities that are at the intersections of two important realms of experience: *being African American* and *becoming a doer of mathematics* (Martin, 1997, 1998, 2000, 2002a, 2002b, 2003a, 2003b, in press). In doing so, I address the following questions: (1) What does it mean to be a learner of mathematics in the context of African American struggle? and (2) What does it mean to be African American in the context of mathematics learning?

The first question acknowledges that African American learners, be they adults or adolescents, do not come to mathematical contexts as blank slates, free of their experiences as African Americans. Any analysis of identity construction and students' becoming doers of mathematics must, in my view, simultaneously consider African American identities as well. The second question raises the possibility that, in the attempt to acquire mathematical literacy, the very nature of African Americans' identities can be affected, positively or negatively. Taken together, these two questions bring together issues having to do with racial-identity development and its role in mathematics participation and learning, as well as the role of mathematical experience in racial-identity development. Methodologically, one challenge is to *document* both episodes of mathematics participation or experience in which racial identity assumes salience, and episodes in an individual's racial-identity development in which prior mathematical experiences assume salience. It is equally important to document and understand how school, peer, family, community, and societal forces contribute to the development of these identities. In my prior research (Martin, 1998, 2000, 2002a, 2003a, 2003b), in-depth interviews conducted with African Americans proved to be an effective method for documenting (1) the intersections of these identities; (2) the forces affecting each of them; (3) the extent to which African Americans view themselves as peripheral participants (Lave and Wenger, 1991) who will increasingly become meaningful participants in mathematics, or as individuals marginalized by virtue of their social identities; and (4) the ways in which their social identities as African Americans are devalued in societal and other contexts.

In this chapter, I restrict my focus to interviews conducted with African American adults and parents, given that they provide a means of documenting the "community context" and that parents and adults are, along with teachers, the most significant influences on the formation of student attitudes, dispositions, and beliefs about mathematics.

The data and analyses that I present are representative cases taken from three studies in which I attempted to address the preceding questions (Martin, 1997, 1998, 2000, 2002a). In these studies, I interviewed more than 100 parents and adolescents, in interviews ranging in length from 1 to 4 hours. In all three studies, thematic analysis of the narratives revealed that issues of racial boundaries, perceived position and devalued social status, meaning-making for mathematics, and identity assume prominence. Most mathematics education research that has focused on African Americans has been concerned with failure and marginality. In contrast, my research has highlighted mathematical success and the ability of African Americans to successfully negotiate boundaries, reposition themselves in mathematics and reconstruct their identities, and exhibit positive agency in the process of doing so.

The first study, reported in Martin (2000), was conducted in a predominantly African American middle school of 600 students, whereas the second and third studies focused on African American parents and other adults in the community college setting where I had taught mathematics courses, ranging from arithmetic to differential equations, for 14 years. The community college is a particularly good context in which to study mathematics resilience among African Americans who may have had negative mathematical socializations in their earlier schooling but who now find it necessary to pursue mathematics for educational and occupational reasons and who have diverse beliefs about the importance of mathematics.

When probed, these students often construct compelling explanations for how they believe their African American status—and the treatment they have received as a result of this status—has hindered their ability to become meaningful participants in mathematics. Participating in mathematics and becoming doers of mathematics in school and nonschool contexts is often framed in terms of struggle and differential treatment (Martin, 2000, 2002a, 2002b, 2003a, 2003b, in press). Given the lack of a research base on these issues, the struggle for mathematics literacy within the context of African American struggle is an important area for further research.

MASTERNARRATIVES, COUNTERNARRATIVES, AND IDENTITY

While underachievement and limited persistence in mathematics among African Americans have received attention from researchers (Johnson, 1989; Secada, 1992; Tate, 1995a, 1997), I contend that the juxtaposition of African American status, underachievement, and marginal participation within the existing literature has unwittingly served to create a *masternarrative* (Giroux, Lanskshear, McLaren, & Peters, 1996) that has continued to dominate discussions and orient research on African Americans and mathematics. This masternarrative has portrayed African Americans as passive in the face of differential treatment and denied opportunity in mathematics, and as lacking in both agency and voice. In addition, this masternarrative often involves interpretations of underachievement and limited persistence that are ahistorical (of both personal and collective histories of the African Americans in mathematics) and that fail to acknowledge academic and mathematics success among African Americans.[2] Peters and Lankshear (1996) stated that such masternarratives often serve as "legitimating stories propagated for specific political purposes to manipulate public consciousness" (p. 2). In the case of African Americans and mathematics, they are presented as inferior to Whites and Asian Americans; failure is constructed as normative; and their struggle to obtain mathematics literacy, despite barriers and obstacles, receives little attention.

Remarkably, very little of the research that has been conducted about African Americans in mathematics has been based on their first-person accounts of their mathematical experiences. My analysis of African American *counternarratives* has revealed important details about their *identities of participation* and *nonparticipation* (Wenger, 1998) in school-based mathematical practices, and in contexts within the larger opportunity structure. These counternarratives, defined by Peters and Lankshear (1996) as the "stories of those individuals and groups whose knowledges and histories have been marginalized, excluded, subjugated or forgotten in the telling of official narratives" (p. 2), serve the purpose of disrupting the notion that African Americans are passive in their socialization experiences. In my view, attention to these counternarratives and resistant behaviors necessitates new research questions and methodological approaches to study mathematics participation and achievement among African Americans.

Although a comprehensive review is beyond the scope of this chapter, I do need to clarify the theory and methods on which my work draws. First, I build on my early ideas about mathematics socialization and identity (Martin, 1993, 1997, 1998, 2000) as well as on the work of scholars who have further extended identity-related issues into situated and sociocultural theories of mathematics learning (e.g., Boaler & Greeno, 2000; Nasir, 2002). Although an increasing number of studies incorporate practice and situated cognition theories into their analyses, there is often a lack of attention to issues of race, closed opportunity structures, power differentials, and differential socialization (Apple, 2000). I address this limitation by highlighting the salience of race and African American experience. Second, I draw on recent research on academic identity development among African American students (e.g., Davidson, 1996; Fordham, 1996; Heath & McLaughlin, 1993; Hilliard, 2003). These works, in turn, draw on a vast literature devoted to the study of ethnic identity in general (e.g., Cornell & Hartmann, 1998) and African American identity development in particular (e.g., Cross, 1991; Sellers, Smith, Shelton, Rowley, & Chavous, 1998; Spencer, 1999). Although an extensive body of scholarship on identity-related issues exists in both the psychological and sociological literatures, no studies in these areas focus specifically on identity development within the context of mathematics. Last, I draw on the work of critical mathematics educators who frame the acquisition of mathematics literacy within social justice frameworks (e.g., Frankenstein, 1990; Gutstein, 2003; Hart, 2003; Moses, 1994; Moses & Cobb, 2001; Skovsmose, 1994; Stanic, 1991; Tate, 1995b; Tate & Rousseau, 2002).

In building on these literatures, one of my primary goals in this chapter is to further elaborate two key concepts developed in my research: *mathematics socialization* and *mathematics identity*. *Mathematics socialization* refers to the experiences that individuals and groups have within a variety of contexts such as school, family, peer groups, and the workplace that legitimize or inhibit meaningful participation in mathematics. *Mathematics identity* refers to the dispositions and deeply held beliefs that individuals develop about their ability to participate and perform effectively in mathematical contexts and to use mathematics to change the conditions of their lives. A mathematics identity encompasses a person's self-understandings and how they are seen by others in the context of doing mathematics. Therefore, a mathematics identity is expressed in narrative form as a *negotiated* self, is always under construction, and results from the negotiation of our own assertions and the external ascriptions of others.

Math socialization and the development of a math identity occur over time as individuals and groups attempt to negotiate access into contexts whose participation is mediated or dictated by knowledge of mathematics (Martin, 1997, 2000). These can be classrooms; instructional units; contexts of mathematical practice found outside of the school; or situations where identity as a learner of mathematics is contested, challenged, or confirmed. A range of agents such as teachers, parents, community members, peers, and the media can all be influential in mathematics socialization and identity formation. As this negotiation of access takes place, overt and implicit messages about participation, constraints, and opportunity are generated, and beliefs about one's ability to perform, one's sense of self, and one's status within various mathematical contexts are formed.

Because mathematics is only one aspect of a person's life, mathematics identities do not develop in isolation from the other identities that people construct (e.g., racial, cultural, ethnic, gender, occupational, academic). For some individuals, these multiple identities may unfold in ways that make them incongruous and can lead to serious personal tensions (e.g., Erikson, 1968; Fordham & Ogbu, 1986). For others, there may be explicit attempts to merge these identities so that they exist in unison. Any challenge or affront to one is then interpreted as a challenge to others: If you challenge or devalue my racial identity, you also challenge or devalue my academic identity (Kohl, 1994).

Theoretically, the perspective on identity adopted in this chapter draws on a *constructionist* approach, taken from the sociological literature, which assumes the following:

> Construction [of identities] involves the passive experience of being "made" by external forces, including not only material circumstances but the claims that other persons or groups make about the group in question, and the active process by which the group "makes" itself. The world around us may "tell" us that we are distinct . . . or our experience at the hands of circumstances may "tell" us that we constitute a group, but our identity is also a product of the claims we make. The claims may build on the messages we receive from the world around us or may depart from them, rejecting them, adding to them, or refining them. (Cornell & Hartmann, 1998, p. 80)

Cornell and Hartmann (1998) identified three key issues within the process of identity construction: *boundary, perceived position,* and *meaning. Boundary* refers to markers or conditions that distinguish between members in a group and those who do not belong. *Perceived position* involves the process of locating a group's or individual's status within in a stratification system or distribution of power. Consideration of boundary and perceived position implies that individuals and groups often develop *relational* or *positional identities* (Holland et al., 1998). In the context of doing school-based mathematics, for example, one group's consistently poor performance on achievement tests relative to other groups often results in that group being assigned a collective identity of "underachievers" or "at-risk."

Cornell and Hartmann (1998) also identified six key sites or contexts where identity construction occurs: politics, labor markets, residential space, social institutions, culture, and daily experiences. Each of these sites can be analyzed in terms of its opportunistic affordances and the degree to which boundary markers, such as race, become salient. For example, Cornell and Hartmann claim that the extent to which social institutions "are available and accessible to all populations within the society, the salience of ethnic boundaries is reduced. . . . To the extent that such institutions are unavailable or inaccessible to one or more populations, or to the extent that special institutions are set aside for them . . . that salience is increased. . . . The fundamental message is that you are denied [or granted] access because you occupy a particular category" (p. 169).

MATHEMATICS LITERACY FOR FREEDOM, FREEDOM FOR MATHEMATICS LITERACY: COUNTERNARRATIVES OF AFRICAN AMERICAN ADULTS

As I have clarified, the two questions that orient my research program are, What does it mean to be African American in the context of mathematics learning? and What does it mean to learn mathematics in the context of African American struggle? The excerpts that I present below highlight the intermingling of *being African American* and *being a doer of mathematics* in the lives and mathematical experiences of two African American adults, Keith and Gina. For both, African American identity (and race) assumes salience and is a boundary or marker that the dominant society uses to position African American on the margins of mathematics. Their (counter)narratives also highlight the agency and resistance that Keith and Gina exhibit in the face of this devaluation and marginalization.

Keith[3]

As described earlier, Keith was a 37-year-old African American male who attended community college after a career in the navy and a nearly 15-year absence from formal schooling. Keith had been married for 18 years and has three children ages 21 (female), 10 (male), and 5 (male). Keith's wife was also 37 years old and was a stay-at-home mom. In addition to taking three college courses at the time of our interview, Keith was employed as a surgical assistant at a local hospital and had worked in the medical field for a number of years. He described his standard of living as working class/middle class. In the context of framing his overall life experiences and identity, Keith characterized himself as someone having a high aptitude for doing well in school but who, early in his life, never really pushed himself, or received the push, to do so.

As his narrative makes clear, Keith was well aware of the boundaries that were imposed on him because of his African American status. Those boundaries were both physical and related to the kinds of opportunities he had in his life. The racialized treatment that Keith experienced had a definite impact on his sense of self and his desire to learn mathematics, both early and later in his life. The quote below highlights the salience of race as a marker for participation in mathematics at a time when Keith's racial, academic, and mathematics identity development were at their formative stages. In particular, being told that he should not aspire to be a physician because of his race, and his subsequent deinvestment in mathematics, supports Cornell and Hartman's (1998) claim that access or denial based on a particular category that a person occupies can lead to the development of a positional identity as a nonparticipant (in mathematics):

> Growing up in Chicago, I was always taught that Whites were better. By the school system itself. "Whites are better. You shouldn't be where Whites are at. You shouldn't be in this part of town. Whites are smarter." . . . When I was in third grade, I was actually the brightest kid in school and that's where my knack for math came from. I actually exceeded all the math that they had there. They had nothing else for me. The children around me didn't exceed in math or do well, so I goofed off. . . . Then when I made it to fifth grade, my mother put me in a Catholic school. . . . I didn't have all the distractions. I pursued math again. And this is in 1968 or 1969. The nun told me at that time that Blacks should not consider professional occupations. It was my goal to become a physician. So, I gave up. . . . So, I just did enough to get through school. That [became] my goal.

Keith's struggle against differential treatment and the devaluation of his African American status was an ongoing one that continued into his adult life. Derailed in his attempt to become a physician, Keith eventually became a surgical assistant. But even in that role, he is thought of as less than able. However, in contrast to when he was in his youth when he *appeared* to acquiesce and internalize messages about his African American status, now he invoked the belief that, rather than accept his "place" as subordinate or as a nonparticipant, he had to be that much better than Whites. This provides a clear indication of his willingness to resist challenges to his identity from those in power:

> *Danny Bernard Martin:* Would you say that over your life, you have been treated fairly in society?
>
> *Keith:* No. It hasn't been fair. I found that as an African American I've generally had to be sharper, quicker, and brighter. In the operating room, I tend to find that if there is a White who is not as skillful as I am in certain areas, he or she isn't picked on as much. . . . So, I've always got to defend myself. I've always got to be sharper, brighter, quicker. . . . The pressure of just being African American on top of doing your job. You have to be at times, three or four times sharper than your White counterpart because they already feel that you're inadequate.

Despite the messages Keith received about his "place," it is worth pointing out that he never lost confidence in his math ability and did not form the kind of African American or mathematics identity that reflected subjugation. Keith's narrative also makes evident his belief in the value of mathematics and his profound realization that not having the opportunity to learn more mathematics or to assume meaningful participation in mathematics changed the course of his life. In Keith's view, the lack of encouragement in mathematics and low expectations was a direct result of his devalued African American status (as a male, in particular):

> I'd say because the expectations were low. . . . Because most African American males don't come through there wanting or having the desire to pursue mathematics. . . . I didn't have anyone around me saying, "[If] you do math, you're going to go here [in life]. You can be a doctor if you just hang in there. Take a science class. . . . You have potential, Keith. If you work, do you realize that you won't be able to get your algebra homework done?" . . . No one took the time to say, "Why don't you join the math club? You know, they got a special program for African American students at Illinois Institute of Technology." . . . Could you imagine? My whole world would be different. I wouldn't even be sitting here with you having this conversation. No one told me. No one took the time. No one really cared. . . . I always wanted to be a physician but I never had a path.

Although Keith could vividly recall the negative messages that he received, he began to reject and resist the idea that his African American status rendered him less talented than others. He was able to develop positive agency and reinvest in mathematics and education, not only for himself but also for his children. Keith's primary goal was to make sure that he and his wife did everything that *they* could to ensure that their children gained access to the kind of educational activities that would give them the greatest opportunity in life (i.e., literacy for freedom). Keith's belief that one's sense of self and identity could be fundamentally changed as a result of the quality of one's experiences reinforces the point that some African American parents and adults resist the devaluing of their racial status by forging strong identities (racial and mathematical). What is most remarkable about Keith's reflection on his life is that despite attempts to marginalize him, he came to believe that mathematical knowledge was key in one's life chances:

> I felt a struggle at one time but what I began to find through the years of working and exposure is that Whites are not smarter than me. . . . But we have never had the opportunity or exposure that Whites have. For example, my children sleep, eat, and drink education. My wife is at home specifically for the raising of the children. . . . The point I'm making is that when you're exposed to things early on and have role models and this is just banged in your head early on, you turn out to be a completely different

person. There's no guarantee but at least you have the tools. . . . I honestly feel that through my struggles and working and living as long as I have so far that math is an essential foundation for everything.

Gina

Gina was a 42-year-old single woman born and raised in an African American community in Oakland, California. She came from a two-parent home and attended a local high school in the early 1970s, a few years after the civil rights movement. Her experiences as an African American student and as a learner of mathematics resulted in her forming a mathematics identity that, for many years in her life, placed her on the margins of mathematics. Indicative of Perry's (2003) notion of literacy for freedom and freedom for literacy, Gina's later reinvestment in mathematics stemmed from a desire to liberate herself from the idea that she was incapable of doing mathematics, *not* from reasons related to jobs or socioeconomics.

After attending the University of California, Berkeley, for one year and leaving on academic probation, Gina enrolled in a local community college and then attended a local state university, earning a degree in social work. She later served as an air force officer for 13 years and then worked in a post office until she was unable to perform her duties because of a work-related injury. She had not been employed since that time and considered her standard of living to be "low poverty."

At the time of the interview she was pursuing her teaching credential. She had already completed Algebra II and statistics, earning the grades of A and B, respectively, and was enrolled in precalculus at the community college where I taught. Reflecting on her early educational experiences, Gina described herself as a quiet student who never asked her (mostly White) teachers for help in mathematics because she felt that she had no cultural connections with them. From the time that Gina was in the seventh or eighth grade, she tried to avoid math and took only one other math course, Business Math, before graduating from high school. She was, however, a good student in her other courses.

In Gina's view, her avoidance of math after her initial negative and unsuccessful experiences was partly a result of the messages that were being sent by school officials and the lack of connection to her teachers. Moreover, the racialized social context and racialized enrollment and tracking patterns in mathematics classes at her schools sent their own messages about the relative status and position of African American students in mathematics. A core aspect this message was that math was for others, not for African Americans:

[The counselors] really didn't connect with the students, not with me or whatever. . . . I was never around White people or whatever. I really didn't know how to approach them so I never did ask the teacher for help. I just did the best I could and I can remember in math class I had got a D. That was in the seventh or eighth grade, and I don't recall taking another math course unless it was part of the stuff you needed for graduation or whatever. . . . [In high school], the counselors would do racial steering, try to steer all the minorities into art and cooking and stuff like that. So if you mentioned math, they were like, "No. No." And they really didn't tell me anything about college preparation and stuff because this was way back in '74. So at that time, you know, it's just right after the civil rights. You know, you really feel segregated even though they place you in a school with different races and stuff like that. Chinese people or Whites or whoever go into the math probably, hardly any Blacks. So when I got older, I just said that whatever fears I had, I was going to try to overcome them. One of them was math.

Gina's negative experiences with mathematics had become so internalized that in selecting a career area, she avoided areas where mathematics was a requisite form of knowledge. This provides a clear indication that she had developed a very negative mathematics identity in her formative years. And because she earlier cited race as a factor in determining who received access to mathematics and who did not, I would argue that the development of her mathematics identity and racial identity were intertwined. Her decision to avoid mathematics was a reflection not only of her mathematics identity but also of her early beliefs about the status of African Americans in mathematics:

> *Gina:* I didn't have any aspirations [in high school]. I said, well, I'm just going to keep going to school since I'm doing good. I kept going and then I noticed you have to pick a major. The ones with math and science, I can't choose that because I know I'm going to fail.
> *DBM:* Why did you figure you were going to fail?
> *Gina:* Because I know I did bad in math and I never went back and took courses. I didn't even take algebra when I graduated from [the university]. . . . The reason why I majored in social work not because I was interested in it, it was because it was the only thing I could do that didn't include math or science.

It was not until years later that Gina decided to reinvest in mathematics by enrolling at the community college. She had completed beginning algebra and intermediate algebra and was enrolled in a precalculus course at the time of the interview. The motivation that she described for reenrolling in mathematics was primarily for her own greater sense of self and accomplishment:

> I didn't take it just to get in a profession, I took it because I wanted to. I took it because I wanted to learn it the right way and I had confidence in myself. . . . I know that math and science is important. . . . I mean they have other professions too but the ones to me that are more respected are the ones that require more math and science.

Like Keith, Gina believed that mathematics knowledge was an arbiter in one's life chances and that a range of agents were instrumental in a student's mathematical development, particularly parents and teachers. When asked to provide her opinion on African American underrepresentation in mathematics, Gina responded as follows:

> *Gina:* But somehow we get lost in these classes, whether it's not being able to succeed and not taking the right ones, not getting help, that's three things right there that prevent you from achieving your goals.
>
> *DBM:* And who's fault do you think that is?
>
> *Gina:* Parents are not helping them. It's the parents, they don't teach the kids to go and be motivated, to talk to teachers and say, "I'm having a problem, can you help me?" And the parents may not be educated. It's more than just the parents. And the teachers are not motivating the kids. Nobody in that chain of the mother, the teacher, the person, the mentor. If somebody in that chain falls short, the person is not going to succeed.

CONCLUSION

I predict that further research into identity issues will reveal that cases similar to those of Keith and Gina are representative of large numbers of African Americans. Keith's and Gina's narratives demonstrate that the struggle for mathematics literacy among African Americans is more complicated than the accounts often found in the literature. This struggle cannot be separated from the life experiences of African Americans as African Americans. Conversely, unfolding experiences of participation and nonparticipation in mathematics affect the development of African American identities. Yet as the two cases I have presented show, African Americans are not passive. They invoke agency, resist, and contest their experiences in both contexts.

The resistance and contestation demonstrated by Gina and Keith is illustrative of Perry's (2003) notion of literacy for freedom, freedom for literacy. I would argue that life experience as an African American, often characterized by struggle and social devaluation, makes it difficult to maintain a positive identity in the pursuit of mathematics knowledge. Yet the same struggles typifying much of African Americans' experience can be transformative in terms of one's identity when those struggles are put in the context of liberation and freedom, and these become the motivators to pursue mathematics knowledge and meaningful participation. Cast in this light, one can envision that when African Americans encounter barriers and obstacles in their attempts to become doers of mathematics, their higher appeal to their African American identities has the potential to render these obstacles less potent. Keith and Gina's comments indicate that the "attraction" of pursuing mathematics knowledge for many African Americans may lie more in its relationship to forging a stronger African American identity than for occupational or socioeconomic advancement related to social systems and institutions that often denigrate their African American status in any case.[4]

Based on both the case studies presented above and my prior research, I would also argue that the analysis of the individual and collective mathematical socializations and identities of African American adults has important implications for addressing success and failure in mathematics among African American students. For example, in looking to those in their homes or communities for messages about the importance of mathematics, African American students may find few people around them who have benefited from mathematical knowledge. These realities may send mixed messages about being African American, participating in mathematics, and the benefit of mathematics knowledge thereby tempering their in-school efforts and the formation of their own mathematics identities.

The findings that I have presented in this chapter have important implications for further research. There is a growing awareness among mathematics educators that studies of mathematics content and problem-solving behavior must be complemented by studies of the contexts in which those behaviors take place. In my view, research that focuses on mathematics socialization and identity offers a way to bridge content and context by enabling us to gain a greater understanding of the process of how mathematics and its importance comes to be situated in the lives of students, how some students become marginalized, how this marginalization in mathematics is rooted in their marginalization as "minorities," and how students can build on an awareness of their social struggles and history to overcome barriers imposed on them as they attempt to become doers of mathematics. Unfortunately, few researchers have engaged in detailed analyses of socialization and identity-related issues within the context of mathematics learning, and very little research on mathematics learning has focused on the co-construction of African American identity (e.g., Martin, 2000; Moody, 2001; Nasir, 2002). In my view, understanding what happens at the intersections of these two realms of experience, being African American and becoming a doer of mathematics, should be a goal for future research.

NOTES

1. Sellers, Smith, Shelton, Rowley, & Chavous (1998) define racial identity in African Americans as the significance and qualitative meaning that individuals attribute to their membership in the Black racial group within their overall self-concepts.

2. In Martin (2000), I offer an extended critique of these perspectives.

3. A profile of Keith also appears in Martin (2003a) and Martin (in press).

4. This is not to deny that socioeconomic concerns cannot be a powerful motivator. However, the very fact of limited African American presence in mathematics and science-related fields makes questionable appeals that are based solely on socioeconomics.

11

Culture, Identity, and Equity in the Mathematics Classroom

Paul Cobb & Lynn Liao Hodge

The motivation for this chapter stems in part from the relatively marginalized status of issues of diversity and equity within mathematics education research (Lubienski, 2002). As Secada (1995) observes, the relatively limited number of studies in mathematics education with an equity focus have, for the most part, been constituted as peripheral to the field. Against this background, we have struggled with the challenge of making a concern for issues of diversity and equity integral to our ongoing research for the past several years. We do not pretend that we have either the experience or the expertise to make a seminal contribution to research on diversity and equity in mathematics education. Instead, the issue that we have sought to address is how a focus on diversity and equity can become part and parcel of mainstream research that involves the development of instructional designs and the analysis of the learning and teaching of significant mathematical ideas.

In this chapter, we first offer a definition of equity that reflects our focus on classroom processes of mathematics learning and teaching. We then differentiate between two views of culture that can be discerned in the mathematics education literature. In one view, culture is treated as a characteristic of readily identified and thus circumscribable communities, whereas in the other view it is treated as a set of locally instantiated practices that are dynamic and improvisational. We clarify the relation between these two characterizations of culture and argue that both are relevant to the goal of ensuring that all students have access to significant mathematical ideas. We then focus on the second view of culture as local and improvisational in the remainder of the chapter and consider its potential relevance. We argue that the manner in which this perspective brings the identities and interests that students develop in mathematics classrooms to the fore make it directly relevant to researchers who focus on instructional design, learning, and teaching at the classroom level. We then go on to develop this perspective in the latter part of the chapter by proposing an interpretive scheme for analyzing the identities that students develop in mathematics classrooms that can inform instructional design and teaching.

A PROVISIONAL DEFINITION OF EQUITY

As R. Gutiérrez (2002, this volume) observes, ongoing debates over how equity might be usefully construed in mathematics education constitute important contexts within which to articulate both immediate and longer-range goals in the field. The concept of equity encompasses a complex range of concerns that emerge when people who are members of various local communities and broader groups within society act and interact in the mathematics classroom. Foremost among these is the issue of students' access to opportunities to develop forms of mathematical reasoning that, as Bruner (1986) puts it, have clout. Bruner goes on to clarify that, in his view, forms of reasoning have clout to the extent that they enable students to participate in significant out-of-school practices in relatively substantial ways. As an illustration, it is apparent that public policy discourse increasingly involves the formulation and critique of data-based arguments. Students' development of the relatively sophisticated forms of statistical reasoning that are implicated in such arguments therefore have clout in that they enable them to participate in a type of discourse that is central to what Delpit (1988) termed the *culture of power* (cf. Cobb, 1997; Cobb, 1999).

In offering this perspective on what it means for particular forms of reasoning to have clout, Bruner viewed the societal function of schools to be inducting students into what he referred to as *culture as lived*. In developing a working definition of equity, it is essential that we also consider a second societal function of schooling, that of comparing and differentiating between students in ways that have direct consequences for their future educational and economic opportunities. The pervasiveness of this function of schooling indicates the need to broaden what it means for forms of reasoning to have clout by taking account of criteria that are internal to the school (cf. Secada, 1995). Foremost among these is that of students' access to future mathematics courses (Tate & Rousseau, in press). As an illustration, Moses and Cobb (2001) clarify that the goal of the Algebra Project is to make it possible for *all* students to have access to and succeed in high school algebra courses that function as gatekeepers to college-preparatory tracks. Moses and Cobb also alert us to a third aspect of equity that concerns the cultivation of students' interests in and feelings of efficacy about the future study of mathematics. As we discuss later in this chapter, this aspect of equity brings to the fore the identities that students develop as they engage in classroom mathematical activities. For the present, it suffices to note that a perspective on equity is inadequate if it is limited to students' participation in out-of-school practices and to their access to particular school mathematics courses. The definition that we propose also includes what are traditionally referred to as students' motivations to continue to study mathematics and their persistence while doing so. Thus, equity as we construe it encompasses students' development of a sense of efficacy (empowerment) in mathematics together with the desire and capability to learn more about mathematics when the opportunity arises.

TWO VIEWS OF CULTURE

Two lines of scholarship that are grounded in differing views of culture can be discerned in research on issues of equity in mathematics education. The first line of research reflects the view of culture as a *way of life* that is characteristic of a bounded community. In this view, culture comprises a network of relatively stable practices that capture daily life within a group or community that are passed on from one generation to the next. This view of culture is prominent in the mathematics education literature and is consistent with the typical use of the term in everyday discourse. The second line of research reflects a more recent view of culture that has emerged within the past 20 years to capture the changing aspects of contemporary life. In this second view, culture is viewed as a network of locally instantiated practices that are dynamic and improvisational (Bauman, 1999; Calhoun, 1996; Gutierrez, Baquedano-Lopez, & Tejeda, 1999; Eisenhart, 2001). This perspective emphasizes people's participation in multiple communities or groups and considers the boundaries between these groups or communities to be blurred and permeable.

The changes that precipitated the emergence of the second view of culture include technological advances in communication and travel that have made the world a much smaller place. These advances have made possible a dramatic increase in immigration in many parts of the world, thereby altering demographic patterns that once seemed relatively stable. A second set of changes concerns the role of women and the composition of the workforce. Children frequently grow up in a variety of social settings (e.g., in day care, with babysitters, in school, and among peer groups) that function together with the family and home communities to raise them (Gutierrez & Rogoff, 2003). As Eisenhart (2001) observes, it is difficult to capture these and other aspects of contemporary life when culture is viewed as a way of life within a bounded community.

> It is no longer straight-forward for anthropologists to plan to study "cultural groups," i.e., designated groups of people with coherent, shared value systems, households or communities with clearly defined boundaries, or shared funds of knowledge transmitted primarily from adults to their children. Conventional assumptions of culture as coherent and co-terminus with social background, language use, region, religion, or ethnicity have become impossible to sustain. (p. 16)

In this more recent view, culture is grounded in shifting social networks and relationships as people who are members of a variety of communities present themselves to and are recognized by others (Clifford, 1986; Eisenhart, 2001). It is in the course of often-contested interactions that people identify themselves and are identified by others. As Calhoun (1996) notes, an explicit concern for issues of identity both in everyday life and in the social sciences is a defining aspect of the modern age.

> It is not simply—or even clearly the case—that it matters more to us than to our forebears to be who we are. Rather, it is much harder for us to establish who we are and maintain this own identity satisfactorily in our lives and in the recognition of others. (p. 32)

Calhoun goes on to clarify that the difficulties that we frequently face in establishing who we are stems both from the disintegration of all-encompassing identity schemes and from changes in discourse about identity. The modern age has brought about a questioning of social categories and social networks that were once taken for granted, thereby problematizing the process of determining who we are in relation to others. Calhoun demonstrates that this process is further complicated by socially sustained discourses that center on identity. It is not merely that how we are recognized often does not fit with who we consider ourselves to be. Discourse about who it is important to be and who it is possible to become is continually changing and may be in conflict with who people view themselves to be and who they want to become. A number of scholars have in fact coined the metaphor of people existing in the *borderlands* of various communities to capture their struggle to construct or maintain who they are (Gutierrez et al., 1999; Rosaldo, 1989).

The first view of culture as a way of life within a bounded community is far more prominent in the mathematics education research on equity. Research oriented by this view typically identifies discontinuities between the out-of-school practices in which students participate and those established in the mathematics classroom as the primary source of inequities. In more sophisticated investigations of this type, the significance of the discontinuities is clarified by locating them within the context of broader sociostructural process that encompass race, ethnicity, and social class and that account for the major fault lines within society. Researchers who take this approach emphasize that the relative value attributed to a particular practice in school typically reflects the differential position that the group with which the practice is associated occupies in society (cf. Abreu, 1995, 2000). The work of Moll (1997) and Civil (1998, this volume) is paradigmatic of one body of research that attempts to reorganize traditional patterns in schooling by taking the practices of students' home communities as its point of reference for classroom design. Civil describes how she and her colleagues collaborate with the mathematics teachers of predominantly Latino students to reduce conjectured sources of inequities by analyzing the practices of the students' home communities in terms of funds of knowledge. The goal in doing so is to develop innovative instructional activities and practices that build on students' out-of-school mathematical experiences.

Willis's (1977) seminal analysis of how British working-class students typically end up in working-class jobs is paradigmatic of investigations oriented by the second view of culture as local and dynamic. His ethnographic analysis of a group of working-class boys demonstrates how manifestations of the boys' working-class backgrounds were devalued in school. Like Moll and Civil, Willis places discontinuities in practices in the context of sociostructural processes. However, in contrast to researchers who are oriented by the view of culture as a way of life, Willis did not assume that the delegitimization of out-of-school practices in school necessarily leads to lack of academic success. It was not self-evident to him, for example, why the boys and their families did not demand better treatment so that they could move into the middle class. Rather than assuming that the boys were passive bearers of a working-class culture that had been passed down to them by their parents, he examined the meaning that the discontinuities he identified had for the boys. His analysis focused on the boys' identities and revealed that they could not reconcile accommodation to the school's expectations with who they were and who they wanted to be. He documents that the boys actively constructed a positive sense of their lives in school by drawing on a number of sources that included popular culture and their parents' shop-floor culture. Willis therefore concludes that the boys' resistance to the school was not predetermined by their socialization into a monolithic working-class culture. Instead, the boys actively contributed to the reproduction of their relatively low status in society by constructing a local counterculture and fashioning oppositional identities that involved a sense of self-worth and status. As he makes clear, this local culture was both dynamic and improvisational.

LOCAL CULTURES AND BROADER DISCOURSES

An issue that arises when culture is viewed as local and dynamic is that of how to account for the types of relatively broad and enduring macro patterns in people's individual and collective activity that are of interest to sociologists. Willis's analysis is again relevant as he did not set out to develop a narrative about a particular group of boys in Britain in the 1970s. Rather, he framed the boys' activity as a paradigm case to understand students' resistance to schooling more generally. Two aspects of his analysis contribute to its potential generalizability. First, he took account of the boys' position within class-stratified British society and documented that the school devalued manifestations of their working-class backgrounds. Second, he stressed that the cultural resources on which the boys could draw as they constructed their local counterculture and their oppositional identities were constrained by their positioning within broader sociostructural processes, the most evident of which is social class. On this basis, he argued that working-class students in other British high schools might be treated similarly and that some would attempt to make positive sense of their lives in school by drawing on similar cultural resources to create local countercultures that, while not identical, shared family resemblances. For Willis, the resulting pattern of resistance in different schools is an emergent phenomenon situated within but not directly caused by class stratification in British society. As Erickson (1992) notes, an explanation of this type would appear to be relevant to societies such as that of the United States in which the major sociostructural distinctions fall along lines of race and ethnicity as well as class (Erickson, 1992).

In this account of the production of relatively stable macro patterns, it is tempting to interpret the resources such as popular culture and their parents' shop floor culture on which the boys drew as ways of life that are characteristic of bounded communities. However, we have argued elsewhere (Cobb & Hodge, 2002) that it is more useful to treat these broader and more enduring practices as aspects of a Discourse. It is important to stress that a Discourse involves much more than linguistic practices. Gee (1997) offers the following definition:

> Discourses are sociohistorical coordinations of people, objects (props), ways of talking, acting, interacting, thinking, valuing, and (sometimes) writing and reading that allow for the display and recognition of socially significant identities, like being a (certain type of) African American, boardroom executive, feminist, lawyer, street-gang member, theoretical physicist, 18th-century midwife, 19th-century modernist, Soviet or Russian, schoolchild, teacher, and so on through innumerable possibilities. If you destroy a Discourse (and they do die), you also destroy its cultural models, situated meanings, and its concomitant identities. (pp. 255–256)

The crucial differences between culture and Discourse as theoretical constructs concerns their origins and what they take as central. The notion of culture has its origins in anthropology and sociology and emphasizes activities that transform the world and that involve the use of physical and symbolic artifacts. In contrast, the notion of a Discourse has its origins in linguistics and semiotics and emphasizes communication together with everything that makes it possible. Our proposal to follow Gutierrez et al. (1999) in viewing culture as a set of locally instantiated practices that are dynamic and improvisational in nature emphasizes people's mutual engagement in joint activities that involve the directly negotiated use of artifacts. In viewing broader practices that extend beyond the scope of mutual engagement as constituting a Discourse, we bring processes of communication beyond direct interaction to the fore.

As an illustration close to the experience of most mathematics educators, the various Standards documents produced by the National Council of Teachers of Mathematics ([NCTM] 1989, 1991, 2000) can be viewed as proposing an educational Discourse. Thus, a group of teachers who are members of a local professional teaching community might also view themselves as members of the broader community of mathematics education reformers. In such a case, the Standards documents serve as a primary resource on which the teachers draw as they jointly construct a local culture of mathematics teaching. As this illustration indicates, Discourses such as that of reform teaching tie local communities of practice into broader configurations (Wenger, 1998). It is only as people actively draw on a Discourse as a resource when improvising a local culture that the Discourse can touch their experience and be given new life (Holland et al., 1998; Wenger, 1998). On the one hand, Discourses constitute resources for the construction of local cultures. On the other hand, people contribute to both the vitality of a Discourse and to its ongoing evolution as they use it as a resource.

STRUCTURAL AND SITUATIONAL RATIONALES
FOR LEARNING IN SCHOOL

Erickson (1992) clarifies that achievement and motivation in school are explicitly political processes "in which issues of institutional and personal legitimacy, identity, and economic interest are central" (p. 33). For his part, D'Amato (1992) distinguishes between two ways in which learning in school can have value for students. D'Amato refers to the first of these ways as extrinsic value or *structural significance*, in that achievement in school has instrumental value as a means of attaining other ends such as entry to college and high-status careers, or acceptance and approval in the household and other social networks. D'Amato contrasts this source of value with what he terms intrinsic value or *situational significance*, in which students view their engagement in classroom activities as a means of maintaining valued relationships with peers and of gaining access to experiences of mastery and accomplishment. The crucial point to note for our purposes is that students' participation in Discourses that give them access to a structural rationale varies as a consequence of family history, race or ethnic history, class structure, and caste structure within society (D'Amato, 1992; Erickson, 1992; Mehan et al., 1994).

> Where school success has been associated with social mobility, as in the case of the middle and upper classes, the need to succeed in school [and in mathematics in particular] is emphasized in home-life networks, and children take for granted the value to their futures and to present social relationships of positive teacher evaluations and other markers of school success. . . . School, however, tends to have little credible structural significance for castelike minority children (Ogbu, 1978) and for the majority of children of lower socioeconomic strata. (D'Amato, 1992, p. 191)

In our terms, Discourses that inscribe the achievement ideology wherein society is seen to reward hard work and individual effort with future educational and economic opportunities constitute a resource on which some students but not others can draw as they attempt to make positive sense of their lives in school. From our perspective as mathematics educators interested in instructional design, the resulting inequities in motivation (Nicholls, 1989) emphasize the importance of ensuring that all students have access to a situational rationale for learning mathematics. It is here, we contend, that issues of equity can potentially intersect with mathematics educators' traditional focus on instructional design, teaching, and learning. In our view, supporting students' development of a sense of affiliation with mathematics as it is realized in their classrooms should be an explicit goal of both instructional design and teaching. Elsewhere, we have reported an initial attempt to address issues of instructional design by documenting an approach for cultivating students' mathematical interests (Cobb & Hodge, 2003a). In the remainder of this chapter, we focus on the challenge of analyzing classroom actions and interactions in a manner that can feed back to inform the improvement of such designs. The interpretive scheme that we outline focuses on the identities that students develop in mathematics classrooms.

IDENTITY AND LEARNING

The notion of identity has become increasingly prominent in the mathematics education research literature in recent years (Abreu, 1995; Boaler & Greeno, 2000; Cobb & Hodge, 2002; Gutstein, 2002a, 2002b; Sfard, 2002). Part of the appeal of this construct is that it enables researchers to broaden the scope of their analyses beyond an exclusive focus on the nature of students' mathematical reasoning by also considering the extent to which they have developed a sense of affiliation with and have come to see value in mathematics as it is realized in their classrooms. The notion of identity as it is used in mathematics education therefore encompasses a range of issues that are typically subsumed under the heading of affective factors. These include students' persistence, interest in, and motivation to engage in classroom mathematical activity. As Nasir (2002) clarifies, the development of students' classroom identities is intimately related to the development of their mathematical reasoning.

> [On the one hand,] as members of communities of practice experience changing (more engaged) identities, they come to learn new skills and bodies of knowledge, facilitating new ways of participating which, in turn, helps to create new identities relative to their community. . . . [On the other hand,] increasing identification with an activity or with a community of practice motivates new learning. In this sense, identities can act as a motivator for new learning, prompting practice participants to seek out and gain the new skills they need to participate in their practice more effectively. (pp. 239–240)

This interrelation underscores the importance of cultivating students' identification with mathematical activity as a goal for both instructional design and teaching.

The interpretive scheme that we propose for analyzing the identities that students develop in mathematics classrooms involves three primary constructs: normative identity, core identity, and personal identity. In this scheme, the *normative identity* as a doer of mathematics established in a particular classroom indicates the identity that students would have to develop in order to affiliate with mathematical activity as it is realized in that classroom (cf. Boaler & Greeno, 2000). To develop this sense of affiliation, a student would have to identify with the obligations that he or she would have to fulfill in order to be an effective and successful mathematics student in that classroom. The process of analyzing the normative identity established in a classroom therefore involves documenting the obligations that the teacher and students interactively constitute and continually regenerate in the course of their ongoing classroom interactions. The obligations that proved relevant in a previously completed investigation (Cobb & Hodge, 2003b) include general norms for classroom participation as well as several sociomathematical mathematical norms that are specific to mathematical activity: (1) norms for what counts as an acceptable mathematical argumentation, (2) normative ways of reasoning with tools and written symbols, (3) norms for what counts as mathematical understanding, and relatedly, (4) the normative purpose for engaging in mathe-matical activity. It is important to note that these specifically mathematical norms collectively serve to specify what counts as mathematical competence in a particu-lar classroom, and are *jointly constituted* by the teacher and students.

The process of delineating classroom norms involves identifying patterns or regularities in the teacher's and students' ongoing interactions. Consequently, the conjectures that are substantiated or refuted in the course of an analysis apply not to individual students' actions but to patterns in collective activity and to students' obligations as they contribute to the regeneration of these patterns. We would there-fore question accounts in which the teacher is portrayed as inviting students to adopt a normative identity as a doer of mathematics that exists independently of their classroom participation. Instead, in the perspective that we propose, students are seen to develop their personal identities in particular classrooms as they con-tribute to (or resist) the initial constitution and ongoing regeneration of the nor-mative identity as doers of mathematics.

Normative identity is concerned with the immediate social context of the class-room, whereas *core identity* is concerned with students' more enduring sense of who they are and who they want to become. We developed the notion of core iden-tity by drawing directly on the work of Gee (2001, 2003). Gee observes that stu-dents each have a unique trajectory of participation in the activities of various groups and communities both in and out of school. As a consequence of this per-sonal history of engagement, they have had a unique sequence of specific experi-ences of presenting themselves and being recognized in particular ways, some of which have recurred. "This trajectory and the person's narrativization . . . of it are what constitute his or her (never fully formed and always potentially changing) 'core identity'" (Gee, 2001, p. 111). Two aspects of this definition make it particu-larly relevant to our purposes as mathematics educators. First, in emphasizing stu-dents' active role in developing their life stories, Gee acknowledges personal agency as well as the social structures inherent in the activities in which they participate. It is therefore conceivable that students with similar life histories might develop markedly different core identities at any particular point in time. Second, Gee emphasizes that students' development of new personal identities in particular settings can involve changes in their core identities. This is important and alerts us to the possibility that students' development of particular personal identities in specific classroom settings might, over time, influence their more enduring sense of who they are and who they want to become.

A primary consideration when documenting students' core identities in rela-tion to schooling is to determine whether they have access to a structural rationale for learning in school and subscribe to an achievement ideology. Investigating this issue might involve using questionnaires or interviews that focus on a range of issues including (1) students' long-term aspirations, (2) their commitment to learning in school and in their mathematics classes, and (3) their assessments and explanations of other students' commitment to and perceptions of the benefits of succeeding in school and in their mathematics classes. As this proposal for data generation indicates, we question the common assumption that students' core identities can be equated with their membership of particular racial and ethnic groups (Gutierrez & Rogoff, 2003). Our intent in doing so is not to deny that a sense of affiliation with the common ancestry and cultural patterns of an ethnic group can be an important source of identity (Nasir & Saxe, 2003). Instead, it is to highlight students' personal agency in constructing multifaceted core identities while also acknowledging that their core identities are informed by who others say they are based on racial and ethnic group membership (Gee, 2003).

In taking this approach, we follow Martin (2000) in questioning Ogbu's (1992b, 1999) influential thesis that children of historically oppressed groups become skeptical about their prospects for social advancement as they are socialized into a collective cultural identity. In developing his thesis, Ogbu adopted the view of culture as a way of life characteristic of a bounded community. This view is apparent in his contention that historically oppressed groups have developed a monolithic cultural identity in opposition to institutions such as schools that are equated with assimilation into dominant social groups. His thesis is sociostructurally deterministic in that it implies that children of marginalized groups will resist instruction regardless of the teacher's actions in order to maintain a sense of affiliation with their cultural group. However, as Martin (2000) notes, Ogbu's appeal to the family as the locus of socialization into cultural values does not adequately account for the manner in which successful African American students come to identify with academic achievement. In contrast to Ogbu's notion of a collective cultural identity, the notion of core identity that we have presented reflects the view that cultures are local and dynamic and are constructed by using broader Discourses as resources. This perspective capitalizes on Ogbu's crucial insight about the importance of sociostructural processes but also acknowledges personal agency and treats the classroom as the immediate social context in which sociostructural processes play out in face to-face interaction. It is therefore a perspective that offers some hope to the instructional designer and the teacher by questioning the claim that interactions in mathematics classrooms necessarily have to unfold in a sociostructurally determined manner.

While core identity is concerned with students' relatively enduring sense of who they are and who they want to become, *personal identity* is concerned with who students are becoming in particular mathematics classrooms. The goal in analyzing students' personal identities is to document the extent to which they have reconciled their core identities with participation in the ongoing regeneration of the normative identity as a doer of mathematics established in their classroom. Personal identity as we define it is therefore an ongoing process of being a particular kind of person in the local social world of the classroom. The data generated might include questionnaires, surveys, and interviews that focus on students' understandings of both their general and their specifically mathematical obligations in the classroom, and on their valuations of those obligations. The intent in generating these data is to document (1) students' understandings of what counts as effectiveness and mathematical competence in their classrooms, and (2) whether and to what extent they identify with those forms of effectiveness and competence. The analysis of these data can therefore inform the interpretation of additional data that document students' assessments of their own and other students' mathematical competence in the classroom.

We can glean several distinctions in the types of personal identities that students might develop in their mathematics classes by synthesizing the available literature in mathematics education and related fields (Cobb & Hodge, 2003b). For example, students might reconcile their core identities with participation in the ongoing regeneration of the normative identity as doer of mathematics established in the classroom, thereby identifying with classroom mathematical activity (Cobb & Hodge, 2003b; Gutstein, 2002a, 2002b; Nasir & Hand, 2003). A second possibility is that students might reconcile their core identity with a broader goal for which succeeding in their mathematics classes is the means, such as going on to college and having a high-status career (Martin, 2000; Mehan et al., 1994; Nasir & Hand, 2003). In this case, striving to succeed in mathematics classes may not involve an experienced conflict, but neither does it involve identification with mathematical activity. A third possibility is that students might be unable to reconcile their core identity with the normative classroom identity but might nonetheless be willing to cooperate with the teacher in order to maintain relationships at home or with the teacher. In such cases, students experience an inner conflict or tension even as they strive to succeed in their mathematics classes, in the process becoming disenchanted with or alienated from mathematical activity (Boaler & Greeno, 2000; Cobb & Hodge, 2003b). A final possibility is that students might actively resist contributing to the establishment of the normative identity as a doer of mathematics, in the process developing oppositional classroom identities (Gutierrez, Rymes, & Larsen, 1995; Martin, 2000).

The first three of these four possibilities correspond to key distinctions made by self-determination theorists (Deci & Ryan, 2000; Grolnick, Deci, & Ryan, 1997; Ryan & Deci, 2000). Self-determination theory seeks to account for the inner adaptations that occur in the course of socialization such that children eventually accept and endorse the values and behaviors advocated by parents, experiencing them as their own. The three corresponding distinctions are (1) *regulation through integration*, in which the value of the activity has been fully integrated with the person's core identity; (2) *regulation through identification*, in which the person sees the activity as instrumentally important for his or her own goals; and (3) *introjected regulation*, in which the source of regulation is internal but has not been integrated with the self and thus gives rise to tensions and inner conflicts. To these distinctions, we add *regulation through opposition* to take account of the fourth possibility, in which students develop oppositional classroom identities. We should acknowledge that there are significant theoretical difference between self-determination theory and the perspective on identity that we have presented. Self-determination theory focuses on core identity and accounts for its development in terms of the internalization of preestablished norms. We, in contrast, differentiate between core identity and the personal identities that people construct as they participate in the activities of particular groups and communities. In our view, people reconstruct their core identities as they attempt to reconcile who they are and who they want to be with participation in particular groups and communities. Despite these differences, the parallels between the forms of regulation identified by self-determination theorists and the types of personal classroom identities that we have discerned add credibility to the latter.

To conclude this discussion of the interpretive scheme, we note that most prior investigations of the personal identities that students are developing in mathematics classrooms have restricted their focus to general norms of participation and to the degree of openness of instructional tasks. Although these analyses open up new, potentially productive lines of inquiry, the constructs employed are not specific to mathematics and could be employed to analyze the learning environments established in science or in social studies classes. The resulting characterizations of classroom environments are therefore relatively global and provide only limited guidance for instructional design and the improvement of mathematics instruction. In contrast, the analytic scheme that we have outlined focuses on the extent to which students have reconciled their core identities with several specifically mathematical norms. The scheme is therefore designed to produce analyses of students' engagement (or the lack thereof) in the mathematics classrooms that take account of both their core identities and of critical features of the learning environments established in those classrooms. The relatively detailed, targeted nature of the analyses contributes to their potential to inform instructional designers' and teachers' efforts to support students' development of a sense of affiliation with classroom mathematical activity.

CONCLUSION

We have said little about instructional design in this chapter, as our primary focus has been on understanding who students are becoming in mathematics classrooms. We can clarify the general implication of the perspective we have developed for design by noting with Dewey that the process of identifying with an activity is synonymous with the development of what he termed a true interest in that activity. Dewey (1913/1975) explicated this relation between students' interests and their personal identities in a particular settings by observing that "true interests are signs that some material, object, mode or skill (or whatever) is appreciated on the basis of what it actually does in carrying to fulfillment some mode of action with which a person has identified him[- or her]self" (p. 43). He also emphasized that motivation "expresses the extent to which the end foreseen is bound up with an activity with which the self is identified" (p. 60). In conceptualizing interests in this way,

Dewey took an explicitly developmental perspective and repeatedly emphasized that the evolution of students' interests is a deeply cultural process. This viewpoint implies that the cultivation of students' interest in engaging in mathematical activity should be an explicit goal of instructional design. Elsewhere, we have followed diSessa (2001) in making an initial contribution to the development of a theory of this type (Cobb & Hodge, 2003a). A theory of this type would orient the development of designs, whereas the perspective that we have presented on identity guides analyses that inform the improvement of such designs.

In the first part of this chapter, we noted that research on equity has generally been marginalized within mainstream mathematics education research. The interpretive scheme we have outlined is the product of our efforts to make a concern for issues of equity integral to our ongoing research. Theoretically, it is premised on the view of broad Discourses as resources on which people draw to construct local, dynamic cultures. It therefore reflects a shift away from the more established view of culture as a way of life that is characteristic of a bounded community. Pragmatically, the interpretive scheme is premised on the assumption that supporting students' development of a sense of affiliation with classroom mathematical activity should be an explicit goal of instructional design and teaching. Although this proposal complicates the process of developing instructional designs, the potential payoff is substantial. In complementing the traditional focus on students' mathematical reasoning with a concern for who they are becoming in mathematics classrooms, we necessarily make an interest in issues of equity an integral aspect of mainstream research in mathematics education. In our view, this opportunity is too important to pass up.

NOTE

The analysis presented in this chapter was supported by the National Science Foundation under Grant Nos. REC 9902982 and REC 0231037 and by the Office of Educational Research and Improvement under Grant No. R305A60007. The opinions expressed in this chapter do not necessarily reflect the position, policy, or endorsement of the foundation.

References

Abreu, G. de. (1993). *The relationship between home and school mathematics in a farming community in rural Brazil.* Doctoral dissertation, University of Cambridge, UK.

Abreu, G. de. (1995). Understanding how children experience the relationship between home and school mathematics. *Mind, Culture and Activity: An International Journal, 2*(2), 119–142.

Abreu, G. de. (1999). Learning mathematics in and outside school: Two views on situated learning. In J. Bliss, R. Saljo, & P. Light (Eds.), *Learning sites: Social and technological resources for learning* (pp. 17–31). Oxford: Elsevier Science.

Abreu, G. de (2000). Relationships between macro and micro socio-cultural contexts: Implications for the study of interactions in the mathematics classroom. *Educational Studies in Mathematics, 41,* 1–29.

Abreu, G. de. (2002). Mathematics learning in out-of-school contexts: A cultural psychology perspective. In L. D. English (Ed.), *Handbook of international research in mathematics education* (pp. 323–353). New Jersey: Lawrence Erlbaum.

Abreu, G. de, & Cline, T. (2003a). *Parents' representations of their children's mathematics learning in multiethnic primary schools.* University of Luton, UK: Department of Psychology.

Abreu, G. de, & Cline, T. (2003b). Schooled mathematics and cultural knowledge. *Pedagogy, Culture and Society, 1*(1), 11–30.

Abreu, G. de, Cline, T., & Cowan, L. (2000). Investigating children's social representations of mathematics. International Conference on Communication, Problem Solving and Learning, June 25–29, University of Strathclyde, Glasgow, Scotland.

Abreu, G. de, Cline, T., & Radia-Bond, B. (2001). The mediating role of language use and home background in children's mathematical learning: The perspectives of monolingual and bilingual teachers. Paper presented at the 9th European Conference for Research on Learning and Instruction, Fribourg, Switzerland.

Abreu, G. de, Cline, T., & Shamsi, T. (1999). *Mathematics learning in multiethnic primary schools* (ESRC-R000 222 381). Luton, UK: Department of Psychology, University of Luton.

Abreu, G. de, Cline, T., & Shamsi, T. (2002). Exploring ways parents participate in their children's school mathematical learning: Case studies in a multi-ethnic primary school. In G. de Abreu, A. Bishop, & N. Presmeg (Eds.), *Transitions between contexts of mathematical practices* (pp. 123–147). Dordrecht: Kluwer.

Abreu, G. de, & Lambert, H. (2003). *The education of Portuguese students in England and the Channel Islands schools. Final Report.* Luton, UK: Department of Psychology, University of Luton.

Addington, S. L., & Lipka, J. (2000, September). *Representations of multiplicative concepts in Yupiik culture.* Paper presented at a conference on equity in mathematics education. Northwestern University, Chicago.

Adler, J. (1998). A language of teaching dilemmas: Unlocking the complex multilingual secondary mathematics classroom. *For the Learning of Mathematics, 18*(1), 24–33.

Anderson, G., Herr, K., & Nihlen, A. (1994). *Studying your own school: An educator's guide to qualitative practitioner research.* Thousand Oaks, CA: Corwin Press.

Anderson, S. (1990). World mathematics curriculum: Fighting Eurocentrism in mathematics. *Journal of Negro Education, 59,* 348–359.

Anyon, J. (1981). Social class and school knowledge. *Curriculum Inquiry, 11,* 3–42.

Apple, M. (1995a). Taking power seriously: New directions in equity in mathematics education and beyond. In W. Secada, E. Fennema, & L. B. Adajian (Eds.), *New directions for equity in mathematics education* (pp. 329–348). Cambridge: Cambridge University Press.

Apple, M. (1995b). Taking power seriously. In W. Secada, E. Fennema, & M. Apple, *Cultural politics and education.* New York: Teachers College Press.

Apple, M. (2000). Mathematics reform through conservative modernization? Standards, markets, and inequality in education. In J. Boaler (Ed.), *Multiple perspectives on mathematics teaching and learning* (pp. 243–259). Westport, CT: Ablex.

Apple, M. (2001). *Educating the right way: Markets, standards, god, and inequality.* New York: RoutledgeFalmer.

Bakhtin, M. (1981). *The dialogic imagination: Four essays by M. M. Bakhtin.* Austin: University of Texas Press.

Ball, D. (1993). With an eye on the mathematical horizon: Dilemmas of teaching elementary school mathematics. *Elementary School Journal, 93*(4), 373–397.

Banks, J. (1988). Ethnicity, class, cognitive, and motivational styles: Research and teaching implications. *Journal of Negro Education, 57,* 452–466.

Bateson, G. (2000). *Steps to an ecology of mind.* Chicago: University of Chicago Press.

Bauman, Z. (1999). *Culture as praxis.* London: Sage.

Benacerraf, P., & Putnam, H. (Eds.). (1983). *Philosophy of mathematics: Selected readings* (2nd ed.). New York: Cambridge University Press.

Benbow, C., & Stanley, J. (1980). Sex differences in mathematical ability: Fact or artifact. *Science, 210,* 1262–1264.

Bernstein, B. (1975). *Class, codes, and control* (Vol. 3). Boston: Routledge & Kegan Paul.

Blachowicz, C., & Fisher, P. (2000). Vocabulary instruction. In M. Kamil, P. Mosenthal, P. D. Pearson, & R. Barr (Eds.), *Handbook of reading research* (Vol. 3, pp. 503–523). Mahwah, NJ: Lawrence Erlbaum Associates.

Bloor, D. (1994). What can the sociologist of knowledge say about 2 + 2 = 4? In P. Ernest (Ed.), *Mathematics, education, and philosophy: An international perspective* (pp. 21–32). London: Falmer Press.

Boaler, J. (1997a). Equity, empowerment, and different ways of knowing. *Mathematics Education Research Journal, 9,* 325–342.

Boaler, J. (1997b). *Experiencing school mathematics: Teaching styles, sex, and setting.* Philadelphia: Open University Press.

Boaler, J. (1997c). Reclaiming school mathematics: The girls fight back. *Gender and Education, 9*(3), 285–305.

Boaler, J. (1999). Participation, knowledge, and beliefs: A community perspective on mathematics learning. *Educational Studies in Mathematics, 40*(3), 259–281.

Boaler, J. (2000a). Exploring situated insights into research and learning. *Journal for Research in Mathematics Education, 31*(1), 113–119.

Boaler, J. (2000b). Mathematics from another world: Traditional communities and the alienation of learners. *Journal of Mathematical Behavior, 18*(4), 379–397.

Boaler, J. (2002a). *Experiencing school mathematics: Traditional and reform approaches to teaching and their impact on student learning.* (Rev. and exp. ed.) Mahwah, NJ: Lawrence Erlbaum Association.

Boaler, J. (2002b). Learning from teaching: Exploring the relationship between reform curriculum and equity. *Journal for Research in Mathematics Education, 33*(4), 239–258.

Boaler, J. (2002c). Paying the price for sugar and spice: Shifting the analytical lens in equity research. *Mathematical Thinking and Learning, 4*(2 & 3), 127–144.

Boaler, J., & Greeno, J. (2000). Identity, agency, and knowing in mathematical worlds. In J. Boaler (Ed.), *Multiple perspectives on mathematics teaching and learning* (pp. 171–200). Westport, CT: Ablex.

Bohlin, C. (1994). Learning style factors and mathematics performance: Sex-related differences. *International Journal of Educational Research, 21*, 387–398.

Bourdieu, P. (1973). Cultural reproduction and social reproduction. In R. Brown (Ed.), *Knowledge, education, and cultural change* (pp. 71–112). London: Tavistock.

Bourdieu, P. (1982). The school as a conservative force: Scholastic and cultural inequalities. In E. Bredo & W. Feinberg (Eds.), *Knowledge and values in social and educational research* (pp. 391–407). Philadelphia: Temple University Press.

Bourdieu, P. (1986). The forms of capital. In J. Richardson (Ed.)., *Handbook of theory and research for the sociology of education* (pp. 241–258). New York: Greenwood Press.

Brenner, M. (1994). A communication framework for mathematics: Exemplary instruction for culturally and linguistically diverse students. In B. McLeod (Ed.), *Language and learning: Educating linguistically diverse students* (pp. 233–268). Albany: State University of New York Press.

Brown, J. S., Collins, A., & Duguid, P. (1989). Situated cognition and the culture of learning. *Educational Researcher, 18*(1), 32–42.

Brown, T. (1994). Describing the mathematics you are part of: A post-structuralist account of mathematical learning. In P. Ernest (Ed.), *Mathematics, education, and philosophy: An international perspective* (pp. 154–162). London: Falmer Press.

Bruner, J. (1975). Poverty and childhood. *Oxford Review of Education, 1*, 31–50.

Bruner, J. (1986). *Actual minds, possible worlds.* Cambridge, MA: Harvard University Press.

Burkhardt, H., & Schoenfeld, A. (2003). Improving educational research: Toward a more useful, more influential, and better funded enterprise. *Educational Researcher, 32*(9), 3–14.

Burton, L. (1990). *Gender and mathematics: An international perspective.* London: Cassell.

Burton, L. (1994). Whose culture includes mathematics? In S. Lerman (Ed.), *Cultural perspectives on the mathematics classroom* (pp. 69–83). Kluwer Academic.

Butler, J. (1993). *Bodies that matter: On the discursive limits of sex.* London: Routledge.

Cain, C. (n.d.). *Personal stories: Identity acquisition and self-understanding in Alcoholics Anonymous.* Unpublished manuscript.

Calhoun, C. (1996). Social theory and the politics of identity. In C. Calhoun (Ed.), *Social theory and the politics of identity* (pp. 9–36). Cambridge, MA: Blackwell.

Campbell, P. (1986). What's a nice girl like you doing in a math class? *Phi Delta Kappan, 67*(7), 516–520.

Campbell, P. (1991). So what do we do with the poor, non-White female? Issues of gender, race, and social class in mathematics and equity. *Peabody Journal of Education, 66*(2), 95–112.

Campbell, P., & Clewell, B. C. (1999, September 15). Science, math and girls: Still a long way to go. *Education Week*, pp. 50, 53.

Carraher, T. (1986). From drawings to buildings: Working with mathematical scales. *International Journal of Behavioral Development, 9*, 527–544.

Chazan, D., & D. L. Ball (1999). Beyond being told not to tell. *For the Learning of Mathematics, 9*(20), 2–10.

Civil, M. (1993). Household visits and teachers' study groups: Integrating mathematics to a sociocultural approach to instruction. In J. R. Becker & B. J. Pence (Eds.), *Proceedings of the Fifteenth Annual Conference of the North American Chapter of the International Group for the Psychology of Mathematics Education* (Vol. 2, pp. 49–55). Pacific Grove, CA: San Jose State University.

Civil, M. (2000, September). *Bridging in-school and out-of-school mathematics*. Paper presented at a conference on equity in mathematics education. Northwestern University, Chicago, IL.

Civil, M. (2002a). Culture and mathematics: A community approach. *Journal of Intercultural Studies, 23*(2), 133–148.

Civil, M. (2002b). Everyday mathematics, mathematicians' mathematics, and school mathematics: Can we bring them together? In M. Brenner & J. Moschkovich (Eds.), *Everyday and academic mathematics in the classroom* (Journal of Research in Mathematics Education Monograph No. 11) (pp. 40–62). Reston, VA: National Council of Teachers of Mathematics.

Civil, M., & Andrade, R. (2002). Transitions between home and school mathematics: Rays of hope amidst the passing clouds. In G. de Abreu, A. J. Bishop, & N. C. Presmeg (Eds.), *Transitions Between contexts of mathematical practices* (pp. 149–169). Boston: Kluwer.

Civil, M., & Andrade, R. (2003). Collaborative practice with parents: The role of the researcher as mediator. In A. Peter-Koop, V. Santos-Wagner, C. Breen, & A. Begg (Eds.), *Collaboration in teacher education: Examples from the context of mathematics education* (pp. 153–168). Boston: Kluwer.

Civil, M., & Kahn, L. (2001). Mathematics instruction developed from a garden theme. *Teaching Children Mathematics, 7*, 400–405.

Civil, M., & Planas, N. (2004). Participation in the mathematics classroom: Does every student have a voice? *For the Learning of Mathematics, 24*(1), 7–12.

Clark, K., & Clark, M. (1950). Emotional factors in racial identification and preference in Negro children. *Journal of Negro Education, 19*, 341–350.

Clifford, J. (1986). Introduction: Partial truths. In J. Clifford & G. Marcus (Eds.), *Writing culture: The poetics and politics of ethnography* (pp. 1–26). Berkeley: University of California Press.

Cline, T., Abreu, G., Fihosy, C., Gray, H., Lambert, H., & Neale, J. (2002). *Minority ethnic pupils in mainly white schools*. London: Department for Education and Skills.

Cobb, G. (1997). Mere literacy is not enough. In L. S. Steen (Ed.), *Why numbers count: Quantitative literacy for tomorrow's America*. New York: College Examination Board.

Cobb, P. (1994). Constructivism in mathematics and science education. *Educational Researcher, 23*(7), 4.

Cobb, P. (1999). Individual and collective mathematical learning: The case of statistical data analysis. *Mathematical Thinking and Learning, 1*, 5–44.

Cobb, P., & Bauersfeld, H. (Eds.). (1995). *The emergence of mathematical meaning: Interaction in classroom cultures*. Hillsdale, NJ: Lawrence Erlbaum Associates.

Cobb, P., & Hodge, L. (2002). A relational perspective on issues of cultural diversity and equity as they play out in the mathematics classroom. *Mathematical Thinking and Learning, 4,* 249–284.

Cobb, P., & Hodge, L. (2003a, April). *An initial contribution to the development of a design theory of mathematical interests: The case of statistical data analysis.* Paper presented at the annual meeting of the American Educational Research Association, Chicago.

Cobb, P., & Hodge, L. (2003b, August). *An interpretive scheme for analyzing the identities that students develop in mathematics classrooms.* Tenth conference of the European Association for Research on Learning and Instruction, Padua, Italy.

Cobb, P., Wood, T, & Yackel, E. (1993). Discourse, mathematical thinking, and classroom practice. In E. Forman, N. Minick, & C. A. Stone (Eds.), *Contexts for learning: Sociocultural dynamics in children's development* (pp. 91–119). New York: Oxford University Press.

Cobb, P., & Yackel, E. (1996). Constructivist, emergent, and sociocultural perspectives in the context of developmental research. *Educational Psychologist, 31*(3/4), 175–190.

Cohen, M. (1999). A habit of 'healthy idleness': Boys' underachievement in historical perspective. In J. Elwood, D. Epstein, & V. Hey (Eds.), *Failing boys? Issues in gender and achievement* (pp. 19–34). Buckingham, U.K.: Open University Press.

Cole, M. (1977). An ethnographic psychology of cognition. In P. N. Johnson-Laird & P. C. Wason (Eds.), *Thinking* (pp. 468–482). Cambridge: Cambridge University Press.

Cole, M. (1996). *Cultural psychology: A once and future discipline.* Cambridge: Harvard University Press.

Cole, M. (1995). Culture and cognitive development: from cross-cultural research to creating systems of cultural mediation. *Culture & Psychology, 1,* 25–54.

Cole, M., & Bruner, J. S. (1971). Cultural differences and inferences about psychological processes. *American Psychologist, 26*(10), 867–876.

Cooper, B., & Dunne, M. (2000). *Assessing children's mathematical knowledge: Social class, sex, and problem-solving.* Philadelphia, PA: Open University Press.

Cornell, S., & Hartmann, D. (1998). *Ethnicity and race: Making identities in a changing world.* Thousand Oaks, CA: Pine Forge Press.

Cross, W. (1991). *Shades of Black: Diversity in African-American identity.* Philadelphia: Temple University Press.

Cuevas, G. (1983). Language proficiency and the development of mathematics concepts in Hispanic primary school students. In T. H. Escobedo (Ed.), *Early childhood bilingual education: A Hispanic perspective* (pp. 148–163). New York: Teachers College Press.

Cuevas, G., Mann, P., & McClung, R. (1986, April). *The effects of a language process approach program on the mathematics achievement of first, third, and fifth graders.* Paper presented at the annual meeting of the American Educational Research Association, San Francisco.

Dale, T., & Cuevas, G. (1987). Integrating language and mathematics learning. In J. Crandall (Ed.), *ESL through content area instruction: Mathematics, science, and social studies* (pp. 9–54). Englewood Cliffs, NJ: Prentice Hall.

D'Amato, J. (1992). Resistance and compliance in minority classrooms. In E. Jacobs & C. Jordan (Eds.), *Minority education: Anthropological perspectives* (pp. 181–208). Norwood, NJ: Ablex.

D'Ambrosio, U. (1985). Ethnomathematics and its place in the history and pedagogy of mathematics. *Educational Studies in Mathematics, 5,* 44–48.

D'Ambrosio, U. (1990). The role of mathematics education in building a democratic and just society. *For the Learning of Mathematics, 10,* 20–23.

D'Ambrosio, U. (1999). Literacy, matheracy, and technocracy: A trivium for today. *Mathematical Thinking and Learning, 1,* 131–153.

Darder, A. (2002). *Reinventing Paulo Freire: A pedagogy of love.* Boulder, CO: Westview Press.

Davidson, A. L. (1996). *Making and molding identities in schools: Student narratives on race, gender, and academic engagement.* Albany: State University of New York Press.

Davis, F. (1990). Assessing science education: A case for multiple perspectives. In G. Hein (Ed.), *The assessment of hands-on elementary science programs.* Grand Forks: University of North Dakota Press.

Davis, F. (1998). Assessment, evaluation, mathematics education reform, and African-American students: A framework. In C. Malloy & Brader-Araje (Eds.), *Challenges in the mathematics education of African-American students.* Reston, VA: National Council of Teachers of Mathematics.

Davis, F. (2003). *A framework for understanding how mathematical meaning is transacted between teacher and students in classrooms.* Paper presented at the annual meeting of the American Educational Research Association, Chicago.

Davis, F., & West, M. (2000). *The impact of the Algebra Project on mathematics achievement.* Cambridge, MA: Program Evaluation & Research Group, Lesley University.

De Corte, E., Greer, B., & Verschaffel, L. (1996). Mathematics learning and teaching. In D. Berliner & R. Calfee (Eds.), *Handbook of educational psychology* (pp. 491–540). New York: Macmillan.

Deci, E., & Ryan, R. (2000). The what and why of goal pursuits: Human needs and the self-determination of behavior. *Psychological Inquiry, 11,* 227–268.

Delon, F. (1995). The French experience: The effects of de-segregation. In P. Rogers & G. Kaiser (Eds.), *Equity in Mathematics Education* (pp. 141–146). London: Falmer Press.

Delpit, L. (1988). The silenced dialogue: Power and pedagogy in educating other people's children. *Harvard Educational Review, 58*(3), 280–298.

Delpit, L. (1995). *Other people's children: Cultural conflict in the classroom.* New York: New Press.

Delpit, L. (2002). No kinda sense. In L. Delpit & J. K. Dowdy (Eds.), *The skin that we speak.* New York: New Press.

Devlin, K (1998). *The language of mathematics.* New York: W. H. Freeman.

Dewey, J. (1913/1975). *Interest and effort in education.* Carbondale: Southern Illinois University Press.

diSessa, A. (2001). *Changing minds: Computers, learning, and literacy.* Cambridge, MA: MIT Press.

Dowling, P. (1998). *The sociology of mathematics education: Mathematical myths/pedaogic texts.* Washington, DC: Falmer Press.

Duberman, L. (1976). *Social inequality: Class and caste in America.* Philadelphia: J. B. Lippincott.

Dweck, C. (1986). Motivational processes affecting learning [*Special issue: Psychological science and education*] *American Psychologist, 41,* 1040–1048.

Eisenhart, M. (2001). Changing conceptions of culture and ethnographic methodology: Recent thematic shifts and their implications for research on teaching. In V. Richardson

(Ed.), *The Handbook of Research on Teaching* (4th ed.). Washington, DC: American Educational Research Association.

Engestrom, Y. (1999). Activity theory and individual and social transformation. In Y. Engestrom, R. Miettinen, & R. Punamaki (Eds.), *Perspectives on activity theory* (pp. 19–38). New York: Cambridge.

Engle, R., & Conant, F. (2002). Guiding principles for fostering productive disciplinary engagement: Explaining an emergent argument in a community of learners classroom. *Cognition and Instruction, 20,* 399–483.

Erickson, F. (1992). Transformation and school success: The politics and culture of educational achievement. In E. Jacobs & C. Jordan (Eds.), *Minority education: Anthropological perspectives* (pp. 27–51). Norwood, NJ: Ablex.

Erikson, E. (1968). *Identity, youth, and crisis.* New York: Norton.

Ernest, P. (Ed.). (1994). *Mathematics, education, and philosophy: An international perspective.* Washington, DC: Falmer Press.

Fennema, E. (1981). Women and mathematics: Does research matter? *Journal for Research in Mathematics Education, 12,* 380–385.

Fennema, E., & Carpenter, T. (1998a). New perspectives on gender differences in mathematics: An introduction. *Educational Researcher, 27*(5), 4–5.

Fennema, E., & Carpenter, T. (Eds.). (1998b). New perspectives on gender differences in mathematics. Special issue of *Educational Researcher, 27*(5).

Fennema, E., Carpenter, T., Jacobs, V., Franke, M., & Levi, L. (1998). A longitudinal study of gender differences in young children's mathematical thinking. *Educational Researcher, 27*(5), 6–11.

Fennema, E., & Hart, L. (1994). Gender and the JRME. *Journal for Research in Mathematics Education, 25*(6), 648–659.

Fordham, S., (1996). *Blacked out: Dilemmas of race, identity, and success at Capitol High.* Chicago: University of Chicago Press.

Fordham, S., & Ogbu, J. (1986). Black students and school success: Coping with the burden of acting white. *Urban Review, 18*(3), 176–206.

Forman, E. (1996). Learning mathematics as participation in classroom practice: Implications of sociocultural theory for educational reform. In L. Steffe, P. Nesher, P. Cobb, G. Goldin, & B. Greer (Eds.), *Theories of mathematical learning* (pp. 115–130). Mahwah, NJ: Lawrence Erlbaum Associates.

Forman, E. (2003). A sociocultural approach to mathematics reform: Speaking, inscribing, and doing mathematics within communities of practice. In J. Kilpatrick, W. G. Martin, & D. Schifter (Eds.), *A research companion to the NCTM Standards* (pp. 333–353). Reston, VA: National Council of Teachers of Mathematics.

Frankenstein, M. (1987). Critical mathematics education: An application of Paulo Freire's epistemology. In I. Shor (Ed.), *Freire for the classroom: A sourcebook for liberatory teaching* (pp. 180–210). Portsmouth, NH: Boyton/Cook.

Frankenstein, M. (1990). Incorporating race, gender, and class issues into a critical mathematical literacy curriculum. *Journal of Negro Education, 59,* 336–347.

Frankenstein, M. (1998). Reading the world with math: Goals for a critical mathematical literacy curriculum. In E. Lee, D. Menkart, & M. Okazawa-Rey (Eds.), *Beyond heroes and holidays: A practical guide to K–12 anti-racist, multicultural education and staff development* (pp. 306–313). Washington DC: Network of Educators on the Americas.

Freire, P. (1970). *Pedagogy of the oppressed.* New York: Continuum.

Freire, P. (1970/1998). *Pedagogy of the oppressed.* (M. B. Ramos, Trans.). New York: Continuum.

Freire, P. (1994). *Pedagogy of hope: Reliving* Pedagogy of the Oppressed (R. R. Barr, Trans.). New York: Continuum.

Freire, P. (1998). *Pedagogy of freedom: Ethics, democracy, and civic courage.* New York: Roman & Littlefield.

Freire, P., & Faundez, A. (1992). *Learning to question: A pedagogy of liberation* (T. Coates, Trans.). New York: Continuum.

Freire, P., & Macedo, D. (1987). *Literacy: Reading the word and the world.* Westport, CT: Bergin & Garvey.

Friedman, L. (1989). Mathematics and the gender gap: A meta-analysis of recent studies on sex differences in mathematical tasks. *Review of Educational Research, 59,* 185–213.

Friedman, L. (1995). Assisting women to complete graduate degrees. In P. Rogers & G. Kaiser (Eds.), *Equity in mathematics education* (pp. 49–58). London: Falmer Press.

Garcia, E., & Gonzalez, R. (1995). Issues in systemic reform for culturally and linguistically diverse students. *Teachers College Record, 96*(3), 418–431.

Gay, G. (2000). *Culturally responsive teaching: Theory, research, and practice.* New York: Teachers College Press.

Gee, J. (1996). *Social linguistics and literacies: Ideology in discourses* (3rd ed.). London: Falmer Press.

Gee, J. (1997). Thinking, learning, and reading: The situated sociocultural mind. In D. Kirshner & J. A. Whitson (Eds.), *Situated cognition: Social, semiotic, and psychological perspectives* (pp. 235–260). Mahwah, NJ: Lawrence Erlbaum Associates.

Gee, J. (1999). *An introduction to discourse analysis: Theory and method.* New York: Routledge.

Gee, J. (2001). Identity as an analytic lens for research in education. In W. Secada (Ed.), *Review of research in education* (Vol. 25, pp. 99–126). Washington, DC: American Educational Research Association.

Gee, J. (2003). *What do video games have to teach us about learning literacy?* New York: Palgrave/Macmillan.

Geertz, C. (2000). *The interpretation of cultures.* New York: Basic Books.

Gibson, J. (1986). *The ecological approach to visual perception.* Hillsdale, NJ: Lawrence Erlbaum.

Gibson, M. (1988). *Accommodation without assimilation: Sikh immigrants in an American high school.* Ithaca: Cornell University Press.

Gillborn, D., & Mirza, H. S. (2000). *Educational inequality: Mapping race, class and gender—a synthesis of research evidence* . London: Office for Standards in Education.

Gilligan, C. (1982). *In a different voice: Psychological theory and women's development.* Cambridge, MA: Harvard University Press.

Ginsberg, H, & Russell, R. (1981). Social class and racial influences on mathematical thinking. *Monographs for the Society for Research in Child Development, 46*(6), 1–68.

Giroux, H., Lankshear, C., McLaren, P., & Peters, M. (1996). *Counternarratives: Cultural studies and critical pedagogies in postmodern spaces.* New York: Routledge.

González, N. (Ed.). (1995a). Educational innovation: Learning from households. *Practicing Anthropology, 17*(3), 3–24.

González, N. (1995b). Processual approaches to multicultural education. *Journal of Applied Behavioral Science, 31*(2), 234–244.

González, N. (1996). Applied anthropology as educational innovation: Learning from households. In L. Moll, N. Gonzalez, M. Civil (Principal investigators), *Final Report: Funds of knowledge for teaching.* Unpublished report

González, N. (1999). What will we do when culture does not exist anymore? *Anthropology and Education Quarterly, 30*(4), 431–435.

González, N., Andrade, R., Civil, M., & Moll, L. C. (2001). Bridging funds of distributed knowledge: Creating zones of practices in mathematics. *Journal of Education for Students Placed at Risk, 6*(1 & 2), 115–132.

González, N., Moll, L., & Amanti, C. (Eds.). (2005). *Funds of knowledge: Theorizing practice in households, communities, and classrooms.* Mahwah, NJ: Erlbaum Associates.

Goodnow, J. J. (1990). The socialization of cognition: What's involved? In J. W. Stiegler, R. A. Shweder, & G. Herdt (Eds.), *Cultural Psychology* (pp. 259–286). Cambridge: Cambridge University Press.

Goodnow, J. J. (2000). Combining analysis of culture and of cognition. *Human Development, 43,* 115–125.

Graham, S., Taylor, A., & Hudley, C. (1998). Exploring achievement values among ethnic minority early adolescents. *Journal of Educational Psychology, 90*(4), 606–620.

Gravemeijer, K., Cobb, P., Bowers, J., & Whitenack, J. (2000). Symbolizing, modeling, and instructional design. In P. Cobb, E. Yackel, & K. McClain (Eds.), *Symbolizing and communicating in mathematics classrooms.* Mahwah, NJ: Erlbaum.

Greeno, J. (1994, August). *The situativity of learning: Prospects for syntheses in theory, practice, and research.* Paper presented at the annual meeting of the American Psychological Association, Los Angeles.

Greeno, J. (1998). Trajectories of participation and practice: Some dynamic aspects of the thinking practices of teaching, educational design, and research. In J. Greeno & S. Goldman, *Thinking Practices in Mathematics and Science Learning.* Mahwah, NJ: Lawrence Erlbaum.

Greeno, J. (2001). *Students with competence, authority and accountability: Affording intellective identities in classrooms.* New York: College Board.

Greeno, J., & MMAP. (1998). The situativity of knowing, learning, and research. *American Psychologist, 53*(1), 5–26.

Gresalfi, M. (2004). *Taking up opportunities to learn: Examining the construction of mathematical identities in middle school classrooms.* Palo Alto: Stanford University.

Gresalfi, M., Martin, H. T., Hand, V., & Greeno, J. G. (In preparation). *Constructing competence: An analysis of student participation in the activity systems of mathematics classrooms.* Available from Melissa Gresalfi, Vanderbilt University, 250-2 Wyatt Center, Nashville, TN 37203.

Grolnick, W., Deci, E., & Ryan, R. (1997). Internalization within the family: The self-determination theory perspective. In J. E. Grusec & L. Kuczynski (Eds.), *Parenting and children's internalization of values* (pp. 135–161). New York: Wiley.

Gutierrez, K., Baquedano-Lopez, P., & Tejeda, C. (1999). Rethinking diversity: Hybridity and hybrid language practices in the third space. *Mind, Culture, and Activity, 41,* 286–303.

Gutierrez, K., & Rogoff, B. (2003). Cultural ways of learning. *Educational Researcher, 32*(5), 19–25.

Gutierrez, K., Rymes, B., & Larson, J. (1995). Script, counterscript, and underlife in the classroom: James Brown versus *Brown v. Board of Education. Harvard Educational Review, 65*(3), 445–471.

Gutiérrez, R. (1996). Practices, beliefs, and cultures of high school mathematics departments: Understanding their influence on student advancement. *Journal of Curriculum Studies, 28,* 495–529.

Gutiérrez, R. (1999a). Advancing urban Latino youth in mathematics: Lessons from an effective high school mathematics department. *Urban Review, 31,* 263–281.

Gutiérrez, R. (1999b). *The politics of implementing an equity-based reform: The role of teacher community.* Unpublished manuscript.

Gutiérrez, R. (2000a). Advancing African American, urban youth in mathematics: Unpacking the success of one mathematics department. *American Journal of Education, 109*(1), 63–111.

Gutiérrez, R. (2000b, April). *Advancing urban Latina/o youth in mathematics: The power of teacher community.* Paper presented at the annual meeting of the National Council of Teachers of Mathematics, Chicago.

Gutiérrez, R. (2000c). Enabling the practice of mathematics teachers in context: Toward a new research agenda. *Mathematical Thinking and Learning, 4,* 145–189.

Gutiérrez, R. (2000d). Is the multiculturalization of mathematics doing us more harm than good? In R. Mahalingam & C. McCarthy (Eds.), *Multicultural curriculum: New directions for social theory, practice, and policy* (pp. 199–219). New York: Routledge.

Gutiérrez, R. (2002). Enabling the practice of teachers in context: Toward a new equity research agenda. *Mathematical Thinking and Learning, 4*(2 & 3), 145–187.

Gutiérrez, R. (2003) Beyond essentialism: The complexity of language in teaching Latina/o students mathematics. *American Educational Research Journal, 39*(4), 1047–1088.

Gutstein, E. (2002a, April). *Roads towards equity in mathematics education: Helping students develop a sense of agency.* Paper presented at the annual meeting of the American Educational Research Association, New Orleans.

Gutstein, E. (2002b, April). *Teaching and learning mathematics for social justice in an urban Latino school.* Paper presented at the research presession of the annual meeting of the National Council of Teachers of Mathematics, Las Vegas.

Gutstein, E. (2003). Teaching and learning mathematics for social justice in an urban, Latino school. *Journal for Research in Mathematics Education, 34*(1), 37–73.

Gutstein, E. (2005). *Reading and writing the world with mathematics.* Manuscript in preparation.

Gutstein, E., Lipman, P., Hernandez, P., & de los Reyes, R. (1997). Culturally relevant mathematics teachers in a Mexican-American context. *Journal for Research in Mathematics Education, 28,* 709–737.

Habibullah, S. (1995). Gender inequity in education: A non-Western perspective. In P. Rogers & G. Kaiser (Eds.), *Equity in Mathematics Education* (pp. 126–128). London: Falmer Press.

Halliday, M. (1978). Sociolinguistics aspects of mathematical education. In M. Halliday, *The social interpretation of language and meaning* (pp. 194–204). London: University Park Press.

Hammersley, M., & Atkinson, P. (1983). *Ethnography: Principles in practice.* London: Tavistock.

Hart, B., & Risley, T. R. (1995). *Meaningful differences in the everyday experience of young American children.* Baltimore: Brookes.

Hart, L. (2003). Some directions for future research on equity issues and justice in mathematics education. In L. Burton (Ed.), *Which way social justice in mathematics education?* Westport, CT: Praeger.

Heath, S. (1983). *Ways with words: Language, life, and work in communities and classrooms.* Cambridge: Cambridge University Press.

Heath, S. B., & McLaughlin, M. (Eds.). (1993). *Identity and inner-city youth: Beyond ethnicity and gender.* New York: Teachers College Press.

Heibert, J., & Carpenter, T. (1990). Learning and teaching with understanding. In Grouws (Ed.), *Handbook of teaching and learning mathematics.* New York: Macmillan.

Hess, R. D., & Shipman, V. (1965). Early experience and the socialization of cognitive modes in children. *Child Development, 36,* 869–886.

Hilliard, A. (2003). No mystery: Closing the achievement gap between Africans and excellence. In T. Perry, C. Steele, & A. G. Hilliard (Eds.), *Young, gifted, and Black: Promoting high achievement among African-American students.* Boston: Beacon.

Holland, D., Lachiotte, W., Skinner, D., & Cain, C. (1998). *Identity and agency in cultural worlds.* Cambridge, MA: Harvard University Press.

Holland, J. (1981). Social class and changes in orientation to meaning. *Sociology, 15,* 1–18.

hooks, b. (1994). *Teaching to transgress: Education as the practice of freedom.* London: Falmer Press.

Hyde, J. (1993). Gender differences in mathematics ability, anxiety and attitudes: What do meta-analyses tell us? In L. A. Penner, G. M. Batsche, H. A. Knoff, & D. L. Nelson (Eds.), *The challenge in mathematics and science education: Psychology's response* (pp. 251–274). Washington DC: American Psychological Association.

Hymes, D. (1996). *Ethnography, linguistics, narrative inequality: Toward an understanding of voice.* London: Taylor & Francis.

Jacob, E. (1998, April). *Anthropological perspectives for research in mathematics education: Beyond cultural groups.* Invited address to the Research in Mathematics Education Special Interest Group at the annual meeting of the American Educational Research Association, San Diego, CA.

Johnson, M. (1984). Blacks in mathematics: A status report. *Journal for Research on Mathematics Education, 15,* 145–153.

Johnson, M. (1989). Minority differences in mathematics. In M. M. Lindquist (Ed.), *Results from the fourth mathematics assessment of the National Assessment of Education Progress* (pp. 135–148). Reston, VA: National Council of Teachers of Mathematics.

Kahn, L., & Civil, M. (2001). Unearthing the mathematics of a classroom garden. In E. McIntyre, A. Rosebery, & N. González (Eds.), *Classroom diversity: Connecting school to students' lives* (pp. 37–50). Portsmouth, NH: Heinemann.

Kaur, B. (1995). Gender and mathematics: The Singapore perspective. In P. Rogers & G. Kaiser (Eds.), *Equity in mathematics education* (pp. 129–134). London: Falmer Press.

Kenway, J., Willis, S., & Junor, A. (1994). *Telling tales: Girls and schools changing their ways.* Canberra: Department of Employment, Education and Training.

Khisty, L. (1995). Making inequality: Issues of language and meanings in mathematics teaching with Hispanic students. In W. G. Secada, E. Fennema, & L. B. Adajian (Eds.), *New directions for equity in mathematics education* (pp. 279–297). Cambridge: Cambridge University Press.

Khisty, L., McLeod, D., & Bertilson, K. (1990). Speaking mathematically in bilingual classrooms: An exploratory study of teacher discourse. *Proceedings of the Fourteenth*

International Conference for the Psychology of Mathematics Educator, 3, 105–112. Mexico City: CONACYT.

King, J. E. (1991). Dysconscious racism: Ideology, identity, and the miseducation of teachers. *Journal of Negro Education, 60,* 133–146.

Kohl, H. (1994). I won't learn from you: Confronting student resistance. In *Rethinking our classrooms: Teaching for equity and justice* (pp. 134–135). Milwaukee: Rethinking our Schools.

Kohn, M. (1963). Social class and parent-child relationships: An interpretation. *American Journal of Sociology, 68,* 471–480.

Kohn, M. (1983). On the transmission of values in the family: A preliminary formulation. *Research in Sociology of Education and Socialization, 4,* 1–12.

Kozol, J. (1992). *Savage inequalities: Children in America's schools.* New York: HarperPerennial.

Ladson-Billings, G. (1994). *The Dreamkeepers: Successful teachers of African American children.* San Francisco: Jossey-Bass.

Ladson-Billings, G. (1995a). Making mathematics meaningful in multicultural contexts. In W. G. Secada, E. Fennema, & L. B. Adajian (Eds.), *New directions for equity in mathematics education* (pp. 126–145). Cambridge: Cambridge University Press.

Ladson-Billings, G. (1995b). Toward a theory of culturally relevant pedagogy. *American Educational Research Journal, 32,* 465–491.

Ladson-Billings, G. (1997). It doesn't add up: African American students' mathematics achievement. *Journal for Research in Mathematics Education, 28*(6), 697–708.

Ladson-Billings, G. (2001). *Crossing over to Canaan: The journey of new teachers in diverse classrooms.* San Francisco: Jossey-Bass.

Ladson-Billings, G., & Tate, W. (1995). Toward a Critical Race Theory of education. *Teachers College Record, 97*(1), 47–68.

Lampert, M. (1985). How do teachers manage to teach? Perspectives on problems in practice. *Harvard Educational Review, 55,* 178–194.

Lampert, M. (1990). When the problem is not the question and the solution is not the answer: Mathematical knowing and teaching. *American Educational Research Journal, 27*(1), 29–63.

Lareau, A. (2002). Invisible inequality: Social class and childrearing in Black families and White families. *American Sociological Review, 67*(5), 747–776.

Lave, J. (1988). *Cognition in practice: Mind, mathematics, and culture in everyday life.* New York: Cambridge University Press.

Lave, J. (1996). Teaching, as learning, in practice. *Mind, Culture, and Activity: An International Journal, 3*(3), 149–164.

Lave, J., & Wenger, E. (1991). *Situated learning: Legitimate peripheral participation.* Cambridge: Cambridge University Press.

Leder, G. (1990). Gender differences in mathematics: An overview. In E. Fennema & G. Leder (Eds.), *Mathematics and gender* (pp. 10–26). New York: Teachers College Press.

Leder, G. (2001). Pathways in mathematics towards equity: A 25 year journey. In M. van den Heuvel-Panhuizen (Ed.), *Proceedings of the 25th conference of the International Group for the Psychology of Mathematics Education* (Vol. 1, pp. 41–54). Utrecht, The Netherlands: Utrecht University.

Lee, C. (1995). A culturally based cognitive apprenticeship: Teaching African American high school students skill in literacy interpretation. *Reading Research Quarterly, 30,* 608–630.

Lee, C. (2001). Is October Brown Chinese? A cultural modeling activity system for under-achieving students. *American Educational Research Journal, 38*(1), 97–142.

Lee, C. (2003a). Every shut eye ain't sleep: Studying how people live culturally. *Educational Researcher, 32*(5), 6–13.

Lee, C. (2003b). Why we need to re-think race and ethnicity in educational research. *Educational Researcher, 32*(5), 3–5.

Lee, C. D., Spencer, M. B., & Harpalani, V. (2003). "Every shut eye ain't sleep": Studying how people live culturally. *Educational Researcher, 32*(5), 6–13.

Lensmire, T. (1993). Following the child, socioanalysis, and threats to community: Teacher response to children's texts. *Curriculum Inquiry, 23*(3), 265–299.

Leontiev, A. (1978). The problem of activity in psychology. In J. V. Wertsch (Ed.), *The concept of activity in Soviet psychology* (pp. 37–71). New York: Sharpe.

Lesh, R., & Doerr, H. (2000). Symbolizing, communicating, and mathematizing: Key components of models and modeling. In P. Cobb, E. Yackel, & K. McClain (Eds.), *Symbolizing and communicating in mathematics classrooms.* Mahwah, NJ: Erlbaum.

Lipka, J., & Adams, E. (2004). *Culturally based math education as a way to improve Alaska Native students' math performance:* The Appalachian Collaborative Center for Learning, Assessment, and Instruction in Mathematics. Athens, Ohio.

Lipman, P. (2004). *High stakes education: Inequality, globalization, and urban school reform.* New York: Routledge.

Lipsitz, G. (1998). *The possessive investment in whiteness: How white people profit from identity politics.* Philadelphia: Temple University Press.

Lockheed, M., Thorpe, M., Brooks-Gunn, J., Casserly, P., & McAloon, A. (1985). *Sex and ethnic differences in middle school mathematics, science, and computer science: What do we know?* (Report submitted to the Ford Foundation). Princeton, NJ: Educational Testing Service.

Lubienski, S. T. (1997). Class matters: A preliminary excursion. In *Multicultural and gender equity in the mathematics classroom: The gift of diversity, 1997 yearbook.* Reston, VA: National Council of Teachers of Mathematics.

Lubienski, S. (2000a). Problem solving as a means toward mathematics for all: An exploratory look through a class lens. *Journal for Research in Mathematics Education, 31*(4), 454–482.

Lubienski, S. (2000b). A clash of class cultures? Students' experiences in a discussion-intensive seventh-grade mathematics classroom. *Elementary School Journal, 100,* 377–403.

Lubienski, S. (2002). Research, reform, and equity in U.S. mathematics education. *Mathematical Thinking and Learning, 4*(2 & 3), 103–125.

Lubienski, S. (2003). Celebrating diversity and denying disparities: A critical assessment. *Educational Researcher, 30*–38.

Lubienski, S., & Bowen, A. (2000). Who's counting? A survey of mathematics education research 1982–1998. *Journal for Research in Mathematics Education, 31*(5), 626–633.

Lubienski, S., McGraw, R., & Strutchens, M. (2004). NAEP findings regarding gender: Mathematics achievement, student affect, and learning practices. In P. Kloosterman, & F. K. Lester, Jr. (Eds.), *Results and interpretations of the 1990 through 2000 mathematics assessments of the National Assessment of Educational Progress* (pp. 305–336). Reston, VA: National Council of Teachers of Mathematics.

Lubienski, S., & Stilwell, J. (2003). Teaching low-SES students mathematics through problem solving: Tough issues, promising strategies, and lingering dilemmas. In H. Schoen

& R. I. Charles (Eds.), *Teaching mathematics through problem solving: 6–12* (pp. 207–218). Reston: National Council of Teachers of Mathematics.

Luria, A. (1976). *Cognitive development: Its cultural and social foundations.* Cambridge, MA: Harvard University Press.

Mac an Ghaill, M. (1994). *The making of men: Masculinities, sexualities, and schooling.* Philadelphia: Open University Press.

Macedo, D. (2000). The colonialism of the English only movement. *Educational Researcher, 29,* 15–24.

MacGregor, M., & Moore, R. (1992). *Teaching mathematics in the multicultural classroom.* Melbourne, Australia: Institute of Education, University of Melbourne.

Mannheim, B., & Tedlock, D. (1995). Introduction. In D. Tedlock & B. Mannheim (Eds.), *The dialogic emergence of culture* (pp. 1–32). Urbana: University of Illinois Press.

Manor, R. (2002, October 5). *Mortgage OKs tougher for local Blacks, Latinos. Chicago Tribune,* pp. 1–2.

Martin, D. (1993). *Mathematics socialization among African Americans.* Project proposal funded by the Graduate Division of the University of California at Berkeley.

Martin, D. (1997). *Mathematics socialization and identity among African Americans: Community forces, school forces, and individual agency.* Unpublished doctoral dissertation, University of California, Berkeley.

Martin, D. (1998). *Mathematics socialization and identity among African Americans: A multilevel analysis of community forces, school forces, and individual agency.* Proposal submitted to National Academy of Education/Spencer Postdoctoral Fellowship competition.

Martin, D. (2000). *Mathematics success and failure among African American youth: The roles of sociohistorical context, community forces, school influence, and individual agency.* Mahwah, NJ: Lawrence Erlbaum Associates.

Martin, D. (2002a). *Mathematics socialization and identity: A sociocultural analysis of African American information technology workforce participation.* Project proposal funded by the National Science Foundation.

Martin, D. (2002b). *Situating self, situating mathematics: Issues of identity and agency among African American adults and adolescents.* Paper presented at the annual meeting of the National Council of Teachers of Mathematics, Las Vegas.

Martin, D. (2003a). *Guardians and gatekeepers: African American parents' responses to mathematics and mathematics education reform.* Paper presented at the annual meeting of the American Educational Research Association, Chicago.

Martin, D. (2003b). Hidden assumptions and unaddressed questions in Mathematics for All rhetoric. *The Mathematics Educator, 13*(2), pp. 7–21.

Martin, D. (2004a). *Advocating for equity and diversity within the context of standards-based reform.* To appear in Proceedings of NCTM catalyst conference.

Martin, D. (2004b). *Mathematics Learning as Racialized Experience: African American Parents Speak on the Struggle for Mathematics Literacy.* Manuscript submitted to *Mathematical Thinking and Learning.*

Martin, D. (in press). Mathematics learning and participation as racialized forms of experience: African American parents speak on the struggle for mathematics literacy. Manuscript submitted to *Mathematical Thinking and Learning.*

Masingila, J. (1994). Mathematics practice in carpet laying. *Anthropology and Education Quarterly, 25*(4), 430–462.

Masingila, J., & King, K. J. (1997). Using ethnomathematics as a classroom tool. In *Multicultural and gender equity in the mathematics classroom: The gift of diversity, 1997 yearbook.* Reston, VA: National Council of Teachers of Mathematics.

McDermott, R., & Webber, V. (1998). When is mathematics or science? In J. G. Greeno & S. V. Goldman (Eds.), *Thinking practices in mathematics and science learning* (pp. 321–340). Mahwah, NJ: Lawrence Erlbaum.

McIntosh, P. (1989, July/August). White privilege: Unpacking the invisible knapsack. *Peace and Freedom,* pp. 10–12.

McIntyre, D., Bhatti, G., & Fuller, M. (1997). Educational experiences of ethnic minority students in Oxford. In B. Cosin & M. Hales (Eds.), *Families, education and social differences* (pp.197–220). London: Routledge.

McLaren, P. (1998). Revolutionary pedagogy in post-revolutionary times: Rethinking the political economy of critical education. *Educational Theory, 48,* 431–463.

Means, B., & Knapp, M. S. (1991). Cognitive approaches to teaching advanced skills to educationally disadvantaged students. *Phi Delta Kappan, 73,* 282–289.

Mehan, H., Hubbard, L., & Villanueva, I. (1994). Forming academic identities: Accommodation without assimilation among involuntary minorities. *Anthropology and Education Quarterly, 25(2),* 91–117.

Mellin-Olsen, S. (1987). *The politics of mathematics education.* Dordrecht, The Netherlands: Reidel.

Mestre, J. (1981). Predicting academic achievement among bilingual Hispanic college technical students. *Educational and Psychological Measurement, 41,* 1255–1264.

Mestre, J. (1988). The role of language comprehension in mathematics and problem solving. In R. Cocking & J. Mestre (Eds.), *Linguistic and cultural influences on learning mathematics* (pp. 201–220). Hillsdale, NJ: Lawrence Erlbaum Associates.

Meyer, M. (1991). Equity: The missing element in recent agendas for mathematics education. *Peabody Journal of Education, 66,* 6–21.

Millroy, W. (1992). An ethnographic study of the mathematical ideas of a group of carpenters [Monograph]. *Journal for Research in Mathematics Education, 5.*

Moll, L. (1997). The creation of mediating settings. *Mind, Culture, and Activity, 4,* 191–199.

Moll, L., Amanti, C., Neff, D., & Gonzalez, N. (1992). Funds of knowledge for teaching: A qualitative approach to developing strategic connections between homes and classrooms. *Theory into Practice, 31(2),* 132–141.

Moll, L., & González, N. (2004). Engaging life: A funds-of-knowledge approach to multicultural education. In J. A. Banks & C. A. Banks (Eds.), *Handbook of research on multicultural education* (2nd ed.) (pp. 699–715). San Francisco: Jossey Bass.

Moll, L., & Greenberg, J. (1990). Creating zones of possibilities: Combining social contexts for instruction. In L. C. Moll (Ed.), *Vygotsky and education.* Cambridge: Cambridge University Press.

Moody, V. (2001). The social constructs of the mathematical experiences of African-American students. In B. Atweh, H. Forgasz, & B. Nebres (Eds.), *Sociocultural research on mathematics education* (pp. 255–278). Mahwah, New Jersey: Lawrence Erlbaum Associates.

Morrow, C., & Morrow, J. (1995). Connecting women with mathematics. In P. Rogers & G. Kaiser (Eds.), *Equity in mathematics education: Influences of feminism and culture* (pp. 13–26). London: Falmer Press.

Moschkovich, J. (1996). Moving up and getting steeper: Negotiating shared descriptions of linear graphs. *The Journal of the Learning Sciences, 5*(3), 239–277.

Moschkovich, J. (1998). Resources for refining conceptions: Case studies in the domain of linear functions. *The Journal of the Learning Sciences, 7*(2), 209–237.

Moschkovich, J. (1999). Supporting the participation of English language learners in mathematical discussions. *For the Learning of Mathematics, 19*, 11–19.

Moschkovich, J. (2000). Learning mathematics in two languages: Moving from obstacles to resources. In W. G. Secada (Ed.), *Changing the faces of mathematics: Perspectives on multiculturalism and gender equity* (pp. 85–93). Reston, VA: National Council of Teachers of Mathematics.

Moschkovich, J. (2002a). An introduction to examining everyday and academic mathematical practices. In M. Brenner & J. Moschchovich (Eds.), *Everyday and academic mathematics in the classroom.* JRME Monograph No. 11. Reston, VA: National Council of Teachers of Mathematics.

Moschkovich, J. (2002b). A situated and sociocultural perspective on bilingual mathematics learners. *Mathematical Thinking and Learning, 4*(2 & 3), 189–212.

Moses, R. (1994). Remarks on the struggle for citizenship and math/science literacy. *Journal of Mathematical Behavior, 13*, 107–111.

Moses, R. (2004). *Algebra Project high school-university network for mathematics literacy: Concept paper.* Unpublished manuscript, Cambridge, MA.

Moses, R., & Cobb, C. (2001). *Radical equations: Math literacy and civil rights.* Boston, MA: Beacon Press.

Moses, R., Kamii, M., Swap, S. M., & Howard, J. (1989). The Algebra Project: Organizing in the spirit of Ella. *Harvard Educational Review, 59*(4), 423–444.

Murrell, P. (2002). *African-centered pedagogy.* Albany: State University of New York Press.

Nasir, N. (1996). *Statistics in Practice: African-American Youth in the Play of Basketball.* Unpublished master's thesis, University of California, Los Angeles.

Nasir, N. (2000). Points ain't everything: Emergent goals and average and percent understandings in the play of basketball among African-American students. *Anthropology & Education Quarterly, 31*(3), 283–305.

Nasir, N. (2002). Identity, goals, and learning: Mathematics in cultural practice. *Mathematical Learning: Mathematical Thinking and Learning, 4*(2&3), 213–248.

Nasir, N., & Cobb, P. (2002). Diversity, equity and mathematical learning. *Mathematical Thinking and Learning, 4*(2 & 3), 91–102.

Nasir, N., & Hand, V. (2003, July). *From the court to the classroom: Managing identities as learners in basketball and classroom mathematics.* Paper presented at the Tenth Conference of the European Association for Research on Learning and Instruction, Padua, Italy.

Nasir, N., & Saxe, G. (2003). Ethnic and academic identities: A cultural practice perspective on emerging tensions and their management in the lives of minority students. *Educational Researcher, 32*, 14–18.

National Academy of Education. (1999, March). *Recommendations regarding research priorities: An advisory report to the National Educational Research Policy and Priorities Board.* New York: National Academy of Education.

National Center for Educational Statistics (NCES). (2004). *The nation's report card mathematics highlights 2003* (2004–451). Washington, DC: U.S. Department of Education.

National Council of Teachers of Mathematics. (1989). *Curriculum and evaluation standards for school mathematics.* Reston, VA: Author.

National Council of Teachers of Mathematics. (1991). *Professional standards for teaching mathematics.* Reston, VA: Author.

National Council of Teachers of Mathematics. (1995). *Assessment standards for school mathematics.* Reston, VA: Author.

National Council of Teachers of Mathematics. (2000). *Principles and standards for school mathematics.* Reston, VA: Author.

National Research Council. (2001). *Adding it up: Helping children learn mathematics.* Report prepared by the Mathematics Learning Study Committee. Washington, DC: National Academy Press.

Newmann, F., & Wehlage, G. (1995). *Successful school restructuring: A report to the public and educators.* Washington, DC: Office of Educational Research and Improvement.

Nicholls, J. (1989). *The competitive ethos and democratic education.* Cambridge, MA: Harvard University Press.

Nieto, S. (1996). *Affirming diversity: The sociopolitical context of multicultural education.* New York: Longman.

Nunes, T. (1999). Mathematics learning as the socialization of the mind. *Mind, Culture, and Activity: An International Journal, 6*(1), 33–52.

Nunes, T., Schliemann, A., & Carraher, D. (1993). *Street mathematics and school mathematics.* Cambridge: Cambridge University Press.

Oakes, J. (1985). *Keeping track: How schools structure inequality.* New Haven: Yale University Press.

Oakes, J. (1990). *Multiplying inequalities: The effect of race, social class, and tracking on opportunities to learn mathematics and science.* Santa Monica, CA: RAND.

Oboler, S. (1995). *Ethnic labels, Latino lives: Identity and the politics of (re)presentation in the United States.* Minneapolis: University of Minnesota Press.

O'Connor, M. C. (1992). *Negotiated defining: The case of length and width.* Unpublished manuscript, Boston University.

O'Cadiz, M., Wong, P., & Torres, C. (1998). *Education and democracy: Paulo Freire, social movements, and educational reform in Sao Paulo.* Boulder, CO: Westview Press.

Ogbu, J. (1978). *Minority education and caste: The American system in cross-cultural perspective.* New York: Academic Press.

Ogbu, J. (1987). Variability in minority school performance: A problem in search of an explanation. *Anthropology & Education Quarterly, 18*(4), 312–334.

Ogbu, J. (1992a). Adaptation to minority status and impact on school success. *Theory into Practice, 31,* 287–295.

Ogbu, J. (1992b). Understanding cultural diversity and learning. *Educational Researcher, 21*(8), 5–14.

Ogbu, J. (1999). Beyond language: Ebonics, proper English, and identity in a Black-American speech community. *American Educational Research Journal, 36,* 147–184.

Olivares, R. (1996). Communication in mathematics for students with limited English proficiency. In P. C. Elliott & M. J. Kenney (Eds.), *Communication in mathematics: K–12 and beyond—1996 Yearbook* (pp. 219–230). Reston, VA: National Council of Teachers of Mathematics.

Oliver, M., & Shapiro, T. (1997). *Black wealth, white wealth: A new perspective on racial inequality.* New York: Routledge.

Osbourne, J. (1997). Race and academic disidentification. *Journal of Educational Psychology*, *89*(4), 728–735.

Pask, G. (1976). *The Cybernetics of Human Learning and Performance*. London: Hutchinson.

Pepper, S. (1942). *World hypotheses: A study in evidence*. Berkeley: University of California Press.

Peressini, D. (1997). Building bridges between diverse families and the classroom: Involving parents in school mathematics. In *Multicultural and gender equity in the mathematics classroom: The gift of diversity, 1997 yearbook*. Reston, VA: National Council of Teachers of Mathematics.

Perry, T. (2003). Up from the parched earth: Toward a theory of African-American achievement. In T. Perry, C. Steele, & A. Hilliard (Eds.), *Young, gifted and black: Promoting high achievement among African-American students* (pp. 1–87). Boston: Beacon Press.

Peters, M., & Lankshear, C. (1996). Critical literacy and digital texts. *Educational Theory*, *46*(1), 51–70.

Pickering, A. (1995). *The mangle of practice: Time, agency, and science*. Chicago: University of Chicago Press.

Pimm, D. (1987). *Speaking mathematically: Communication in mathematics classrooms*. London: Routledge.

Powell, A., & Frankenstein, M. (Eds.). (1997). *Ethnomathematics: Challenging Eurocentrism in mathematics education*. New York: State University of New York Press.

Pressley, M. (2000). What should comprehension instruction be the instruction of? In M. Kamil, P. Mosenthal, P. D. Pearson, & R. Barr (Eds.), *Handbook of reading research* (Vol. 3, pp. 545–561). Mahwah, NJ: Lawrence Erlbaum Associates.

Rampton Committee. (1981). *West Indian children in our schools*. London, HMSO.

Restivo, S. (1994). The social life of mathematics. In P. Ernest (Ed.), *Mathematics, education, and philosophy: An international perspective* (pp. 209–220). London: Falmer Press.

Reyes, L., & Stanic, G. (1988). Race, sex, socioeconomic status, and mathematics. *Journal for Research in Mathematics Education*, *19*, 26–43.

Rodriguez, A. (1998). Strategies for counterresistance: Toward sociotransformative constructivism and learning to teach science for diversity and understanding. *Journal of Research in Science Teaching*, *35*, 589–622.

Rogers, L. (1999). *Sexing the brain*. London: Weidenfeld & Nicolson.

Rogers, P., & Kaiser, G. (Eds.). (1995). *Equity in mathematics education: Influences of feminism and culture*. London: Falmer Press.

Rogoff, B. (1990) *Apprenticeship in thinking*. New York: Oxford University.

Rogoff, B. (1994). Developing understanding of the idea of communities of learners. *Mind, Culture, and Activity: An International Journal*, *1*, 209–229.

Rogoff, B., & Angelillo, C. (2002). Investigating the coordinated functioning of multifaceted cultural practices in human development. *Human Development*, *45*, 211–225.

Rosaldo, R. (1989). *Culture and truth: The remaking of social analysis*. Boston: Beacon Press.

Rosebery, A., Warren, B., & Conant, F. (1992). Appropriating scientific discourse: Findings from language minority classrooms. *The Journal of the Learning Sciences*, *2*(1), 61–94.

Rubenstein, R. (1996). Strategies to support the learning of the language of mathematics. In P. C. Elliott & M. J. Kenney (Eds.), *Communication in mathematics: K–12 and beyond—1996 yearbook* (pp. 214–218). Reston, VA: National Council of Teachers of Mathematics.

Ryan, R., & Deci, E. (2000). Self-determination theory and the facilitation of intrinsic motivation, social development, and well-being. *American Psychologist, 55*, 68–78.

Sandoval-Taylor, P. (2005). Home is where the heart is: Planning a funds of knowledge-based curriculum module. In N. Gonzalez, L. Moll, & C. Amanti (Eds.), *Funds of knowledge: Theorizing practice in households, communities, and classrooms*. Mahwah, NJ: Lawrence Erlbaum.

Savignon, S. (1991). Communicative language teaching: State of the art. *TESOL Quarterly, 25*(2), 261–277.

Saxe, G. B. (1982). Culture and the development of numerical cognition: Studies among the Oksapmin of Papua New Guinea. In C. G. Brainerd (Ed.), *Children's logical and mathematical cognition* (pp. 157–176). New York: Springer-Verlag.

Saxe, G. (1991). *Culture and cognitive development: Studies in mathematical understanding*. Mahwah, NJ: Lawrence Erlbaum.

Saxe, G. (1999). Cognition, development, and cultural practices. In E. Turiel (Ed.), *Culture and development: New directions in child psychology*. San Francisco: Jossey-Bass.

Schliemann, A. (1995). Some concerns about bringing everyday mathematics to mathematics education. In L. Meira & D. Carraher (Eds.), *Proceedings of the 19th PME conference* (Vol. 1, pp. 45–60). Recife, Brazil: Universidade Federal de Pernambuco.

Schwartz, D., & Martin, T. (2004). Inventing to prepare for future learning: The hidden efficiency of encouraging original students production in statistics instruction. *Cognition and Instruction, 22*, 129–184.

Scribner, S. (1984). Studying working intelligence. In B. Rogoff & J. Lave (Eds.), *Everyday cognition*. Cambridge, MA: Harvard.

Secada, W. (1989). Educational equity versus equality of education: An alternative conception. In W. G. Secada (Ed.), *Equity and education* (pp. 68–88). New York: Falmer.

Secada, W. (1991a). Agenda setting, enlightened self-interest, and equity in mathematics education. *Peabody Journal of Education, 66*, 22–56.

Secada, W. (1991b). Diversity, equity, and cognitivist research. In E. Fennema, T. P. Carpenter, & S. J. Lamon (Eds.), *Integrating research on teaching and learning mathematics* (pp. 17–53). Albany: State University of New York Press.

Secada, W. (1992). Race, ethnicity, social class, language, and achievement in mathematics. In D. A. Grouws (Ed.), *Handbook of research on mathematics teaching and learning* (pp. 623–660). New York: Macmillan.

Secada, W. (1994). Towards a consciously multicultural mathematics curriculum. In F. L. Rivera-Batiz (Ed.), *Reinventing urban education: Multiculturalism and the social context of schooling* (pp. 235–255). New York: Institute for Urban and Minority Education.

Secada, W. (1995). Social and critical dimensions for equity in mathematics education. In W. G. Secada, E. Fennema, & L. B. Adajian (Eds.), *New directions for equity in mathematics education* (pp. 146–164). Cambridge: Cambridge University Press.

Select Committee on Race Relations and Immigration. (1977). *The West Indian community*. London, HMSO.

Sellers, R., Smith, M., Shelton, N., Rowley, S., & Chavous, T. (1998). Multidimensional model of racial identity: A reconceptualization of African American racial identity. *Personality and Social Psychology Review, 2*(1), 18–39.

Sfard, A. (2002, June). *Telling identities: Conceptualizing diversity in terms of identity*. Paper presented at the Fifth Congress of the International Society for Cultural Research and Activity Theory, Amsterdam, The Netherlands.

Silva, C., & Moses, R. (1990). The Algebra Project: Making middle school mathematics count. *Journal of Negro Education, 59*, 375–391.

Silver, E., Smith, M. S., & Nelson, B. S. (1995). The QUASAR Project: Equity concerns meet mathematics education reform in the middle school. In W. G. Secada, E. Fennema, & L. B. Adajian (Eds.), *New directions for equity in mathematics education* (pp. 9–56). Cambridge: Cambridge University Press.

Singh Kaeley, G. (1995). Culture, gender and mathematics. In P. Rogers & G. Kaiser (Eds.), *Equity in mathematics education* (pp. 91–97). London: Falmer Press.

Skovsmose, O. (1994). *Toward a philosophy of critical mathematics education.* Dordrecht: Kluwer Academic Publishers.

Sleeter, C. (1997). Mathematics, multicultural education, and professional development. *Journal for Research in Mathematics Education, 28*, 680–696.

Sowder, J. (1998). Perspectives from mathematics education. *Educational Researcher, 27*(5), 12–13.

Spanos, G., & Crandall, J. (1990). Language and problem solving: Some examples from math and science. In A. M. Padilla, H. H. Fairchild, & C. M. Valadez (Eds.), *Bilingual education: Issues and strategies* (pp. 157–170). Beverly Hills, CA: Sage.

Spanos, G., Rhodes, N. C., Dale, T. C., & Crandall, J. (1988). Linguistic features of mathematical problem solving: Insights and applications. In R. Cocking & J. Mestre (Eds.), *Linguistic and cultural influences on learning mathematics* (pp. 221–240). Hillsdale, NJ: Lawrence Erlbaum Associates.

Spencer, M. B. (1999). Social and cultural influences on school adjustment: The application of an identity-focused cultural ecological perspective. *Educational Psychologist, 34*(1), 43–57.

Stanic, G. (1991). Social inequality, cultural discontinuity, and equity in school mathematics. *Peabody Journal of Education, 66*, 57–71.

Stenning, K., Greeno, G., Hall, R., Sommerfeld, M., & Wiebe, M. (2002). Coordinating mathematical with biological multiplication: Conceptual learning as the development of heterogeneous reasoning systems. In M. Baker, P. Brna, K. Stenning, & A. Tiberghien (Eds.), *The role of communication in learning to model* (pp. 3–48). Mahwah, NJ: Erlbaum.

Stevens, R. (2000). Who counts what as mathematics? Emergent and assigned mathematics problems in a project based classroom. In J. Boaler (Ed.), *Multiple perspectives on mathematics teaching and learning* (pp. 105–144). Westport, CT: Ablex.

Stevenson, H. W., & Stigler, J. W. (1992). *The learning gap: Why our schools are failing and what we can learn from Japanese and Chinese education.* New York: Simon and Schuster.

Strutchens, M., Thomas, D., & Perkins, F. D. (1997). Mathematically empowering urban African-American students through family involvement. In *Multicultural and gender equity in the mathematics classroom: The gift of diversity, 1997 yearbook.* Reston, VA: National Council of Teachers of Mathematics.

Sukthankar, N. (1995). Gender and mathematics in Papua New Guinea. In P. Rogers & G. Kaiser (Eds.), *Equity in mathematics education* (pp. 135–140). London: Falmer Press.

Swain, M. (2001). Integrating language and content teaching through collaborative tasks. *Canadian Modern Language Review, 58*(1), 44–63.

Swann Committee. (1985). *Education for all: Report of the committee of inquiry into the education of children from ethnic minority groups.* London, HMSO.

Tajfel, H. (1978). Social categorisation, social identity and social comparison. In H. Tajfel (Ed.), *Differentiation between social groups: Studies in social psychology of intergroup relations* (pp. 61–76). London: Academic Press.

Tajfel, H. (1981). *Human groups & social categories.* Cambridge: Cambridge University Press.

Tate, W. (1995a). Economics, equity, and the national mathematics assessment: Are we creating a national toll road? In W. Secada, E. Fennema, & L. Byrd Adajian (Eds.), *New directions for equity in mathematics in mathematics education* (pp. 191–206). Cambridge, U.K.: Cambridge University Press.

Tate, W. (1995b). Returning to the root: A culturally relevant approach to mathematics pedagogy. *Theory into Practice, 34,* 166–173.

Tate, W. (1997). Race-ethnicity, SES, gender, and language proficiency in mathematics achievement: An update. *Journal for Research in Mathematics Education, 28,* 652–679.

Tate, W. (2002). African American students and algebra for all. In S. J. Denbo & L. M. Beaulieu (Eds.), *Improving schools for African American students.* Springfield, IL: Charles Thomas.

Tate, W., & Rousseau, C. (in press). Access and opportunity: The social context of mathematics education. In L. English (Ed.), *International handbook of research in mathematics education.* Mahwah, NJ: Lawrence Erlbaum Associates.

Valdés-Fallis, G. (1978). Code switching and the classroom teacher. *Language in education: Theory and practice* (Vol. 4). Wellington, VA: Center for Applied Linguistics.

Valsiner, J. (2000). *Culture and human development.* London: Sage.

Valsiner, J. (2001). The first six years: Culture's adventures in psychology. *Culture & Psychology, 7*(1), 5–48.

van Oers, B. (1996). Learning mathematics as a meaningful activity. In L. Steffe & P. Nesher (Eds.), *Theories of mathematical learning* (pp. 91–113). Mahwah, NJ: Lawrence Erlbaum.

van Oers, B. (2000). The appropriation of mathematical symbols: A psychosemiotic approach to mathematics learning. In P. Cobb, E. Yackel, & K. McClain (Eds.), *Symbolizing and communicating in mathematics classrooms.* Mahwah, NJ: Erlbaum.

Varenne, H., & McDermott, R (1999). *Successful failure: The school America builds.* Boulder, CO: Westview Press.

Vithal, R., & Skovsmose, O. (1997). The end of innocence: A critique of ethnomathematics. *Educational Studies in Mathematics, 34,* 131–157.

Volmink, J. (1994). Mathematics by all. In S. Lerman (Ed.), *Cultural perspectives on the mathematics classroom* (pp. 51–67): Kluwer Academic.

Vygotsky, L. (1962). *Thought and language* (E. Hanfmann & G. Vakar, Eds. and Trans.). New York: John Wiley. (Original work published in 1934)

Vygotsky, L. (1978). *Mind in society: The development of higher psychological processes.* Cambridge, MA: Harvard University Press.

Wagner, L., Roy, F. C., Ecatoiu, E., & Rousseau, C. (2000). Culturally relevant mathematics teaching at the secondary school level: Problematic features and a model for implementation. In M. Strutchens, M. L. Johnson, & W. F. Tate (Eds.), *Changing the faces of mathematics: Perspectives on African Americans* (pp. 107–122). Reston, VA: National Council of Teachers of Mathematics.

Walker, E., & McCoy, L. (1997). Students' voices: African-Americans and mathematics. In *Multicultural and gender equity in the mathematics classroom: The gift of diversity, 1997 yearbook.* Reston, VA: National Council of Teachers of Mathematics.

Walker, P. C., & Chappell, M. F. (1997). Reshaping perspectives on teaching mathematics in diverse urban schools. In *Multicultural and gender equity in the mathematics classroom: The gift of diversity,* 1997 yearbook. Reston, VA: National Council of Teachers of Mathematics.

Walkerdine, V. (1990). Difference, cognition, and mathematics education. *For the Learning of Mathematics, 10*(3), 51–56.

Walkerdine, V. (1998a). *Counting girls out: Girls and mathematics* (2nd ed.). London: Falmer Press.

Walkerdine, V. (1998b). *The mastery of reason: Cognitive development and the production of rationality.* London: Routledge.

Walkerdine, V., & Girls and Mathematics Unit (Eds.). (1989). *Counting girls out.* London: Virago.

Watkins, W. (2001). *The White architects of Black education: Ideology and power in America, 1865–1954.* New York: Teachers College Press.

Weis, L. (Ed.). (1988). *Class, race, and gender in American education.* Albany: State University of New York Press.

Wenger, E. (1998). *Communities of practice: Learning, meaning, and identity.* Cambridge: Cambridge University Press.

Wertsch, J. V. (1991). *Voices of the mind.* Cambridge, MA: Cambridge University Press.

West, M. M., Davis, F. E., Lynch, M., & Atlas, T. (1998). *The Algebra Project's middle school intervention in 1997–98: An evaluation report.* Cambridge, MA: Program Evaluation & Research Group, Lesley College.

Willis, P. (1977). *Learning to labor: How working class kids get working class jobs.* New York: Columbia University Press.

Woodson, C. G. (1933/1990). *The mis-education of the Negro.* Trenton, NJ: Africa World Press.

Yackel, E., & Cobb, P. (1996). Sociomathematical norms, argumentation, and autonomy in mathematics. *Journal for Research in Mathematics Education, 27,* 458–477. New York: Cambridge University Press.

Young, B. (2002). *Characteristics of the 100 largest public elementary and secondary school districts in the United States: 2000–01* (NCES 2002–351). Washington, DC: U.S. Department of Education, NCES.

Zaslavsky, C. (1979). *Africa counts: Number and pattern in African culture.* New York: Lawrence Hill Books.

Zaslavsky, C. (1994). Africa counts and ethnomathematics. *For the Learning of Mathematics, 14,* 3–7.

Zaslavsky, C. (1996). *The multicultural mathematics classrooms: Bringing in the world.* Portsmouth: Heinemann.

Zevenbergen, R. (1996). Constructivism as a liberal bourgeois discourse. *Educational Studies in Mathematics, 31,* 95–113.

About the Contributors

Guida de Abreu is a cultural developmental psychologist at Oxford Brookes University. She has studied culture and mathematical cognition over a period of 20 years and has conducted studies in Brazil, Portugal, and England. She is also interested in the social-psychological development of immigrant children. She was the director of the largest project to date on the experiences of Portuguese children in British schools. Her recent publications include *Transitions Between Contexts of Mathematical Learning* (Abreu, Bishop, & Presmeg, 2002, Kluwer); and a special issue of the *European Journal of Psychology of Education*, "The Social Mediation of Learning in Multiethnic Schools" (Abreu & Elbers, 2005).

Jo Boaler is a professor at Stanford University, specializing in mathematics education. She is a former secondary school teacher of mathematics and has taught in diverse, inner London comprehensive schools, across the 11–18 age range. Her PhD won the national award for educational research in the United Kingdom and she is the author of numerous articles and four books. Dr. Boaler specializes in the impact of different mathematics teaching approaches upon student understanding, achievement, and equity. Her book *Experiencing School Mathematics* won the Outstanding Book of the Year award for education in Britain. Her latest book, with Cathy Humphreys, *Connecting Mathematical Ideas*, is a collection of video cases and accompanying lesson notes and analyses.

Marta Civil is a professor in the Department of Mathematics at the University of Arizona, where she teaches mathematics courses for K–8 teachers and graduate courses in mathematics education. Her research encompasses teacher education, cultural and social aspects in mathematics teaching and learning, equity, and parental engagement in mathematics, primarily in working-class, Latino communities. She has presented her research at national and international conferences and has several publications. Currently, she is the principal investigator for CEMELA (Center for the Mathematics Education of Latinos/as), a multi-university consortium focused on research and practice on the connections between mathematics education and the cultural, social, and linguistic contexts of Latino/a students.

Tony Cline is professor of educational psychology at the University of Luton and codirector of the doctorate program in educational psychology at University College, London. He has chaired the editorial board of the National Association of Special Educational Needs. His 70-plus publications have covered a wide range of subjects, including bilingualism, dyslexia, inclusive education, and selective mutism. His recent research projects have focused on minority ethnic pupils in mainly White schools, training routes into teaching, and young people's representations of child development.

Paul Cobb has spent the past 20 years researching issues related to mathematics teaching and learning; he has focused on the identities that students develop in mathematics classrooms and the process of cultivating their interest in mathematics for the past 5 years. He has written more than 120 articles and book chapters and is invited to give lectures on mathematics education around the world. He is a member of the National Academy of Education and an invited fellow at the Center for Advanced Study in the Behavioral Sciences at Stanford.

Marian Currell is assistant principal at Dr. Martin Luther King Jr. Academic Middle School in San Francisco, and an Algebra Project teacher and trainer. She worked as staff developer and teacher in collaboration with other teachers and Principal James Taylor as the school revamped their mathematics program and fulfilled, in 1996, the Algebra Project's goal that all Grade 8 students take Algebra I. This program continues to succeed despite changing state and district mandates, and the school is seen as a model for advancing mathematics literacy for African American and other students of color.

Frank E. Davis is professor and director of the PhD program in educational studies at Lesley University and has been a mathematics educator for more than 30 years. He is co–principal investigator with Mary West and James Greeno of a National Science Foundation (NSF) research grant on improvement of mathematics literacy for African American students and has evaluated numerous mathematics and science education projects funded by the NSF and others. He serves as advisor on two NSF evaluation research grants. He was a research fellow for the American Educational Research Association (AERA)/NSF and was a visiting scholar at Stanford University.

James G. Greeno is a cognitive scientist whose research has focused on conceptual understanding and learning, most recently in classroom discourse activities. His contributions include a mathematical model of learning and transfer of verbally mediated categorical concepts, computer simulation models of conceptual understanding in mathematical problem solving, and interaction-analytic studies of conceptual understanding and learning in classrooms. He recently contributed "Theoretical and Practical Advances Through Research on Learning" to *Complementary Methods for Research in Education*. He is a member of the National Academy of Education and the Society of Experimental Psychologists and is visiting professor of education, University of Pittsburgh, and emeritus professor of education, Stanford University.

Melissa S. Gresalfi is a postdoctoral scholar at Vanderbilt University. In her research she considers context and social interaction by studying students' learning as a function of participation in activity settings. She examines how opportunities to learn get constructed in mathematics classrooms and how, when, and why different students take up those opportunities. With this focus, she has explored the extent to which classroom practices are equitable with regard to categories such as race and gender.

Rochelle Gutiérrez is an associate professor of mathematics education at the University of Illinois at Urbana-Champaign, where she has been since 1996. Her research focuses on the structural and pedagogical factors involved in equity for marginalized students, especially African American and Latino/a students. She has also focused upon understanding the organizational, cultural, and pedagogical aspects of high school mathematics departments that support students of color and students in poverty taking high levels of mathematics by Grade 12. She has been a Spencer Foundation postdoctoral fellow and has served on numerous national committees, including the RAND National Study Panel on Mathematics.

Eric Gutstein, known as "Rico," teaches mathematics education at the University of Illinois, Chicago. He taught mathematics for social justice for several years in a Chicago public school. He now works with the first Chicago public high school for social justice, which opened in fall 2005, and with the Young People's Project, youth arm of the Algebra Project, where he teaches and helps develop social-justice mathematics projects. He is the author of *Reading and Writing the World with Mathematics* (Routledge, 2005), is a cofounder of Teachers for Social Justice (Chicago), and is a longtime activist.

Sarah Theule Lubienski is an associate professor in curriculum and instruction, University of Illinois, Urbana-Champaign. Her scholarship centers around intersections of education and equity, focusing on mathematics achievement, instruction, and reform. Her most recent work involves examinations of race/ethnicity-, gender- and SES-related trends in mathematics data from the National Assessment of Educational Progress (NAEP). She currently serves as chair of the Research Using NAEP Data Special Interest Group of the American Educational Research Association, as well as chair of the editorial panel of the *Journal for Research in Mathematics Education.*

Danny Bernard Martin is an associate professor of mathematics education and mathematics at the University of Illinois at Chicago. Prior to coming to UIC, he was professor in the Department of Mathematics at Contra Costa College for 14 years and was a National Academy of Education/Spencer Foundation postdoctoral fellow from 1998 to 2000. His primary research interest is equity issues in mathematics education, with a focus on mathematics socialization and the construction of mathematics identities among African American adults and adolescents. He is currently developing a perspective that frames mathematics learning and participation as racialized forms of experience. Dr. Martin is author of the book *Mathematics Success and Failure Among African Youth.*

H. Taylor Martin joined the faculty at the University of Texas at Austin in 2003. Her primary research interest is how people learn content in complex domains from active participation, both physical and social. She is cooperating with local elementary schools to improve assessment tools for young children's mathematics and to examine how hands-on activities affect mathematics learning. She is also investigating the development of adaptive expertise through cooperation with the VaNTH Engineering Research Center in Bioengineering Educational Technologies.

Judit Moschkovich is an associate professor of mathematics education at the University of California, Santa Cruz. In her research she examines students' understanding of linear functions, mathematical discourse practices, and bilingual mathematics learners. She has conducted research for more than 10 years in secondary mathematics classrooms with large numbers of Latino/a students. She is a past member of the *Journal for Research in Mathematics Education* and *Journal of the Learning Sciences* editorial panels and is currently senior chair of the Research in Mathematics Education Special Interest Group for American Educational Research Association. She was the principal investigator of the National Science Foundation project Mathematical Discourse in Bilingual Settings: Learning Mathematics in Two Languages and is currently one of the principal investigators for the Center for the Mathematics Education of Latinos funded by the National Science Foundation (2004–2009).

Robert P. Moses is the founder and president of the Algebra Project and is Eminent Scholar at the Center for Urban Education and Innovation, Florida International University. After studying philosophy at Harvard's graduate school, he directed the Student Non-violent Coordinating Committee's voter registration in Mississippi and taught secondary mathematics in Tanzania. Since 1982, he has been curriculum developer, mathematics educator, and teacher trainer for the Algebra Project. He has been awarded a MacArthur Fellowship and numerous honorary doctorates. He is coauthor of *Radical Equations: Math Literacy and Civil Rights* and is collaborating with several mathematicians in high school curriculum development.

Na'ilah Suad Nasir is an assistant professor at Stanford University in the School of Education, where she has been since 2000. Her research interests center on exploring the relation between learning, development, and culture, particularly in relation to youth in urban communities. She has examined the relation between the in-school and out-of-school mathematics learning of African American children in urban schools and describes the complex cognitive strategies that some children employ in out-of-school practices such as basketball and dominoes, as well as how identities as "doers" and learners get formed in these practices. She has published widely in such journals as *Harvard Education Review* and *Educational Researcher.*

Mary Maxwell West is a senior research associate at Lesley University. She is trained in both cognitive development and anthropology, and she has collaborated with scientists and educators in research and evaluation of mathematics and science education for 25 years. She has been co–principal investigator of four National Science Foundation grants in mathematics education research, was on the staff of the National Commission on Testing and Public Policy, and was a member of the National Working Group on Authentic Assessment in Mathematics, and the National Working Group on Implementation of Reform in Mathematics Education.

Index